The Secret Massuese

Alan Zoltie Publishing inc.

ISBN: 978-1-7374122-0-5

I as a human being am slammed by the thought that everything is temporary except the mark I choose to leave.

Dedicated to ending violence of any kind, everywhere.

Tiana - Premonition

In the tiny town of Tartu, Estonia, she grew up knowing at the tender age of 5 just what she wanted to do and where she wanted to live. She sat in her mother's home, night after night, watching American movies and TV shows. She inhaled every single word, every ounce of a culture she could only dream of, and every one of those fictional characters became her best friends.

Tiana was an introvert, a very talented and gifted child, lacking in nothing but the confidence to make real lasting friendships. She could be a little bit of a loner at times, but her creativity won her many plaudits, even though she never accepted them as anything other than distant admirers. Her mother and father divorced when she was 3, her mother then re-marrying some two years later and Tiana's step-father, who came with two more children of his own and an ability to be regularly intoxicated, just like most men in the Baltic republics, became her nemesis. She despised him beyond all words and in time he would become the catalyst that would send Tiana globetrotting around the planet just after her 16th birthday. But even before that, she had her own career path marked out. Her mother was 5 feet 2 inches, her real father, 5 feet 6 inches, but she had decided that she was going to be 5 feet 9 inches, no matter what it took. She believed! She also believed in her looks, her long naturally red hair, her athletic build, and her incredibly sparkling brown eyes, and her willingness to conform to whatever her life required to progress up the seemingly impossible ladder she was about to climb. Tiana was a fighter, Tiana still is a fighter, but the courage it took to escape to her dreams from her simple beginnings, was a feat that even today seems like a miracle, and probably is.

At 13 she became a model, and fell in love with a man more than double her age. At 14 she was having sex, regular sex, unaware that there was anything wrong with that. At 15 she took part in her first orgy. She was never raped or abused, she was always a willing participant, but now, when thinking back to those early days, perhaps she was just naïve, and the abuse she received was more mental than physical, more directed at her innocence than her looks, but abuse all the same. She has blocked out some of what really happened to her, for good reasons. She wants to move on, to achieve what she set out to achieve and to climb a mountain that once looked taller than Everest, but which now is available to conquer at will. Tiana has courage, courage which stems from an industry she has grown up to dislike, and industry that broke her, sexually, physically, but never mentally and an industry that certainly made her strong and worldly.

Having made good money in her early modeling career, Tiana was sick and tired of Estonia, it's lackluster pace and lack of opportunity. Although she will always be grateful for her upbringing, she had bigger fish to fry and when she turned 16, she fled. Not 'fled' in the literal sense, but she had to get out, and she found a way to leave. She'd discussed this with her mother, who was very much against her leaving to live in London, a place that Tiana longed to go and a place that she felt would be a stepping stone to her dream destination, LA. Her mother was well aware of Tiana's ambitions, but felt, probably quite rightly so, that Tiana was too young to make such monumental decisions regarding her own future, and so, with a heavy heart, Tiana, who knew exactly what she wanted, made haste for the UK and a new life. She never thought she'd return to Estonia, firmly believing that once she was out, she was out. Things never panned out that way though, they never do, and in later years, she and her mother would reconcile and repair their relationship, which at that point in time, was fractious to say the least.

It was now 2003, and Tiana felt as free as a bird as she boarded the British Airways 737 bound for London Heathrow. She recalls looking at the sky as the plane took off and thinking to herself, 'my life just changed for the better, I am now a woman" even though, in truth, she was still just a girl. Tiana had grown up quickly, she'd had to. She had been surrounded by those who wanted to take advantage of her mind, body and soul. She'd survived, she knew she was about to embark on the next stage of her journey and that things could only get better. It was however a premature assumption because as soon as she touched down in London, her life took another turn, and not necessarily one that she'd expected or planned for.

Modeling had been her passion, her outlet and obviously her career to date, and when London beckoned, Tiana already knew where she would start. She had friends in the business and contacts from all over Europe, most of whom were converging on the UK at that time. Her instincts led her to one of those friends, who'd already put down roots in the east end of London. Tiana made haste from Heathrow to an apartment she'd been told about in the hope that she would at least be able to spend a day or two with some of the ladies whom she'd shared the modeling runway with over the past two years. When she'd left her past behind in Estonia, living accommodation was the last thing she'd thought about. Just getting away from everything that had hounded her through her early teenage years was the most important thing on her brief agenda. She'd hated Estonia, she'd disliked the town where she'd grown up. Her family situation bugged her even more and the fact that her mother, quite rightly, had tried to stop her from leaving Tartu, left such a bad taste in Tiana's psyche. She believed, rightly or wrongly, that she was old enough to do anything she wanted. She'd experienced the best and the worst in humanity, and yet she was still only 16. Her life to date had not been 'rough' by any means, but it had been complexly different to most 16-year-old girls. Her looks had carried her thus far, she'd been fucked at 13 by men much older than her, become reliant on drugs from 14 up until now, (she's 31 as I write this), and been able to wear expensive clothes and jewelry to accentuate her looks, even though those items hadn't belonged to her. She'd always felt like a princess, been treated like one, well, most of the time, and now that she was free from her 'close quarters' upbringing, she was ready to party hard, work hard and dream even harder. Tiana was on a mission, a mission to succeed and her first stop, London, was just a small step in the direction she aimed to follow until her success had been guaranteed.

Tiana, arriving tired and hungry from her journey, knocked on the door of the apartment where the other girls lived and when that door opened, and her friend Anastasia, Stassi for short, stood smiling and shocked that Tiana had actually made it there, hugs all round followed by intense happiness amongst these two old friends, perused. The two ladies just looked at one another and hugged, hugged until they hurt, releasing all Tiana's tension and worry in one split second.

The apartment where Stassi resided, was shared by her and 8 other ladies, all who hailed from different countries across Europe, and all of whom had converged on the UK's capital city in order to enhance their modeling careers. Tiana felt immediately at home. She settled in quickly, having been offered a bed in a room occupied by Stassi and one other lady from Italy. As the days went by, she began to relax as the modeling work arrived and the agency she'd joined, the same one that Stassi already belonged to, saw the real potential Tiana had, and offered her more and more work, both in the UK and in Europe. Tiana's life really took off again, although it had never really stalled, she was flying all over Europe, and even back to Estonia, where Tiana had left 'the love of her life, or so she'd thought. Erik was head of the modeling agency in Estonia, where her career had begun, and from the age of 14 the two of them had been deeply involved in an incredible affair that would last until Tiana was 18. Erik was 14 years older than Tiana, but their connection was magical and animalistic. When Tiana moved to the UK, her heart was still with Erik and her trips back to Estonia were welcomed by both of them, and filled with passionate sex which sometimes became so intense, it was hard to separate them, day or night.

Meanwhile in London, her life, after 12 months of living in this apartment with the rest of her 'besties', was becoming mundane and boring. Tiana was beginning to realize that modeling might not be the right career choice for her. She disliked all the bitchiness, the backstabbing and the rivalry that seemed to be a daily occurrence in her living quarters and especially inside the UK modeling agency that booked all of her work. She was sad and angry that things weren't moving in the direction she'd hoped and she missed Erik and sometimes her mother too. She'd been careful not to judge other's, even though they were judging her. She stepped back often from the brink, that precipice where her friends would take advantage of her kindness and then refuse to reciprocate, which led to many squabbles and fall-outs between them all. Tiana thought that perhaps it was time to choose another career path and that modeling, although lucrative, was maybe just not where she wanted to be.

It took another 6 months before she came to the decision that enough was enough. In that 6-month period, she'd made and spent most of the money she'd earned, and her lifestyle was, 'exotic', to say the least. A surplus of drugs, alcohol and sex had fueled her demise, a demise that had perhaps woken her up to the fact that a real job, a proper job, a sensible job, 9 to 5, was where she should start to look and pursue. Her friends were continually bickering, and she wanted no part of that. She and Erik were sort of on their last dance, and she knew that relationship was in serious trouble mainly because of the distance between them and the age gap too. With a heavy heart, but with common sense, Tania made moves to kick start a new career, but one that would only last a few weeks and one that would confirm in her own mind that there was more to life than the status quo.

Fucking Who I Want

Why is it OK for men to brag about how many women they've fucked, but when a woman does the same thing, she's regarded as a slut or a whore? What gives a man the right to add 'conquests' to his belt, and not a woman. When a man pays for sex, it's regarded as something of a rite of passage, but if you ever hear of a woman doing the same thing, it's not only frowned upon, but it's something that is laughed at or rarely spoken about. Tiana never understood that. She was liberated at 13, losing her virginity, not because she was forced, although when she thinks back, perhaps she was coerced gently by a man old enough to be her father, but because she felt it was the right thing to do and wanted to experiment. She'd always been a trend setter, from make up at 8 to clothes at 10, ahead of her years and way ahead of a chasing pack, a pack who could never catch up. She loved sex, from the second Erik entered her and deflowered her, she became obsessed with love making, brutal fucking and oral pleasure. It was in her blood. Yes, she'd been with Erik for some time, but she'd also fucked several other guys, guys she couldn't even remember due to her cocaine highs or her unwillingness to ask their names. When that cock was inside her, she changed. She became the animal she knew she was, enjoying every second of every thrust, no matter whose penis it was. Yes, there was good sex, crap sex and amazing sex, but in general it was just sex and Tiana was into sex in a big way. She loved the pleasure and the highs, she loved the orgasmic endings, if they came, and that of course depended on who was fucking her. She lived for sex, she lived for drugs, she liked to just live, and sex had a way of making her feel alive, very alive. She never concerned herself of any of the adverse consequences that sex could bring, nor did she ever worry about her reputation. She was a complete woman with a body to match, 34c-24-36, perfect and natural. She could have posed for Playboy, she could have shot porn, she could have just married a rich guy, any rich guy and became a trophy wife, but Tiana chose to fuck, and she chose to fuck her way. Her path to modeling was peppered with raunchy parties, and there was always an ample supply of good looking and rich guys to go around. Erik had been her first, but would never be her last. There would be dozens more, perhaps hundreds, all wanting the same thing, all given the chance, all to come back for more, only to be tossed aside as Tiana made her way through life in favor of her ambition and not comfort. She'd always said, 'a woman needs to do what she needs to do to make it to the top', and, even to this day, she's still climbing.

Back in London, she moved out of her shared apartment and into a little flat, (apartment), in Shoreditch. She'd started looking for a 9 to 5 job and soon found one, working as a hotel receptionist at a semi-decent establishment in Earls Court. It lasted 6 weeks. Her take home pay for a month was less than she'd been making per hour doing modeling. The 400 UK pounds she received couldn't feed her insatiable partying habits and before her training was over, she quit. In the meantime, she'd received so many propositions from visiting gentleman she's personally checked in to that hotel, she had a list as long as her arm for prospective dates and other employment. But her first priority was to find another 'normal' job. She started to look in the newspapers, on Craigslist and on other on-line job search engines. It didn't take too long. She'd spotted an Ad for a nanny position, something she'd never tried but as a 18-year-old, thought she'd be quite good at. The family lived in Streatham, another of South London's quaint suburbs, and after calling to arrange an interview, Tiana took only 30 minutes to be offered the job to look after the family's 4-year-old son. The husband and wife both worked and they asked if Tiana would take the position as a live-in nanny. She had no hesitation. They were a middle-class Muslim family, and Tiana believed they were happily married. Moving in would be great for her. No rent, fed when required, and payed to do a job she'd find very simple, and freedom to party on her own time.

Everything was going well for about 6 months when suddenly, the husband started touching Tiana, simple touching, on her shoulder, her waist, all quite innocent at first, or so she thought, but then it became more persistent, more personal and it was accompanied by a few simple words that Tiana found offensive. She knew it was time to leave, but she had to plan her escape knowing she would have another job to go to. His unwanted advances had ruined the perfect job. She was comfortable there, she could do as she pleased. The child was a breeze to look after and the wife just a perfect friend and boss. The husband however, turned out to be very strange and again, Tiana knew from experience that her looks had been the beginning of the end. He just couldn't resist. She began to job hunt once again, Craigslist being her comfort at night as she went from Ad to Ad. "Perhaps another nanny job?" she thought, but then again, perhaps not. And then, one evening, an Ad jumped out at her and hit her bang smack in the middle of her tired face.

"Want to earn a lot of cash?

Flexible schedule

Freedom you deserve

Luxurious apartment

Masseuse/companion required in Central London"

This Ad would change the rest of her life, but she didn't know it just then. She sat back and thought for a while. She'd never performed massage, but how hard could it be? What did it mean, masseuse/companion? Certainly not an Escort, she would never do that, but massage? She picked up the phone and dialed. Two days later, she found herself on the Edgeware road sitting across from one of the classiest ladies she'd ever met. Their next hour of conversation, spent discussing Tiana's possible new career, would probably end up being one of the most lucrative meetings she'd ever had.

The Agency

The office itself was beautifully decorated, but sparse. When she walked in, Julia was sitting behind a glass desk, very modern Tiana thought, and had virtually nothing on the top of that desk other than her cell phone, a regular land line and a notepad. There was also a picture frame, but it was turned towards Julia, so Tiana had no idea who was inside that frame. Julia stood as Tiana approached. Tiana could tell that this lady just oozed class. She was about 40 years old, had shoulder length blondish hair, wonderfully luscious lips, deep blue eyes and, Tiana knew, a ton of Botox to keep the ageing process at bay. Julia was gorgeous, and extremely British. Her dress sense, exquisite and her voice, just darling. Tiana knew immediately that she wanted to be her. She could tellninstantly this woman was just amazingly well grounded, knew how to talk to people, and was tough. Tiana sat.

Julia opened the conversation.

"Tiana, nice name, where are you from?"

"Estonia"

"How old are you?"

"22"

"You look so much younger. I would have put you at 18. Do you have some ID?"

Tiana took out her passport and handed it to Julia. Julia opened it, placed it on her desk and gave Tiana another look, but this time, she looked at her in detail, from top to bottom.

"Please stand up" Julia demanded

Tiana stood. Julia then stood, walking towards Tiana while studying her, just like a trainer would study a thoroughbred filly. Tiana was a little intimidated, but there was something about Julia she absolutely loved, although she had no idea what that was yet.

"Please sit" Julia demanded once more.

Tiana sat and Julia offered her a coffee. Tiana refused, and asked for water, Julia obliged.

Julia began.

"Do you know what sensual massage is Tiana?"

"No" came the response

"Well", Julia continued, "you're about to find out. I am going to explain what we need you to do, how we need you to behave, and how much you can make in a week, and then you, well, you are going to decide if this is for you and if it is, then we will sign a contract together. Understood?"

Tiana could only murmur a faint 'yes'. She was mesmerized by Julia. She didn't know what it was, but this woman had her riveted to the spot. She could barely breath, let alone speak.

"Sensual massage, FBSM as it's known in the trade, is the art of making a man feel loved, without loving him. Making him feel pampered, without loving him. Making him ejaculate, without loving him. In other words, it's a massage with a 'happy ending'. Do you understand?"

Of course she understood. She'd been with so many men in the past 5 years, she knew exactly what they wanted, exactly how to treat them and exactly how to extract every ounce of their attraction for her own personal gain. Tiana had been fucked, massaged, pampered, and then fucked again, many times, so many in fact, she'd lost count and had no desire to sit down and think of how many guys she'd been with to date. She had also learned how to get what she wanted from each of these guys. It was easy, once you gave it up, you got anything you wanted, most of the time.

Julia continued.

"At this 'agency', we advertise your services and the services of other ladies just like you. Our agency owns several apartments all over London, one of which you will be assigned to. We will find you clients, always men, visiting from all over the world and some who are local. You will pamper those clients. You will be naked and they will be naked. You will ask them to lie down on their stomachs, you will massage their backs and chat to them and then, after about 30 minutes, you will flip them over, you will jerk them until they climax, you will clean up and you will then ask them to leave. They will be happy, you will be paid. Got it?"

She was so abrupt. Tiana nodded her head in agreement.

Julia then softened up. It must have been a ploy to be so direct and to the point, just to see what reaction she received in return. Tiana had learned from her modeling career that you always listened and then you did what it took to advance to the next rung on the ladder. Her ability to listen and to progress had done her well over the past 4 years and so she knew in order to make this new job work, she'd have to do the same. Take it all in and then make it her own.

Julia's mood transformed as she continued.

"Before we get into greater detail Tiana, have you ever given a massage before, to anyone?"

"Only my boyfriend" she replied

"OK this is different. These men can be married, single, handsome, ugly, smelly, gorgeous, or just plain stupid. You never know what you are going to get, but no matter who it is, or who they are, whether you find them attractive or ugly, you treat them all the same. They come to you to feel good, they come to you to chat, they come to you because they are bored, they come to you for many reasons, but mostly they come to you for a release. Yes, THAT release. They all think with their dicks, every one of them. They want a beautiful woman like you to rub their cock and make them cum. They will then go home happy and you will go home richer, and hopefully they will have had a wonderful experience and come back again and again for more. We want them to be happy, ecstatic, fulfilled, and most importantly we want them to come back. We charge the 120 Pounds per hour, you get half I get half, and we do nothing but make them happy. Now, one thing you need to know, and you need to listen carefully to me Tiana because if you don't you will regret it and our relationship will be over before it even begins."

Tiana looked at her and she could see that Julia's eyes were now on fire and that whatever she was about to say was serious, so serious in fact, that Julia bent forward and pointed her index finger right at Tiana's face.

"You can jerk them off, you can talk to them, you can sympathize with them, you can cry with them, you can touch them, BUT…" Julia raised her voice for the finale, "…YOU CAN NEVER DATE THEM, SLEEP WITH THEM, OR FUCK THEM IN MY APPARTMENT OR ANY PLACE ELSE FOR THAT MATTER…."

she sat back slightly in her chair, "… do I make myself clear?"

She had made herself very clear, very clear indeed, and Tiana was now certain that Julia was a total professional and that if she stuck to the game plan, her possibilities of making this job a success were endless. She began silently doing the math in her brain. 120 Pounds per head, divided by 2 and then maybe multiplied by 5, 6 or more per day? Was that how it worked? She had so many questions, but Julia wasn't finished.

"Now that the hard part is over, let me explain the benefits. You will share an apartment with 2 other girls. The apartment is spotless, and it WILL be kept that way. We have rules, you will follow the rules. We have a client list that shall remain private. We have a need for discretion, you will follow that need. You will receive a cell phone, this is a company phone and you will treat it that way. You will make no personal calls on my time, not from my phone or your own phone. You will treat all of our clientele as if they are kings from a foreign land, each one being precious. The apartment is their sanctuary and it is your job to ensure complete satisfaction. We will take your picture and post it on-line on our website. If you have any issues with us doing this, you should leave now. There will be no massage training, you can figure the basics out by watching YouTube videos, and I will forward a link. This service lies on the boundaries of legality. You are not a whore, you are not an escort, you are a PROVIDER, do you know what a provider is?

Tiana did not know.

"You are providing a service, a service that most men want. It's not prostitution, but it's legal nonetheless. Do you understand"

She nodded in the affirmative.

"You will be naked with men you have never met before and often never meet again, and they will be naked too. Do you understand?"

'Yes" Tiana replied softly. She was so intimidated by this lady, but yet she loved her, even though she didn't know her.

"You will learn how to tease, how to tempt and how to make them all beg for more, but you will never ever cross any of the boundaries that I mentioned earlier, because once you do, you are finished, not just with me, but with the whole business. This industry is close knit and very incestuous. If I find out you've broken the rules, then the whole town knows within minutes. Understood?"

"Understood" she replied.

"We provide everything. Towels, oils, showers, etc etc, everything to make their experience enjoyable and everything to make it as easy as possible for you to supply a service that will make all their dreams come true. All you need to do is look sexy, stay clean and refreshed for each client and perform the service I have already outlined. Are we clear? Do you think you can do this and make it work according to our rules?"

Tiana looked at Julia, looked her up and down, told herself this job was perfect, and stood. She stuck out her hand, offering it to Julia and said, "where do I sign?"

Julia laughed," There are no contracts Tiana, just our handshake and word and we are good to go. Do you have other work?"

"Yes I model, part time of course. When do I start?" Tiana asked.

"Right now. Follow me"

And with that last command, Tiana entered a world where she would thrive for the next 8 years, a world that would bring her money, comfort, friendships and ultimately bring her to the place she wanted to live, the place she'd always wanted to live, the place of her childhood dreams, Los Angeles. This was the world of FBSM, Full Body Sensual Massage, and Tiana was about to become one of the best in the business and one of the best there had ever been.

The Industry

FBSM, Full Body Sensual Massage

GFE Girlfriend Experience

B2B meaning body to body fully nude, often with mutual touch allowed

Dining at the Y, Oral performed by man on a woman

MSOG, Multiple Shots on Goal, meaning you can fuck and ejaculate as many times as you can inside the same woman

YMV Your Mileage May Vary, meaning the length of your session depends on how your provider feels

BBBJ Bare Back Blow Job, blow job without condom

CBJ Covered blow job or blow job with condom

And so it goes on. There are acronyms for everything. Every position, every service offered, every penny that a man, or woman, and yes, women also go to these providers, although it's not as common, want to spend, it's covered by an acronym. In the UK and most of Europe, this kind of massage is legal, here in the USA however, it's completely illegal. You may be jailed for allowing a nude woman provide massage to you if you too are also nude and get caught by the cops. It's all semantics. Being an Escort isn't illegal, but escorts will have full sex (FS) with you. The difference? They are insinuating that you're paying for their company only and that sex, should it happen, is free and discretionary. With FBSM, the sexual act at the end is expected and paid for in advance, hence each provider stipulating certain criteria in their Ad. 'Please leave the money in a plain open envelope when you enter' is a typical line form any Ad. Or, 'please note that payment for services are for my time only', with no mention of the HJ, hand job realease, as the finale. It's a screwed-up industry in the

USA, controlled by no one in particular. Vice in each city's Police depatments is always undermanned and therefore the thousands of women who practice FBSM are fairly safe as long as they VET their clientele correctly. Ladies who work alone and independently normally ask for references, such as work email, phone number verification, picture verification, employment status. Those who work with agencies or Pimps, and yes, not surprisingly, there are Pimps in this industry, have the vetting process taken care of by those who they split their earnings with. The internet is a good place to vet anyone. Phone numbers, names and ID's are readily available to anyone who takes enough time to check, or double check, so the chances of finding a cop on the prowl to capture one lady is highly unlikely. They are too undermanned, too busy with serious VICE and too uninterested to arrest one housewife/young lady practicing FBSM massage. It's a tough law to enforce so most of the ladies are safe in their career choice.

In the USA, massage, with a happy ending, is classed as a 674B minor charge. A 674B is a citation and is less of a charge than a misdemeanor. A person caught performing FBSM may be cited and then jailed for up to 12 hours, released on their own cognizance, and then, if found guilty, can get up to 6 months' probation and a mandatory AIDS test. And so, those who perform FBSM for a living are driven underground and forced to advertise on sites which are not too well known, or are now being suspended by the FBI, who in most providers opinions, once again, are wasting tax payer's dollars weeding out girls who are just trying to make an honest living. None the less, if charged, a criminal record is an automatic given and is there for life.

A few more facts about the fucked up legal system as it relates to FBSM in the USA. If a man or a woman visits a provider and pays for FBSM and is caught by the police, he or she can be charged with a 647A, which, when translated into simple English, is a charge in relation to offering money to receive a sensual massage or prostitution. Their car can be impounded, only because they drove there to receive this service and yes, a criminal record created in the person's name, for life. The police are also very sneaky and underhand in their pursuit of convictions and it's a common practice for them to make an appointment from an Ad they've seen, show up as if they are a normal John, wired and ready to arrest the masseuse, after trying to trick them into admitting they are providing sexual services. Sometime the officer concerned will be wired and or have a hidden camera. The VICE squad will then crash her apartment and arrest her. In

Orange County California, as an example, there are 9 dedicated officers actively working Sex and Drug investigations. Let me ask you a question? When was the last time you heard of a masseuse committing a serious crime? When was the last time you heard of any serious crime committed by a drug offender or dealer? Exactly! Our system is truly fucked. 9 officers, paid with your tax dollars, making appointments to come to their homes to make arrests just because they pleasure frustrated men?

Backpage.com became huge as a trusted site for these women just because of such scenarios. It was a favorite amongst all providers for many years. Until the middle of 2018, when the Feds moved in and caught them red handed, taking Ad's that involved sex trafficking. Because of this, new laws were drawn up in the USA by congress and with immediate effect, not only was it shut down, Craigslist too had to close all its dating/massage services for the very same reasons.

Backpage.com was unique.

Way back in the day, say 10 years ago, we had Craigslist. Craigslist provided and adequate environment in which ladies could advertise safely and regularly, without issue. All the providers used it. There were very few issues for many years, but then someone got killed going to meet a John, and then it happened again. Safety became a priority and the Feds moved in. This is when Backpage.com, a kind of hole in the wall publication, rose to fame. All the girls switched, if not all, then most, and Backpage.com went from 3 million a year to 150 mil per month in revenue, in the short space of just one year! It was a meteoric rise from nowhere. No one had ever heard of Backpage.com, but now, if you wanted a blow job or a great massage or just a simple date, Backpage.com was the place to get it. They're Ad revenue eclipsed the economies of some small countries, and then, yes you guessed it, the Feds started sniffing around them too. But all was not lost. This was the beginning of Krypto currency, the dawn of a new era, the start of things to come, or so everyone involved believed!

Backpage.com was smart. They determined that if they were being paid in Krypto, it would never be traceable, and they were correct, to a point. The only issue was, they didn't know how to make it happen. And so, as I mentioned already, sometime near the beginning of 2018, the Feds shut it down, leaving tens of thousands of providers without any alternative to advertise their services. Yes, there was Eros.com, HarlotHub.com, TNAboard.com, Adultsearch.com and several other fragmented sites, but Backpage.com was the daddy of all of them and without it, the providers revenues plummeted. Some providers quit, others struggled through bad times not knowing where to turn next. Some new sites came on line, some old ones went bust, but those providers who were determined, survived. And here we are now, in the middle of 2019 and still they await a replacement for the king of all kings, Backpage.com.

The industry itself was thriving and growing exponentially for many years and most of the providers out there had 'shelf lives' of 10 years or more. Since the demise of Backage.com, many ladies are in the business for less than 2 years, find it difficult to gain new clientele and to hang on to repeat customers. When Backpage.com folded, some providers were clever and had kept their repeat client lists on devices they stored in secret places, safety deposit boxes, hard drives etc, but those who didn't suffered. From the UK to Hong Kong to the USA, Backpage.com made a huge difference to all those who used it. The industry now awaits its successor. The King is dead, long live the king.

Fake Names

With Tiana's modeling career still active, although not flourishing as it had been in the years prior to her turning 22, this new job, providing FBSM was a godsend. She could work when she wanted, take time off to model, as required, or just hit the shops or go to a movie if she'd had enough of either profession. First things first though, she was taken by Julia to an apartment she would frequent, on and off, for the next 5 years. It was situated near Baker Street in central London. When Tiana walked into the building, her first impressions were good. It was clean, quiet and central. The entry process was simple, no code required to get in. Once she was inside, and just as Julia was about to show her round the apartment, a door opened from across the inner hallway and out popped a very tiny Asian lady, who, Tiana thought, reminded her of a picture of a Thai goddess she'd once seen hanging at the Tate Gallery in London. Sylvia was stunningly beautiful, so much so, that Tiana felt humbled to be in her presence. Julia introduced them.

"Tiana, this is Sylvia, although she goes by the name of Kitty, for work purposes. Sylvia, this is Tiana, please make her feel at home and show her the ropes and oh, by the way, Tiana, please come up with a work name. We don't want anyone knowing who you really are, do we?"

"Nice to meet you" said Sylvia, as she moved towards Tiana, arms outstretched and gave her a warm hug and kiss on the cheek.

Julia made her excuses and left, and on the way out she turned and said to Tiana, "Oh, Justin will be over later today to take pictures of you for our site. Are you good to hang around for a couple of hours until he arrives?"

"Who's Justin?" Tiana asked

"The BIG BOSS" said Julia, as she rolled her eyes and left, closing the door to the apartment behind her and leaving Tiana in Sylvia's capable hands.

"Let me show you around?" Sylvia suggested, "there are three bedrooms, all with massage tables." She spoke as she walked, opening all 3 doors and taking Tiana into each room. Tiana was really impressed with the cleanliness of this apartment, everything was spotless and fresh looking. Carpets and tile were all clean and sparkling, the bathrooms, one in each bedroom, all 'en-suite', and immaculate, and the kitchen area and living room, nicely decorated and yet again, spotless. 'It was probably cleaned every day', thought Tiana.

"So clean" she said to Sylvia. "yes, we have a cleaner in here three times a day, every day" was her response. 'Wow', thought Tiana, 'that's expensive, but obviously worth it!'

Sylvia then told her that there would be three of them sharing the place. The other lady, Heather, was British and she came in a couple of days a week. Another lovely lady, Sylvia assured her, and one that Tiana would meet in the coming week.

"How long have you been doing this?" Tiana asked.

"3 years, and I am going to keep going until I can afford my yacht!" Sylvia laughed out loud when she said that.

"So the money is good?"

"Extraordinary" said Sylvia, "You will make more in a week here than you would do any other job, unless you are a plastic surgeon or Richard Branson!"

Tiana loved Sylvia's humor. She asked, "Sylvia, since I have never done this before, can you please give me a few pointers to get going?"

"Of course darling. Grab some water from the fridge and take a seat. I know Justin always runs late, so we have time."

"Thanks so much. I am all ears.

And so Sylvia began.

"Let me take you through this from the moment you get the call from a client until the minute the session ends. You will obviously have different requirements for each client as you get to know your regulars, but in general, what I am about to tell you, is common practice for the Agency, so if you stick to this process, not too much can go wrong. I have had some amazing men come in here, some famous, some incredibly good looking, and some," she paused, "well, let's just say taking a bath wouldn't go amiss before they decided showed up." Both ladies laughed out loud and Tiana rolled her eyes towards the back of her head.

"But seriously" Sylvia continued, "it's normally quite good and most of my clients are polite, clean and leave me with enough money to remain happy, content and believing in my yacht."

Sylvia then took Tiana through the routine.

"You take the call from our dispatcher, Madelene, we call her Mads for short, you're then told the time and day they plan to show up. Mads has already vetted them on the phone, remembering this is not an illegal practice, so it doesn't matter here in the UK what they do for a living. We service everyone, doesn't matter creed, color or profession. You just need to insist they treat you with respect.

They arrive, you offer them a beverage, you make some small talk, unless they just want to proceed with their massage, in which case you do the same. Take them into your room, that one over there" she pointed, "tell them to undress and then leave. Give them two to four minutes, come back in by knocking first, and ensuring by that time that you are also fully naked. You can undress in your en-suite, while they undress in the room. You ensure you've told them beforehand to lie on their tummy, then you enter and get your oils, and you begin chatting, if they want to, or you just massage. Now, this next part is entirely up to you. You are very beautiful Tiana, so any man worth his salt will want to stare at your tits, even though they are lying face down on their stomachs. They'll also want to make sure you're fully nude, it's just human nature. They'll steal a glance at your snatch and poossie, so don't be alarmed, they just always behave the same way. You'll also find most men lying on their tummies will not get an erection. This is sometimes changed by you rubbing their balls when they lie in that position, but the secret is not to make them cum too soon. You need to pretend to take your time. They paid for an hour, but 50 mins is the maximum time they get. If you're busy, and the Agency prefers you have back to back appointments, then after 30 min, flip them and make them happy as soon as you can. I've had guys who take 1 minute and guys who take so long, I feel numb from jerking them by the time they decide to ejaculate. Had one guy one time that came after 25 minutes of tossing him off. He was a regular so I didn't mind. The appointment overran by half an hour, Julia was pissed, but my bank account was so happy. That was 2 years ago and he still comes in once a week. You make the judgement call on each one of your clients, don't listen to anyone else's advice, follow your nose so to speak. Then when they cum, and sometimes that is messy as I'm sure you know, you chat with them for a few minutes, cleaning up while you speak and ask them if they'd like to shower. Oh, I completely forgot to tell you, when they arrive, they must leave their payment in the dish on the kitchen counter. You never count it, but you will get a sense over time if you've been short changed. Your tip, should they give you one at the end, you keep on your person or in this room. Once they shower and get dressed, you give them a hug and see them out. Then the fun part begins. You take the sheets from the table, and the towels they used and throw them in the washing machine, taking care to replace them with clean ones from the storage room down the hall. Then you clean the shower, if they've used it, but only after you freshen up. If you have multiple clients you must look and feel fresh to all of them. They all need to believe that they are the first and the last that day. Got it? Any questions?"

Tiana sat and thought, pondering her new career choice and wondering if she'd actually made the right decision. She'd been into all sorts of strange sexual activities over the past few years, so how hard could it be to do this? "Questions?" she said as she looked at Sylvia, 'hmmm, let me think" Just as she was preparing her list, the door opened, and in walked the BIG Boss, Justin.

Justin was 6 feet 2 inches of pure muscle, and Tiana looked at him for a few seconds thinking, 'I wouldn't like to cross this guy" There was something about him that meant trouble, although when he began to chat, he was nice and friendly and Tiana made an immediate connection as her worries of dealing with a tough cookie diminished rapidly. The more Justin spoke, the more comfortable Tiana was. She realized very quickly that this guy was the boss, Julia wasn't as powerful as she'd at first imagined and as Justin explained to her in great detail what was expected of her, Tiana realized that she'd never want to cross this guy. Something inside her knew he would be trouble. "Best to keep on his good side" she thought.

After taking several sexy shots of Tiana, Justin suggested they have a brief chat about expectations. While he'd been taking pictures, he'd been moving her around in and out of erotic poses, to be placed on the company web site. No nude pics were allowed and Tiana was grateful that she didn't have to strip off in front of Justin. She felt that his presence alone made her feel naked.

Justin sat her down on the edge of the massage table in what would eventually be her room.

"T" he began, " I know that Sylvia has gone over most of the things that we expect in the way of conduct, but I would just like to reinforce certain situations so that should you be tempted in any way, you'll think twice before considering going against what we preach"

"OK" She was listening intently.

"1 You never ever have sex with a client. I realize you understand this, but if you do break this rule, not only will they never come back to see you, they got what they wanted, we, as a company, if we ever find out, will terminate you immediately and you will be on your own.

2 You do not date a client. Ever!

3 You have fun and make money"

He was done. He never did speak much, but he was intimidating all the same. He scared Tiana in a way she could not understand. It wasn't fear, it was more respect, a mutual respect. He was good looking, but kind of ordinary in a strange way. He was definitely from someplace in Europe, but she didn't know where. He was, without doubt, strong, both physically and mentally. He was her boss.

"Justin, I completely understand" she said, "I will not let you down." "Good" he replied, "because your first massage will be at 3 PM tomorrow. Do not be late."

And with that he exited the room, the apartment and then the building. It would be weeks before she saw or even spoke to Justin again. Tomorrow would be the beginning of the rest of her life, and she was excited and nervous all in one breath. It was the start of something new and she loved that. She didn't care about anything other than money and she now hoped that she would make enough to do anything she wanted, any time she wanted, for as long as she wanted.

"Roll on 3 PM" she thought, as she walked out of her room and into her future.

Through Tiana's Eyes

I met Alan, the author, on a flight from Seattle to Orange County CA. We sat and chatted for an hour and a half and at the end of our conversation he'd persuaded me to write this book, a book about my life so far, a book that describes all the good and bad that have come from my experiences since I left Estonia as a young lady. I wanted to catalogue everything that had happened to me so that others could learn how I've survived and grown in an industry that swallows girls like me for lunch. It's not been easy, in fact I think it's been a learning experience from the very first day, although some of the learning I've had to endure I would not wish upon any female. My life has now come to a point where I want to try to 'kiss and tell' and make the world aware of what it has taken to be successful in the sex industry. And I use the term 'successful' in the loosest sense of the word. I have been very successful, and to get there I have jumped through many unwanted hoops, rings of fire, and had many other situations that have been uncomfortable, enlightening and undesirable. My stories that follow are all true. They have been handpicked by Alan and I to present you the reader with as close to a first-hand experience of what goes on in the world of FBSM, without actually revealing my true identity or the identity of those who are mentioned in this book. All the characters we have written about have had their names changed, but all these situations were real, very real indeed. Some of the people I have met in the past 8 years are famous, some not so. We have tried to make these stories as accurate as possible, with a little humor thrown in for good measure. It's been a journey that I do not regret, not one single moment, and one that made me an adult well before my time. My sexual exploits have been numerous and when you are reading the following pages, please be aware that we are describing scenes that are normally classed as taboo in most places around the planet. My ideals are varied. I love and always have loved my body. I think I am sensual, I think I am sexy, I know I am attractive, and I have used all these attributes to stay humble but yet move forward in life and make money, lots of money. I am not conceited, I am not big headed and I am not shy in coming forward. I am genuine, as Alan found out when he met me. I believe that sex trafficking should be outlawed and we will get to that either in this book or the books that will follow. I intend to educate any woman who might be thinking of entering this profession, of its up's and downs, and there have been many. I believe in fate, I believe in the energy one creates in one's inner self and that it promotes advancement throughout one's life. I have been blessed to have had such an incredibly unorthodox life, but one which, as I mentioned before, has been financially rewarding. I do realize that life is not all about the money, and honestly, my dream is to have a happy marriage and kids, with the man of my dreams, just like any other woman would want. If that ever happens, then I know my life will have come full circle. Alan asked me at one point, "if you had a daughter would you tell her what you'd done in your past and would you allow her to choose the same career path?" My answer was simple. "If my daughter decided to do what I did, as long as she's happy and safe, I would have no issues at all, and of course, if she wanted to know what I did in my early days, once she's old enough, I would tell her the truth. Same goes for the man who decides to fall in love with me and marry me. He has to know the truth otherwise what kind of marriage would it be?"

Please remember, contrary to what you might believe, I am a normal human being, with normal feelings and a somewhat abnormal lifestyle. Please try not to judge me, but if you do, judge me on merit, not on your own conservative or unconventional beliefs. Sex has been my life and will always be a part of my life, whether I remain single and continue with FBSM, or get married and settle down. Sex is just part of who I am, who we all are, and I have embraced that. My parents do not know what career path I have chosen since ending my modeling career in favor of FBSM, nor do I ever want them to know. That might seem hypocritical to some of you based on what I just said about telling any child of mine in relation to my past but with my mother and father, it's something I do not think they could ever understand. They were brought up in a different era, no internet and no easy access to anything that we all seem to take for granted today. When they grew up, Estonia was part of the Russian empire and also a very poor country. Their understanding of anything that I have done or will do in the future is, in my humble opinion, limited, to say the least. It's best that my exploits in this book are yours to enjoy or to criticize, and not theirs.

FMSM is and always will be part of me. It's now ingrained in my soul. I have stories that will curl your toes in frustration and in angst. I have other stories that will probably disgust you. Some of my experiences have been hilarious, although not at the time they happened, but in general, all of my stories hold some kind of place in my heart, a heart that is beating stronger than ever and hopefully will do so for many years to come.

And so, with all that said, I am going to take you back some 8 years, just after Justin had taken my pictures and placed them on his web site. Just after Julia had told me word for word what their expectations had been and just after Sylvia and I had met. You see, that's when everything became so clear to me, it was like a coming to God, I just knew that this industry was where my future lay and I knew that one day I would write this book and not just 'tell all' but educate, entertain and amaze all of you out there who know it goes on, but were too scared to either try it or learn more about it before you judged. My name is Tiana, you will remember my name for a very long time, longer that you probably care to, but you will remember it all the same. Yes, this book really starts now and it starts with the very first FBSM I ever performed, just 24 hours after signing up for the journey of a lifetime. Enjoy it.

Oliver Arrives On Time

I received my first text message from Maddy in dispatch. It was just like one of those USA cop shows on TV, except this was sexy massage and not "calling car 54, we have a robbery in progress" It was simple and straight to the point.

Tiana, you have Oliver at 3 PM. He has paid by credit card. Good Luck! Mads! xxx

She was hilarious and Mads and I were going to become great friends, but I will leave that story for another chapter. Funnily enough, I wasn't nervous. I'd watched a YouTube video, which frankly was a waste of time. I decided I would be OK with my own version of massage and even though I knew what the ending had to be, I pondered for quite some time if I could put my own slant on a common and garden every day hand job. I'd given my first hand job at 14 and my first blow job at the same age. I used to practice in my bedroom in my parents' home in Tartu. I would take carrots from the pantry in our kitchen and use them to master my technique. At one stage my poor mother thought I was a vegetarian because every time she came in to clean my room, 6 or 7 'used' carrots lay rotting in my trash can. She took me aside one afternoon and asked me why I never ate the carrots. I told her I had tooth ache and that every time I thought it was better, I'd try another one, only to be out matched by recurring pain in my gums. Well, with a sudden jerk she grabbed my hand and marched me to her dentist friend Sergey, who, after looking inside my mouth, and also at my tits, fucking pervert, guaranteed my mother there was nothing wrong with me. After that episode, I decided that after each 'blow job' practice session, I would with eat the carrot or dispose of it outside at a later date. I'm convinced these early episodes in sexual enhancement with veggies led me to be the vegan I am today.

In any event, to put a new slant on a hand job, no matter how hard I tried to be different, just didn't seem possible. And, as I sat and waited for Oliver's arrival, I tried to figure out what else I could do other than rub gently, I mean, erection = ejaculation and after gentle rubbing with lotion for lubrication, nature takes care of the rest. How can it be varied? Unless by oral stimulation, and that was just out of the question. I had been warned.

The doorbell rang, I answered, and in he marched. Mr. Oliver, all dressed up in his Saville Row suit, shirt and tie. "Handsome" I thought, "Very Handsome"

We hugged, like the long-lost friends we were not.

I spoke.

"Oliver, nice to meet you, I am Tiana and I am looking forward to making you happy and relaxed today"

"Tiana, you're not what I expected. You're just more beautiful than your pictures"

"Ha! Flattery will get you everywhere Oliver!" 'but it's not going to get you anything other than a regular hand job', I thought to myself. Geez, if they are all going to flatter me, my head would just grow and grow, so without further adue, I ushered Oliver into my massage room. "Please undress Oliver and I'll be back shortly" I said.

"It's fine Tiana, you can stay, I am happy for you to watch"

'Ok', I thought, 'does his suggestion break any of our rules?' I decided not, and as he took off one piece of clothing at a time, in what seemed like an eternity, I undressed too. I had no qualms about showing off my perky tits and shaved snatch, in fact I can be quite the exhibitionist at times. I watched him remove his last sock as he was rambling on about some stupid taxi driver who'd gone the wrong way and had nearly made him late, and when he'd done undressing and had that stare, you know, THAT stare, all men do it, they try not to be obvious, but they want to be sure your body is as perfect as they'd imagined and that your snatch is cleanly shaved and your tits to their satisfaction, yes, THAT stare, I casually looked at him straight in his eyes and I pouted both of my perfect pert breasts upwards as I stretched my arms readying myself for the action to come. He ogled me for more than a few seconds, decided not to delay and lay face down on my table. 'A true Pro' I thought, and so began my first FBSM session

32

and our, not too strained conversation, which went something like this.

"Have you had a busy day Oliver? I asked

He responded with a grunt, and I knew then, this would not be as enlightening as I believed it should or could be. Oliver was flat on his stomach, not really communicating and not really desirous of any kind of conversation. 'Fine by me' I thought and carried on with the massage. Now, in all the years I have been doing this, I have never once, not once, used a clock to time my clients sessions. I do not want to have clocks, watches or phones visible when doing massage. I want each client to feel unrushed and pampered, even though they might only be with me for 30 minutes, I want them to feel that it's been like an hour and they've had the best time of their life in that 30 minutes. With Oliver, as I was a rookie and had never done this before, I felt that I'd been massaging him for about 35 minutes. My head told me it was 35 minutes, but my arms felt like it had been over an hour. Oliver was engrossed and making all the right noises, so, I asked him to flip. He was hard as a rock, something that made me smile. Either he just loved my tits or he loved my tits and my touch. I certainly hoped it was both. I took out the bottle containing the oil and pretended to look at his chest and his stomach, while all the time reaching for his erection. I massaged it gently, I smiled at him, I massaged it some more. He was so hard, I believed he was going to explode, and sure enough, two or three more strokes and BOOM! There he went, All over my arms and the sheets. It was a fountain of sperm, rounded of by a huge moaning climax, yes, he was a screamer of sorts, which made me even happier. I had hit the jackpot, or should I say the sperm pot, and after a few more seconds, Oliver settled down to just a sigh and look of relief and contentment, spread all over his happy face.

"Are you feeling relaxed now?" I asked

"That was excellent, thank you" he gasped

I was covered in cum, all warm and gooey, but it didn't disgust me as much as I thought it would. I've had warm cum all over my body many times, I have swallowed it many times, too many to remember, but this was different. This was fast, this was, a complete stranger and one who I would probably never see again and this was for money. I really believed that Oliver had had his money's worth, I believed that his paid hour had flown past and with that in mind, I made my way to the kitchen to wash myself and he got up and made his way to the adjacent bathroom to shower. It was only when I got outside of that room and looked at the kitchen clock that I realized we'd only been going 20 minutes! '20 minutes' I thought to myself, 'oh fuck, what am I going to do now? He paid for an hour, they told me get him out in 45 minutes. Fuck, Fuck, Fuck' But while I was washing my arms and my hands, ranting endlessly under my breath, Oliver walked out, semi dressed, (his jacket and tie were under his arm and not on his person), smiling and walking towards me, ready to give me a hug and leave. 'Surely it can't be over?', I thought. But it was. He said his goodbyes, and then he left, straight out the door, no complaints, no regrets. Money was secure in the envelope, so no issues there, but I honestly couldn't believe that there would be no repercussions. After all, I just swindled him out of 40 minutes. I was sure I'd never hear the end of this from Justin or Julia. That being said, before I had time to think any more about what just happened, my phone started to vibrate and Madds was texting me two more appointments, one arriving in the next 30 minutes and then one more two hours later.

Text message: T you have two more on the way. One in 30 and the other at 7. Call me.

I picked up the phone to call her, ready for her onslaught.

I want to tell you about Madds. She's a hoot, a friend and a real character. She sums up what's great about the English culture and yet she typifies none of that culture. She's unique in every way and I will dedicate the next chapter just to her.

My Friend Madds

'It's a warm sunny springtime day here in Anaheim California as Tiana and I sit outside a Starbucks close to the Honda Center, where in about 2 hours' time, 'March Madness' basketball will get underway. There are a few people milling around with Michigan shirts and a few others with what look like Texas shirts, but I'm not really interested in them. My interest lies in Tiana and asking relevant questions that will lead me, I hope, to uncovering exactly what makes this young lady tick. We have covered a lot of ground already, some of which I've written about, but every time I ask another question, it leads us down another path that's more mind-blowing than the previous road we've already traveled. She sips her 'Americana' coffee, black of course, and she looks and acts like any other young lady who is 30 years old, dressed casually in her white tee shirt, no bra and leggings, covering her pretty face with large framed sunglasses and a baseball cap that screams "Hollywood", and indeed has that very word embroidered on the back of the hat. She has no make-up on, she doesn't need it, her natural beauty is one of her greatest assets, but she does wear lip gloss and maybe a smidgeon of eye shadow. I am entertained by her ability to shock me with straight answers to my very direct line of questioning, but today, after we have a little banter and chit chat back and forth, I decide to ask her one or two things that I think might upset her. Being a very direct person myself, it's no big deal for me to just spout out something that comes up in my mind which I feel might be of interest to my readers, and so, with Tiana's attention full on, I ask her,

"How many men would you say you've slept with?"

There's a kind of eerie silence for a few seconds as she ponders that question, throwing her head back and looking towards the sky as if to begin the math. She takes not too much longer to state,

"I lost count a long time ago"

"Is it hundreds?" I persisted

"Oh yes, and probably many hundreds"

"And in all that time Tiana, with all those men, you've never contracted any diseases?"

"Nope" She was blunt and to the point.

"And the drugs, were you addicted? Did you blow all your earnings on that kind of lifestyle?"

"I don't get addicted to anything" she noted, "I take my own body with my own mind and when I have had enough, I stop. Counseling is not for me, I am able to make my body do what I want it to do"

This is something I can relate to myself, although I have never done drugs of any kind, I know what it takes to be self-disciplined and willing to stop something you are addicted to, in my case, chocolate. Tiana then spoke again.

"When I lived in London, and was modeling, drugs was just part of the culture, but when I joined the 'Agency' and began massage, the money I was making was more than I had ever earned before, and the temptation to binge was even greater than when I was modeling. I even joined a site called Sugar Daddy, which Julia told me about and which I will discuss with you another time, but massaging rich men dressed in expensive, and their ability to tip me big bucks without thinking too much about making a dent in their own wallets, drugs, more sex and a raucous life style were inevitable. Which brings me on to Maddie. Maddie was the dispatcher for the Agency. At first I thought she was dispatching from their London office, but soon I realized she lived in Swindon, a town about 40 miles to the west of London. I also didn't know that the agency had 4 or 5 different apartments, some in the City of London, and other's in the suburbs of London. Madds was just one of three dispatchers, but she and I had a strained relationship, to say the least.

Tiana placed her coffee cup on the iron table where we sat, and handed me a recording. "Go home and listen to this and you'll learn a lot about Madds."

So I did, and this is what I learned.

"Madds was a booker/dispatcher, but no one in their right mind should ever have put her in that position. The agency used to place Ad's on various sites such as Backpage.com and Craigslist, where Escorts and Massage ladies were prevalent. The agency had 3 bookers/dispatchers, two in London and Madds, who lived in Swindon. They all had at least 5 cell phones each, one for each of the girls they looked after and when they placed Ad's for all the girls, the phone number for each girl was different. Madds had to remember which phone went with each girl, and as she wasn't the brightest light in the lamp, she decided to number them accordingly. The agency didn't want anyone to know that we, the girls, belonged to an agency, men really wanted to book independent women, I have no idea why, but this is what Justin told us, probably to scare us off taking the clients for ourselves and cutting the agency out, so they made it look like each of us worked alone, with no connection to any company or to any other girl. Two of the bookers were Eastern European, Madds was English. The other two, Jennifer and Desirae, came from Ukraine, and both were very efficient. I was assigned Maddie, and boy did she make my life difficult. I think she was going through menopause, and if not, she was just a total psycho bitch, and a natural one at that. She used to shout at the clients. "You get a massage Babes, you don't get to fuck her. If you want to fuck her, you'll need to be on the billionaire scale and not just the pauper you are and always will be" She couldn't communicate to save her soul. Unorganized, inefficient, rude, moody, and often very nice. She took being bi-polar to a new level. She'd text me while she was driving, and nothing made sense,

Text message; book at 1, horny as fuck, don't make him wait

"I mean, WTF is that supposed to mean, so I would call her. "Madds" I'd say, "WTF is that text supposed to mean??" "Oh hi babes" she loved that word, everyone was Babes, even her dog, "It's a booking," I'd just stare at the phone and think to myself, 'I know it's a fucking booking you stupid bitch, but what is horny as fuck and why would he wait.?' And then I would find out that she's been using her voice to dictate that message and it would really mean

BOOKING AT 1, SHE WAS HORNY AS FUCK And then, Don't be late. Bi-polar to the extreme!

I was exasperated. She'd do this all the time. She made life so difficult. Whoever was last out of the apartment at night had to make sure it was left in pristine condition for the first one in the next morning, we began at 11, so all the candles, the towels, the sheets, had to be replaced the night before, and when the doors opened at 11, there was nothing to do other than greet the first guest. Things didn't always run smoothly though, and we often had issues. I'd arrive at 10.50AM and receive a text from Madds saying I had a client at 11 and when I walked into the apartment the place would be a mess, no one having cleaned up the night before. The guy would show up while I was trying to make the place respectable and Madds would be on the phone asking me why I wasn't letting him in and telling me at the same time that she'd just had her nails done and was going to text me a picture of her new color, all of this while I am in a panic trying to set things up and the buzzer is continually ringing for the guy waiting patiently downstairs to come up. She was a complete mess, from top to bottom. She was also Julia's best friend in life, so there was no way they'd every fire her, but the clients started to get pissed off because of the way she spoke to them, and when they'd show up for their massage, you could tell that they realized it wasn't me they were talking to when they arranged their massage, it was her! Most of them were good about it, after thinking their massage was going to be with a real bitch, but some of them decided not to show up after Madds had abused them on the phone, both by text and by voice. How she ever got away with any of it, I will never know, but the other 2 bookers had no issues like that and no matter how hard I tried to get switched to one of them, my requests always fell on deaf ears. Best story ever though was when one guy showed up expecting to see Sylvia, and got me. His confusion and my confusion was compounded by the fact that Madds was confused too and had inadvertently switched the phones and answered the one that had been number 3, thinking it was number 5. After that experience, she labeled them with names and not numbers, but even that failed to stop her inability to recognize who she was answering for and confusion reigned for many months until all of us got fed up with her and decided to do our own thing, but that story is for another day."

Back at Starbucks, Tiana has finished her coffee, and it's now around 72*, with the sun beating down on my back. She asks me if I know what a prostate massage is? I tell her I have no clue, and so begins another account of a situation she'd found herself in by error.

Julia had called her to tell her that she'd received a message from Sugar Daddy, with some rich guy wanting to take her shopping, something Julia could never refuse. She was a shopaholic, especially when a 'sugar daddy' was paying. "T, can you fill in for me over at the place in Farringdon at 4PM, I am off to shop with a potential 'daddy' and need covering, please, please please?"

Didn't leave me much choice and we always helped one another out, so I agreed. "Anything I should know about him Julia and what do I tell him when he shows up and sees that I am not you?" "You'll be fine darling, we look alike!"

Look alike?? She was blonde, huge fake tits, and bloated lips, I was thin, natural boobs and a redhead!

"He's paid for two hours T, please make him happy" 2 hours was a very long time, longer than Anything I had done in the first two weeks of being with this agency. I had no idea what I could do to pass that amount of time, and with that in mind, I got on the tube to Farringdon, where I'd await this gentleman's arrival.

Very distinguished, grey haired and dressed beautifully, that's how I'd describe the gentleman who arrived at the Farringdon apartment. He was 15 minutes early and immaculate. Shirt neatly pressed, tie, diagonal stripes and in coordination with his jacket color, handkerchief in his top outside jacket pocket, well-groomed mustache, also grey, and the he opened his mouth. One thing that I have always disliked is British dental work. It's just crap. Even Estonia is more up to date in that department, and we are a 3rd world country in comparison to the UK.

"You're not the lady in the picture" he said. He sounded like the Prime Minister, so polite and well spoken, but as soon as I looked at his teeth, his words passed straight though me and into another dimension. '2 hours of looking at that brown disfigured mess?' I nearly puked.

"Well I changed my hair and colored it red. You OK with that Sweetie?" I asked him. I figured he'd be around 75 and so probably had difficulty remembering what he did last night never mind who's pic he was looking at. He sort of hummed and hawed and then acquiesced.

"You'll do I suppose"
Like he was doing me a favor, which technically he was, a 240 UK pounds favor. I asked him very nicely to strip off and take a shower. I wasn't sure if I could handle the stench of his Paco Roban aftershave, so politely I suggested he washes thoroughly because I had an allergy to his choice of scent. He didn't argue much, sort of grumpy uninterested and decidedly offended look as he vanished into the shower. I undressed, slowly, leaving my underwear on, just

in case he decided to abort the massage, which often happened when men showed up and realized I wasn't the girl in the pictures they'd seen on line on our website. In fact, after working with the agency for a couple of months, I decided to Google myself and I found that the images on line were not of me. I have no idea why, nor did I ever ask, and to this day I don't know why Justin even took pictures of me on my first day because he never used them. Same thing applied to the other girls I knew. Standard images of God only knows who, were placed on the internet, so I'm amazed that when guys showed up they didn't cancel more often than they did.

The old guy came out the shower, I asked him to get on the table, the massage table and he looked at me as if to say, 'you know what I want, why am I getting on there?'

"Is something wrong?" I asked

"You said you'd tie me up first!"

Tie him up? Bloody Julia. What a cunt. She'd left me with a man old enough to be my grandfather and now that man wanted to be tied up?? What the fuck was I supposed to do?

"You said you had ropes, and that you'd tie me to the bed and then….."

And then what?? I wanted to leave the room and call Julia, but I couldn't. I had no idea what to do. It was my second week in the job, no one had ever asked to be tied up before, and I had no rope.

"Well can we start with just massage on your back and go from there?" I hoped he'd agree, and yet again, with a huff and a puff, he sort of nodded his head in the affirmative, although I could see he was really disappointed. He'd already left his money in the envelope when he'd arrived so I had no qualms about him walking out. I'd been paid and he couldn't take it back, could he? After 15 minutes of inhaling the aftermath of his Paco scent, I thought to myself, '2 hours of this and I'll be dead. I need to speed it up and kick him out'

"You ever had a prostate massage?" I asked him. He was still face down but from the reaction I could hear, he had no idea what I was talking about. "wait here" I begged, and I left the room to find some towels and a condom.

Prostate massage is a practiced technique and not all providers can do it properly and comfortably. It takes skill and patience, a little like fingering a woman's clit and vagina. Most men will just shoot to the heart of the vagina with their finger or fingers and completely ignore that woman's needs. A gentle persuasion is required around the clitoris and short stimulation around the labia too. This will enhance any woman's expectations and final orgasm, if done properly and carefully. Same applied to prostate massage. Condom on one finger, caress the butt hole before entry and then with one hand on the penis and a finger on the prostate, man in the downward dog position, kaboom! Success 99% of the time with incredible all-round gratification.

I walked back into the room. He was getting antsy.

"OK listen up" I put on my Sargent Major voice, which often intimidated men into submission under any circumstance. It worked a treat. He froze.

I positioned him on the table and told him to relax. There was a certain amount of panic in his voice.

"What are you going to do to me?

"Relax, you'll love this."

Only 15 minutes had passed since he'd arrived. I knew if I did this correctly, another five minutes would be all I'd need.

I placed the condom on my right index finger. He was looking at me as if I was about to strangle him. I began to massage his ageing butt hole, very gently at first and then, after applying some lubricant, with a little more vigor. I could tell from the noises he'd started making that he was enjoying this immensely, and so, without further hesitation, I grabbed his penis with my left hand, entered his butt with my right index finger, locating his prostate and massaging it with a circular clockwise movement, which I knew from experience to be the best way to make him happy. As I tugged his cock, he exploded and screamed out loud, "Fuck, Fuuuuukkkkkkk, FUCK!!!!" and he came, probably with more passion than ever in his entire life before. I thought he was going to have a coronary, but that proved not to be the case. He fell flat on his face on the table. He was done. He couldn't speak. Breathless, he looked back towards me, not angrily, but inquisitively, as if to say, 'what the fuck just happened?' I smiled, and said to him quite casually, "I presume you enjoyed that sir? Shower is over there as you already know. Get cleaned up and dressed and I will be right back" The whole thing had taken 22 minutes, men do tend to cum quickly when I do this procedure to them, and he didn't complain once. He showered and left. He even gave me and extra 100 pounds tip, not bad for 22 minutes work. Julia would never hear the end of this. To leave me in the lurch like that was irresponsible and when eventually I got hold of her and asked her about the tying him up with ropes experience, all she could say was, "Sorry sweets, I forgot"

Bitch.

What Makes Me Tick

I've often wondered what would have happened had I not had the incline to leave Estonia. My parents still live there, but they know nothing about what I do or what I've done. My aim was to get to LA, something I hoped to achieve without the fuss of telling them or involving them in my life, either emotionally or financially. They are simple people, not worldly like me, and they would have their hearts broken if they ever knew what I did after I left them. Modeling for me was my 'get out' and FMSM my financial savior, except I blew everything I made as soon as I made it. I was raking in about 700 UK pounds per day after starting FBSM, and it had only been a few weeks. Yes, there might be days where nothing happened, and sometimes even weeks, I would sit around hoping the phone would ring, but it never did. And on other days, I would be so busy I wouldn't even have time for food. Yes, no food, and that was difficult. I could do 9 or 10 massages in the one day, I think 10 or 11 might be my record, but not once did I ever think I'd be better suited doing it on my own and not once did I ever grudge the agency, Justin, his 50%. I always reckoned that he did all the hard work and covered my ass if anything went wrong, so why 'fix it if it ain't broke', as they say in the movies. Ah yes, Hollywood. The hankering to get there and live there just never went away. London was fine, but to stay sane I used to move home very 12 months. I was claustrophobic in that sense, and felt that a change of scenery would alleviate all my hankerings to run away to America, especially LA, city of all my dreams. Los Angeles had burned a hole in my heart, a good hole and I couldn't take my mind off my ambition to be there full time. But would it ever happen? I sometimes had my doubts, doubts that were amplified every time I would have an American man come in for a massage. It happened once in a while and just the thought of trying to make conversation in the hope they would like me, take me away and marry me so I could live there, was overwhelming. Yes, I am a dreamer, but a solid dreamer and my dreams never turn to nightmares, at least not yet. My ambitions were overtaken by reality, the reality of living in the UK, and living quite comfortably at that, as opposed to throwing in the towel and just boarding a plane to California in the hope that when I arrived, it all just worked out. America was such a difficult place to obtain entry from a foreigner's perspective, and to me, the only way to make it happen would be to marry a citizen, and I was millions of miles away from ever doing that. I was limited to a tourist visa, which gave me 3 months max, and the thought of having to leave once I arrived, was really heartbreaking.

Back in London, I soon discovered I had a real knack for this FBSM gig. All of the men I massaged, without exception, loved me. They loved the way I spoke, they loved my body and they always loved the way I 'jerked' them off at the end. I had been working for about a month before I received my first real proposition, which came by way of an older gentleman who insisted that I should run away with him and be his mistress forever and a day. We clicked the moment we met, but I knew he was married, and he didn't try too hard to hide that fact. He wanted to fuck me so badly. When I flip a guy over to reveal his erection, I of course am fully naked. I always shaved my snatch, just like they told me to do when I joined the agency, and so with my perfect tities and a shaved poosie, there isn't ever much between me and they guy with the erection. I knew they all wanted to fuck me, they knew they wanted to fuck me, but we both knew it was never going to happen. I had no feelings for any of them, well, that was until a certain German walked into my life a few months later, but in the meantime, it was just a job to me, and a fantasy to them. They were all turned on, and I was just… well I was just me. They would lie with their penis at full staff, I would climb on their front, sort of at the top of their legs, holding their hardness, and I would rub, rub them up and down, and rub them against my wetness. Some tried to get more by pushing against me to see if they could 'slip' it inside me, and others would just gaze at my tits. Either way, no one every fucked me and everyone left happy. My repeat clients always thought that by returning they would get to that 'next base', but they had no chance, none at all. I mean I wasn't a virgin, in fact I don't recall if I ever was a virgin! I think I was born without a hymen and God just wanted me to pleasure as many men as I could before I settled down to have babies, should that ever happen. I have no qualms about my sexuality, or who I've fucked, but the guys who were clients did nothing for me, and even though they thought I was wet because of them, I wasn't, it was all just baby oil! I rarely felt dirty, I never felt abused and I always went home happy. That may have been the cocaine, a habit I will come to in this book, and one which started in my mid 20's or it may just have been the cash, most of which I blew on cocaine and wild partying, again something I will discuss later in the book, but for now, my happiness was of my own making and I often had hapenis in my grasp ;-)

That was my joke for the day, sorry if it's an old one. Me and the girls in the apartment were of similar ilk. We just wanted cash, the more the better. I don't think any of us saved money, we spent like it was going out of fashion, but we enjoyed what we did with that money, even though most of it ended up our nose in one magic drug or another. I was often so high, I believed I was on mars. I once said to Sylvia, they should sell morphine suppositories because that way she could stuff one up my ass which would then be higher than my elbows! We had some great nights out and some fun days in. My whole life revolved around this FBSM lark, which is exactly what it had turned into, a lark. The words for that in Estonian were MILLE Lark, and I used that term all the time when I was high, but I was rarely dry. Sex was easy, only because I like to give. I would pick guys up in bars and fuck them. I would meet random guys and do the same, but in general, it was all meaningless sex. Sex is a turn on for me with the right person, but gratuitous sex can also be a turn on, and not just for guys. All the girls loved that kind of competition. Who could or would fuck the most guys that week or weekend. I rarely lost. All of this made me tick. Maybe I was lost in life, just a little, but I always believed I could stop whenever I wanted, and I always had the courage to admit who I was and what I was. People talk about warm-blooded males. I am a super-hot redhead. I know what God presented to me on the day I was born. Great legs, great tits, great personality and a perfect poosie that requires regular fucking by perfect cocks, preferably large. I love to be admired, adored, and spoilt, what woman doesn't, but more than anything, I love to be fucked, and fucked by a real man and not some wimp who tries hard to make it feel like a true love scene and not a porno movie. Fucking is fucking, love making is for wimps, unless I am talking about that German, but again, that's for another day. My other turn-ons are clothes and drugs. Eventually I would cease to desire either as I matured into the woman I have now become. My goals in life were ever changing. When I was a teenager, I craved nothing but attention and fucking. In my twenties, I craved fucking and drugs, so in my 30's, which have just begun, my cravings have yet to be set in stone, but I do still like to be fucked so I'm sure when I get through the 30's and look back, fucking will still be up there.

Inside our little apartment off the Edgeware Road in London, so much went on every day. It would be one drama after another, followed by more of the same. Nonstop fun and games, and when I remember some of the stories I am about to tell you, I still cannot believe we never got into more trouble than we actually did. Indeed, I often think that we were all lucky to survive intact, but really, most of the men who came through that door were super nice and very generous. Yes, they had fetishes, yes, they had perversions, but it was all quite innocent in comparison to the Estonian orgies in my teen years. Those were interesting to say the least, but the guys in London never really pushed me into thinking I would get close to the perversion of those teen years, nor did they force themselves onto me like the Estonians had. It was a really tame profession, with the occasional fountain of cum that some men ejaculated after going months without a release of any kind. I saw good looking guys, ugly guys, old guys, young guys, sad guys, happy guys, black, white, yellow, Muslim, Jewish, Christian, and they all ended up the same, they ejaculated which cum and left happy. Oh, yes, I got paid handsomely to jerk off anyone who wanted a cheap thrill, but the only thrill for me was the money, and it still is!

The Money

50% of something large is better that 0% of nothing at all. Estonia was my schooling, from the tender age of 11, when one of the boys at school tried to kiss me during lunch break. I told him if he paid me 5 Kroon, I would gladly stick my tongue down his throat. He ran! I never got paid, but I got the gist of what it took to get ahead, and then later in life I understood what it meant to give head! Both were the same and had the same meaning to me, defined only by age, money and desire. When I got paid, in my teen years, there wasn't much to buy in Estonia, and so I was lured in by what everyone else was doing, drugs. Hard, soft, pills, powders, it didn't matter. My boyfriend, the one who was old enough to be my father, instigated my love for banned substances and the cash I made fed both our insatiable habits. These were wild times, but yet when I look back, my innocence fueled my ambition to be this person I felt I should be and not the person I was. I just wanted to fit in, be part of the crowd I mingled with and really, get laid, get high and get on with life. Sex really didn't serve a purpose other than to appease my hormones, that were raging like a wildfire inside my head. Drugs didn't serve a purpose other than to help me fit in with people I'd never see again and to look cool, and all of this, before I was 16. Money, money, money. More came and more was spent, and at 16 when I bought my own ticket to fly to London, the money kept on coming. It got better and better, and I really believed at the end of every week, when I had tons of cash in my pockets, under my mattress, in my handbags, that I was a big shot, untouchable and bulletproof. Gosh, when I look back on those days now, from the position in life that I currently occupy, how stupid I was, how naive, how ridiculously immature and lucky not to be in jail, pregnant or just a washed-up druggie.

Fortune shone upon my being, and for that I will always be eternally grateful.

But back to the money. When I had money, it seemed to just disappear. In the beginning, my man in Estonia was instrumental in trying to help me NOT spend it, but I was a lost cause and did so without caring about him or about how much I was blowing on senseless living. I was far too young to understand and I firmly believed that whatever he did for me was the right thing, but I never listened. He wasn't my father by any means, but he acted like one. He was rich and helpful, I just didn't listen, or maybe I just didn't want to. Remember, he was 32, I was 14, but I honestly though I loved him, I still do, he's never far from my thoughts or my feelings, but yet, I have not seen him in 15 years. It's strange how his presence has lingered, and hung around, and I think about him every day, almost. He did what he did, I did what I did, and it all just came together and then petered out. He never took advantage, at least it seemed that way, he never pushed me away, we just grew apart, and now? Well, he's probably found the next Tiana and is screwing her just like he did with me. Who knows? His penis was wonderful by the way, as was our sex, which I mentioned earlier.

I got to London and got my first modeling job and then got paid and it was a shock to me just how much money I had in my pocket that was actually mine, not my parents, not my boyfriend's, just mine. No one was spending it for me, and with that in mind, I decided that something was truly wrong because I shouldn't have that much cash lying around. I never declared any of it, I have paid no taxes in all the years I've been doing this, so what does a pretty 16-year-old do in London with lots of money? Spend it, of course! The parties started, the drugs flowed freely, and life began to spiral out of control, with me thinking I was in full control. I bought clothes, more drugs, fancy dinners, more drugs, champagne, and yet more drugs. I shared the wealth. Yes, there were men, who also contributed, but in general, the other ladies in my shared accommodation, and I, pooled our new-found wealth and just partied all the time. It was fun, exciting and often scary. Scary because we did things that were frowned upon by society but totally accepted by all of us in that house. We shared food, money, cocaine, clothes and yes, even men. There were men who slept with one of us, some of us or all of us, and we paid them to be there! Money was my inspiration, my nemesis, and also my downfall in many ways, but it made me tick, because when I grew up in Estonia, we never had enough to go around, not even for food.

When the massage job with the agency was in full flow, the money was even better, and again, all cash. I felt cool, comfortable, safe, indestructible. Once again, spending willingly and irresponsibly, although I didn't realize it at the time, until I had no money left to burn. When that happened, I went out and made even more, then spent it all again. Hence that vicious cycle of want, want and want.

LA though was still on my mind. I believed, rightly or wrongly, that even though I was doing well, making tons of cash, that when and if, and it was a huge IF, I ever got to LA, that is where I would come into real wealth. My dreams told me this and my ambition carried me all the way into firm belief. That belief never died, it spurred me on and held me true, and so when I spent what I had, and then made it all over again, I had this deep-down knowledge, albeit a dream, that one day in LA, I would be super rich and extremely responsible to boot.

My only concern? It was taking me too long to get to LA, and yet, I was only 22. So young, so mature in many ways, and immature in others, but so committed to getting to my dream destination, with, some cash and some of my mind still in place.

Extraordinary Facts

We're back at our favorite Starbucks, and having written quite a bit since we last met, which was only a few days ago, Tiana shows up chirpy and full of joy. Today she opts for the cropped top and leather jacket with jeans look. Sexy, but also classy. No matter how I look at her, I am always interested to see if there's a dark side to this lady, but so far, I have yet to find one. I know she's just spent the past two days at a beach hotel, practicing FBSM with probably 10 or more clients, some of who would be regulars. It can't be much fun doing that, but she looks content.

"You look happy" I said

"Of course, I just spent 2 days at Marina Del Ray, and I made over $2000 in cash, why wouldn't I be happy?"

Tiana, I have decided, really admires herself. She has certain mannerisms which lead me to believe that she's always been fond of her looks, but none that are more reaffirming than the way she studies her reflection on the glass windows at Starbucks, continually grooming and then re-grooming her red hair. She is very particular when it comes to her appearance, probably a derivative of her modeling days, and on occasion I will receive a certain look, eyes wide open, a sort of gaze in her stare, saying, look at me closely, I am beautiful'

When I tell her these things, she laughs, and brushes my suggestions to one side, denying any culpability towards her, often delightful, behaviors. We move on.

She begins,

"I'd like to tell you about an experience that I had when I was around 19 years of age." I am all ears.

She continues, "I was lonely in London, not lonely, more bored. I wanted a change. My heart had always been in dance, and in acting. I was in a meeting with my UK agent at the time and suddenly out of nowhere he asks me, "You're from Estonia, correct?" I told him of course, but he already knew that. He asked again, "didn't you want to try acting and dance?", again, I told him yes, and then he proceeded to show me an Ad for a position at this school of dance in the city of Tallinn, Estonia. The dance company was famous, I knew that, and after a little thought and discussion that lasted about ten minutes, he agreed he'd put my name forward and see if he could get me a trial. This was kind of a dream for me. To model was wonderful, but to dance…" Her voice tapered off and there again was one of her little mannerisms as I could see her mind slipping right back into her past, and her thoughts of wherever she'd been that particular day, come flooding right bang smack into our conversation.

"I had the money, I knew in my heart I wanted to try this, but my only reservation was leaving London to return to Estonia. I always believed that once you were out, you were out and my dream of LA would be a pipe dream, should I venture to return to where I'd come from, Estonia. But time was of the essence and I never imagined that should I decide to go to this dance school, I'd be stuck in Estonia forever and a day. They must travel the globe as a group, correct? Well I was off. I packed my bags and I left. This next 6 months turned out to have a very influential part to play in my life, both then, and now. It was June in Estonia, so it was warm and the days were long. I loved the fact that I could get up early, and go to bed really late, all in daylight. The dance school was in the center of Tallinn and its classes ran from 8 Am every day, except Sunday, to 6 PM. I found a place to stay, which took no time at all, and went immediately to the school to meet the man who would eventually become one of my closest friends in life.

Maksim was about 20 years older than I was. He was gay, but I didn't know that at first. He was the lead dance instructor for the Tallinna School of Dance. He had over 200 students in this school, all of whom were experienced, or had a background in dance. I was a model, not a dancer, and although I'd practiced dance as a child, this was a long shot for me, hoping to keep up with those who had lived and breathed dance all their lives would be difficult. The students ranged from 12 to 25 years of age, and the competition, as I was about to find out, was tough."

Tiana looking into the windows at Starbucks again, checking her hair and puffing out her chest. I am getting used to these actions, and they are beginning to amuse me, so I asked her outright, "Do you like yourself?" "I LOVE myself" she responded, which I then told her was exactly the answer I was thinking she'd give me. She does love herself and is extremely comfortable with who she actually is. Nothing phases her. Any questions I ask are answered directly and truthfully without shame or embarrassment and this is something I have grown to like about her. She admits that she's done things in life just to 'get ahead', none of which she regrets, and she admits this without the slightest embarrassment. I asked her today, "what's your opinion on sex?" knowing that she's slept with hundreds of men. Her response was this, "sex is a currency for me, I use it to buy what I want or need" Her candor is admirable, to say the least, but her answers are honest, and I can tell that they are completely unrehearsed.

"I was coming home from school one evening, I remember that Maksim and I had this incredible bonding session where he's admitted to me that he was gay and told me other very interesting facts about himself, something that had nothing to do with dance, and I was happy, happier than I'd been in London because I knew that he and I had the possibility to become great friends. He knew it too, but never admitted it until a few weeks later when we went to dinner and pleaded undying love for one another, friends only of course, remember he was gay!" as she said that, she laughed. "So, I was strolling along one of Tallinn's main thoroughfares, the sun was out, the sky was clear, I had on high heels, I always look sexy in heels, and leggings. I had a cropped top on, much like the one I have on today and no bra, remember, women in Europe love to discard their bra's in summer. My tits were bouncing, my headlights were on, code for hard nipples"

I just nodded

"Suddenly, from behind me, I heard these words, blurted out in Russian."

The scene is now set, Tiana licks her lips, as if she's relishing what's to some in the way of a great story, she tilts her head back and begins.

"Let's call him Mr. X."

"Call who" I asked

"You'll see. Just listen." she commanded.

"It was kind of cheesy. He said it in Russian, which was unusual, because not too many men spoke Russian in Estonia, well not in public anyway, oh, and he was getting out of his car at the time. His voice was deep and the words simple. It was sort of, what's a nice girl like you doing in a place like this? But more, nice shoes, nice body kind of thing. I looked round and I was shocked. I knew him! "

"Who was he?" I demanded to know.

"Well, he was one of the most well-known politicians in Estonia. I mean VERY well-known. His face was plastered everywhere. He was on TV every night on the news and on talk shows. He was in newspapers, magazines and blogs. You could see him talking with famous people all the time. I was sure it was him, Mr X, so I walked up to the car he was exiting and took a closer look. Are you....

"Yes I am", I was blushing and I knew it.

"You are very beautiful, I would like to buy you dinner"

"I am not sure that would be a good idea" I knew he was married with kids. But he insisted and I agreed. We went out the following night for dinner and thus began the craziest relationship I have ever had. We kept it so secret, or at least we thought we did. We would go to dinner and weekends away, and he'd be in disguise. We would fuck in his car, his apartment, anywhere we could. It was amazing. All the time, my relationship with Maksim was becoming stronger and stronger. The one thing I was learning was, I could not dance and my modeling career was really where I should return. I tried acting too, Maksim was my mentor in that field, and although I was good at it, the relationship I had with Mr. X was getting wilder and wilder until one afternoon, while we were fucking in his car down a quiet road outside of Tallinn, a country road, we were interrupted by several attempted calls on his cell phone. They were persistent and as he was thrusting his cock in and out of my vagina, such a wonderful cock, the phone seemed to be ringing in unison with his movement. He decided to answer, and that's when we knew it was all over. Someone had seen us, we didn't know where or when or how, but a story was about to break regarding Mr. X's infidelity. He was strangely resigned to his destiny, and asked me if I could take a back seat for a few weeks while it all blew over. Scandal is scandal, and I couldn't. My career was at a turning point. I knew I had to go back to London. It seemed, after further investigation, it was purely a rumor that Mr. X was cheating on his wife, and that no one had any evidence, but politics being politics, wherever he went, he was followed, and we had no opportunities at all to get together, after that afternoon, without someone trying to pin something on him. I could not live that way. I discussed it with Maksim and he agreed, time to get back to the UK and away from this madness. So I left. Just like I did the first time, 3 years earlier. I drove to the airport, got on the first flight to London and left it all behind. I left Maksim, who really was my closest confident at that time, and I left Mr. X, who although I saw him again now and then over the coming years, was one of my greatest loves and someone I had so much respect for, even though that might seem hypocritical since I was having an affair with a cheat, I really did love him and he changed my life in so many ways."

"So you went back to London to carry on modeling?" I asked

"Yes, Mr. X and Maksim had, together, cleaned me up. I was off the drugs, I was off everything illegal. I had been rejuvenated and then I had been off loaded, self- inflicted, but off loaded all the same. I knew Mr. X would never leave his wife, he was in his late 30's at the time, and climbing the Estonian political ladder rapidly, so I knew what we had would never last, but it hurt all the same."

"Back in London, what did you do?"

"Well I stayed on the straight and narrow for a while and then I fell back into my old ways, hence the job in the hotel and then the job as a nanny, before FBSM took over my life. There's more to this story. Maksim came to live with me in London soon after. He was different though. He wanted to travel and I took him in. I even paid for his ticket to London and helped keep him while he found his footing in the UK, but he wasn't the same. He lasted a year and then vanished. I just couldn't understand why he'd come and lived off me for a year and then disappeared. Then about two years later I received a call that he'd died. I went to Estonia for the funeral, he was lying in an open casket, literally half the man I used to know, when someone told me he died of cancer and that it had eaten him alive. I found out eventually that was a lie and Maksim died of AIDS, the onset of which had been when he asked to come to the UK to stay with me. He'd been so withdrawn and incommunicative for a whole year, and now I knew why. He obviously never wanted to discuss it with me, but it ruined our relationship because of his stubbornness. That made me very sad.?"

"And Mr. X?"

"We stay in touch. In fact we met last year in new York, no sex, no funny business, but we were both happy to see one another. His kids are now grown and he'd still married. But his political career never recovered. And, you should know, he's not the only politician I ever fucked"

"He's not?"

No, but the next one came much later on in my life and was completely different in terms of what we did and how we behaved. I will tell you about that sometime soon"

"Back to modeling and FBSM Tiana. When modeling finished and FBSM took over, you said you'd been in an apartment in Edgeware Road at first, and then Farringdon?"

"Yes"

"Were there any other places the agency had apartments? If so, what went on in these places?"

And there another chapter began. Tiana placed her black Americano on the table and started to talk again. I knew this was going to take some time.

The Apartments.

"If you ever had a daughter Tiana, would you tell her everything you're telling me? You've told me your mother knows nothing about what you do or what you've done, you also bear no guilt on any part of your life to date, and I believe you. After all I am sitting opposite you watching your facial expressions, so I'm pretty sure if you were embarrassed or guilty about any part of your life, I could tell"

I was more than intrigued, after all, this was out 3rd session together and on each occasions my questions had become more direct and personal and Tiana had never shirked any of them. She seemed so comfortable in her own skin, not embarrassed about anything she'd done in her life and certainly proud, very proud of what she'd achieved to date. But when I thought about it, I wondered, 'what had she achieved?'

I continued.

"Are you sure you are where you really want to be?"

"Of course, this is the best place on earth. I have performed miracles to get here" she was talking about LA and California in general, "I had an opportunity to come to Orange County after I got out the relationship with Mr. X, I was offered a position as a dispatcher for a cleaning company, through a friend of mine in London. I knew I wanted to live in CA, but at that point in time, remember I was only 19, I was too frightened to come. I don't know why, but I was. But now I am here and I am happy. Just after that approach to make the move at 19, I started the hotel job and then the nanny, and then the agency. The agency then took over my life. Did I tell you they had several apartments? Do you want to know what happened at each one?"

"Absolutely" I said, as I took another sip from the bottled water Tiana had bought me about an hour ago. It was warm, like her personality, and refreshing, like her attitude.

"OK soooooo, " and she fixed her hair again, " I began at Edgeware road, as you know and then I moved to Farringdon, where the clientele were more 'business' like, due to it's proximity to the City of London, where all of the financial institutions are based. Suits, shirts and ties, all nicely groomed, although some were just scruffy and could not dress properly to save themselves. If they paid, or should I say, as long as they paid, then everyone left happy. Oh, remind me to talk to you about the Indians, the Asians, and the smell." "Will do" I interrupted.

"In Farringdon, appointments for massage went from 11AM through to midnight. Day after day. It was truly amazing. Most of these men were married, in fact I'd say 80%. They wanted a release, a hand job, after completing a big deal, or, they wanted to be jerked off because their wife wouldn't do it, or they just wanted to feel my perfect tits, because," she hesitated, "well, because they are perfect!" She smiled and pouted her breasts towards nowhere in particular, but I could tell she loved them. It's hard not to look at them when she does this. Her nipples are always erect, and I believe she might have a nipple ring on the right one, but I don't want to ask.

"These men were not getting anything near what they wanted at home, all of them, or they were not getting anything at all, especially the smelly one's. Let me tell you, smell is an issue with me, and the rest of the ladies who worked with me. We all hated the smelly ones. There's no excuse not to take a shower every day, but some of these guys hadn't bathed in days, maybe weeks, and so when they arrived, no matter what apartment I was working in, first things first, I insisted they shower. They would make all sorts of excuses not do get in, thinking that if they showered, they would have less time to look at my tits and shaved poosie. Well, 'fuck them' was my attitude and once I got into the swing of things, about a month after joining the agency, if the client didn't shower before the massage, and I could smell BO, I would not work on him until he did. Also, did you know that sperm smells? Not only does it smell, it smells differently on each man." I just nodded. I had no idea where this was going.

"I didn't offer blow jobs" she was smiling so I knew something was going to contradict that last statement, "but on occasion" I thought to myself, here we go, "on occasion, I would meet a guy I was totally attracted to and, well, I would go for it. I like oral sex, and I like to please, and I certainly like to please my clients, and there was no issue, in my opinion, giving head to those I would consider dating. I never swallowed. I am vegan, and if they were not vegan, then their protein was not vegan, and I was not swallowing non-vegan protein. I have my standards you know. Vegan sperm is happy sperm."

I chuckled again

"They were happy, my tips were very much larger and everyone went home smiling. When a man ejaculates, just like a woman, they all smell different. I got to the stage where, even if I was just giving a hand job, HJ in the trade, I could smell their scent through their sperm. Sometimes it smelled nice, as in pretty much odorless or sweet, and other times.." She held her nose and closed her eyes, mimicking disgust.

"In the porn industry the male actors drink pineapple juice so that their sperm tastes sweet when the actress swallows it. Did you know that?" she asked me. "Yes" I replied.

"Oh. OK, anyway, my aim was pleasure, no matter what the smell, but pleasure became so mundane from my side as the years went by. When you have tossed off thousands of guys, it gets to be tedious and often boring, especially with the ones who take forever to come. Add a little oil or lotion to an erect dick, let them touch my tits, or my nipples and I can promise you that within moments, 98% of men who do this will cum buckets all over my hands. Let me stick my finger in their ass, massaging their prostate, and it happens even quicker, but, and it is a huge BUT, you get a guy who for some reason won't ejaculate quickly, and you're sitting on top of him rubbing and rubbing, and still nothing happens, well, that is a massive issue not only because you have another client on the way and you need to get this one out of the room and showered and ready to leave, but also your hand becomes numb and his dick doesn't get any softer. One guy I had was hard for 20 minutes before he came. I think he'd taken that little blue pill and was testing me, but that's perhaps just my imagination working overtime. Ideally, I want them in and out, and they want to look at my body and cum and leave. Ideally. Life isn't always ideal though, is it?

I needed more water.

"Anyway, the agency had many more apartments. Farringdon was my next stop, followed my Earls Court, South Kensington, Nottinghill, and eventually

Bond St, which is the place I met the English politician. Again, another story for another time"

"Can you tell me that one now?" I begged
"Sure, why not. But I thought you wanted to know about the apartments?"
"I do, but we seem to be into politics today, so tell me about this one. We know about the Estonian one, but the English one intrigues me"

"Well it was one of those crazy days where Maddy was driving me nuts. She really had no clue. Double bookings, miss communication, and an inability to stay on level keel, mentally. She'd texted to tell me that I needed to get to the Bond St apartment because a guy called Mr. P, was on his way. "For Fucks sake Madds" I told her, "I need more time than this, you have to give me more notice. I'm not the Roadrunner", she was always so flippant, "Come on babes, you'll manage, just make sure you treat him well, he's a regular, but likes to change it up once in a while." I got to Bond St underground station and walked to the apartment and he was already there, waiting patiently outside, Mr.P. I made my apologies and asked him to wait a few minutes longer while I set things up.

"Just like the houses of parliament" he said to me. "Pardon?" I asked. I had no idea what he was talking about. "Unorganized and running behind" he said. "I work there" he continued.

Well frankly I didn't care. I just wanted to go in, set the place up, light a few candles and toss him off, get paid and get him out. Madds had arranged yet another booking less than an hour from that time. I was a woman on a mission, or a masseuse with a cause, as I always liked to say. One thing I've never mentioned was that every one of us ladies at the agency had fake names. We never went by our real name, ever. I was Sally, not Tiana, but my nickname, gained because of my quick turnaround rate with the men coming in and out super-fast, was 'Slow-Hand'" she laughed out loud as she told me this. "Quite funny when you think about it"

I agreed, but wanted to move on. "Tell me more about Mr. P"

"Well, he became impatient waiting outside and while he was doing so he seemed extremely fidgety. I get the nervous one's, sometimes I get the ones who are cocky and self-assured, but fidgety was unusual. I was a little concerned for him so I thought to myself, 'ah, fuck it, just let him come in', so he did. I invited him to shower while I was setting up. He knew where to go, obviously not his first time, and he disappeared into the bathroom. I continued to set up, but suddenly, Mr. P reappeared, naked, shouting, 'there's no bloody hot water!!'

Fuck, was the only word that came to mind. I didn't know what to do, so I improvised. Again, remember I was on a time deadline, number 2 was on his way. I told him I was sorry, and that if he behaved himself, I would make it up to him in another way.

He gave me a quizzical look, and agreed to forgo his shower and get right into his massage. He began asking questions, too many questions, I thought, but sensible one's at that. He was very inquisitive and very self-assured. He gave off a vibe, one that was familiar to me, but I couldn't figure out why. As I massaged, my curiosity was at its peak, so I just blurted out, and I have no idea to this day why I blurted it out, "Are you some kind of politician?" Well, you could have cut the air with a knife. Total silence.

"How'd you know?" he asked, as he pushed himself up and looked round and staring directly at my tits.

"You are, aren't you?"

"Yes, but you can never tell anyone I was here and you must always call me Mr. P and now, now you have to let me take you out to dinner as a punishment"

I laughed at him but I was kind of turned on. He was good looking, confident, smelled lovely and had a certain charm that I normally associated with men who wanted to just fuck me. Mr. P however, wanted to buy me dinner. I accepted. In a matter of moments, I had him turned round, admiring what I believed to be a larger than average cock, began rubbing it and stood back as he screamed with pleasure and his warm cum oozed onto my arm.

"Good start?" I said to him and he just lay there and laughed.

Well, that was just the beginning of a relationship blossomed into very interesting and quite serious over the next three years, and even to this day, Mr. P has a huge influence on my life and we are still good friends. He's no longer in politics, but that doesn't matter, I love him all the same. When our relationship was in full swing he used a false ID for everything outside his work environment, he was married with two kids, but I didn't care. Mr. P became a kind of sugar-daddy for me. He sort of still is, but again, it's something we should expand on at a later date.

Tiana looked at me and asked me if I wanted to hear more now? I told her maybe next time, and asked her to revert back to stories that covered her time in the many apartments she'd worked in. She then said.

"I have an amazing story for you"

As if none of the other stories so far hadn't been amazing!

"You ready?"

That Smell

He arrived, as they all do, keen and ready to be released, which is another term for wanked off, jerked off, tossed off or whatever else you want to describe it as. Masturbated or to be given a HJ, Hand Job. They all seem to have that look on their face when they walk in the door for the first time. Regulars have a different look, but first timers, well, they are filled by dread or excitement or both. It's written clearly between their eyeballs. I know that look, and all the girls knew that look too. We would all play on it. I still do. When a man comes to see me, I try hard to make him feel as welcome as possible and as relaxed as I can. There's nothing worse than a first timer who can't get an erection. It's embarrassing for them, and it's hard work for me, trying to coax them into ejaculation, because in all honesty, that's what they've paid for. The massage is peripheral, and none of us are expert in that profession.

Anyway, this guy shows up, and I see THAT look. He's dressed nicely, obviously just come from his workplace and is ready to get his release. I send him into the shower after we exchanged pleasantries. I hear the water running and then he appears, naked, and lies on the bed, ready for action. I perform my usual gentle first touch and climb up on the massage table to sit on top of him to make it easier on my back and to enable me to rub my tits across him when I feel like it. Men love that, most men, not all men, but most do.

I'm in the process of rubbing the oils onto his back and I smell this awful odder, which I thought at first was coming from the guy on the table. It was vile, but then it would vanish. I had issues in the past with gas leaks, toilets overflowing, sewage in the sink and other normal things that happen to apartments or buildings, which can be remedied by calling a plumber or the building supervisor. But this was different.

I carried on massaging this guy and then turned him over. The smell was getting stronger and becoming viler. He was immersed in my hand strokes, and then he came. I cleaned him off, but then proceeded into the bathroom to get more towels. He'd come all over me, the sheets, and the floor, it was like a fountain, and more action was required. I entered the bathroom, picked up a towel and opened the shower door to make the towel wet with warm water. I looked down and there it was! Shit, shit all over the shower. Every fucking inch of the shower floor was covered in it. The fucker had shit his pants, well not his pants literally, but he'd shit all over the floor, and the stupid bastard had come in for his massage without telling me what he'd done!! I was livid. I stormed back into the main room and as I opened the bathroom door to go back in, he uttered meekly towards my raging face, "I had an accident"

An accident!!! I was shouting. You shit all over the shower and you never told me. What kind of accident was that? "I'm sorry" he said, but I wasn't having any of his innocence. "you need to get up and start cleaning, NOW!"

I had another client due in ten minutes and the whole place smelled of shit, his shit. He got up gingerly and made his way back into the shower and about five minutes later, fully dressed, told me it was done and he walked out, never to be seen again, at least not by me.

I went to take a look, and I was shocked. He'd done nothing. His feeble attempt at cleaning was a complete failure. My phone buzzed. It was Madds.

"Babes, your 8PM is at the door, let him in please." "Madds, my 7 PM shit on the shower floor and I need to clean it up, delay him" "No babes, you sort it, have fun!" and she put down the phone. The door was buzzing, the shit was stinking up the apartment and I had no idea what to do.

I decided to take matters into my own hands. I dressed, walked to the front door, told the waiting client a pipe had burst and asked him if he'd buy me a drink instead of getting a massage.

He looked at me, decided I was worth the effort and then spent two hours trying to get me to fuck him, while we both drank a bottle of vodka in the local pub. In the meantime, Madds stopped answering her phone, no one else was going to assist, so I spent from 11 PM until 1 AM cleaning up the first guys shit. Another typical night in Nottinghill, I thought, but worse was to come. For days, I could not get that smell out of my nostrils or off my body. It was disgusting.

The guy who'd shit his pants vanished, the guy who'd been in the pub trying to fuck me, complained I never gave him his massage, and everyone blamed me, when all the time I was the one trying to appease the shitter and the attempted fucker. I couldn't win. Julian, the agency top dog, gave me a hard time when he found out what happened, and that's when I decided, fuck it, I am not following their rules any longer. I had enough of their BS and went rogue. I didn't go rogue alone though. I went rogue with Alice."

"Who is Alice?", I asked

"Alice and I were great friends. She also worked at the agency, and even up until the middle of last year, 2019, we still were. Smells? Well they were our bonding. You have no idea how humanity smells. Some people smell great, other people don't smell, but some...... Some people smell so bad there should be a government health warning placed on their bodies.

Being in this line of work, FBSM, I get to meet the dregs of society, all the perverts that God created, but I also get to meet lovely people, people who are proud of who they are, who take care of themselves, who do not smell! I used to dread whenever someone knew came into my room for a massage, I have a nose that detects even the slightest of odors, and that first meet and greet, well, it was always difficult for me because all I wanted to do was step in close to the client and take a whiff of what was going to be for the next hour. Even worse are clients who arrive smelly, shower, cannot get rid of their smell and put me through an hour of hell, only to become regulars! I dislike that intensely. I met a guy once, he happened to be Indian, and every time he showed up, he stank of curry. It was disgusting. His whole person was just a curry odor. When he ejaculated, it smelled of Vindaloo, and I could only laugh inside when I had recurring images of his wife swallowing that load and telling him, 'oh darling, you need to add more cumin next time you cook that recipe!' Gross!!! French guys never used deodorant, Italian guys used too much aftershave, American men, well, let's just say their smell is dependent upon ethnicity, and that white is better that yellow, black or brown, most of the time. I apologize to all who are reading for my racial profiling, but you are all out there and you all know it's true.

One massage I did where I was almost finished, the guy was ready to flip and to be 'taken care' of, ended prematurely when he farted so violently, I thought I was going to pass out from the residue of that fart. He wasn't even apologetic, he turned to me and said, 'if you don't fart, you die, so it's over and done with, finish me off" I had completed the massage on his back but that smell was making me sick, so I said to him, "darling, if you want to pay me danger money, I will continue, if not, please just get dressed and leave" he took out 100 UK pounds, waved it in my face, farted again and said, "carry on, I will see if I can fart and cum at the same time, and if I can I will double this donation!"

He couldn't and he didn't, but I needed a long walk in Regents Park once he'd left, to get the smell out of my system. Vile wasn't the right word, and neither was disgusting. His insane farting was pure evil.

And then there's the odor from foreskins, which by the way, I hate. Why isn't every male circumcised? I want to do a whole chapter on men's penis shapes and sizes, but foreskins? God, they are disgusting. That spooky sliver of skin at the end of un uncircumcised dick is weird. It can be small medium or large, but whatever it is, it carries germs and has an insane ability to disgust me like no other part of the human anatomy. I don't know why that is, but if I was ever going to make a scary movie, I would call it Revenge Of The Foreskin. The foreskin in my movie would scare the shit out of every audience, no exceptions. And did I tell you they smell? Of course I did. If I had my choice I would only massage circumcised guys, but then in this day and age, some moron would sue me for penis discrimination, and I'd lose!

Alice And The Italian Bitch

In Camden town, opposite that famous concert venue, the Roundhouse, sat our nicest apartment. One which I didn't frequent very often, but on this occasion, a nice summers day in my second year of working with the agency, I was asked to go to collect all the money from the previous day's takings. I didn't have much booked that morning and needed to get out and about, so I agreed and I took the tube (underground train) to Camden Town station, a very short journey for me, and stepped out into bright London sunshine, a rarity, ready for this new day.

I arrived at the apartment and opened the door, where I found two girls I'd never met before. One was Alice, from London, and the other, Francesca, who was from Italy. Alice was very standoffish, Franny, as I decided to call her, was just a sick bitch who loved herself more than anyone else I'd met in my entire life. At first, both were just unfriendly and uninterested in conversation, but as time went by, Alice and I became incredible friends, while Franny and I used to butt heads daily.

Franny was a total lunatic. She'd told all of us that the reason she'd become a masseuse was because she'd dated a very famous Italian soccer player, who's name escapes me, and that he'd dumped her, after promising to marry her. She was drop-dead gorgeous, and she just sat around all day admiring herself. No word of a lie, she'd look herself up and down in every mirror we had, at least ten times an hour. She had perfect large breasts, a thin and curvy figure and a face that would enhance the cover of any fashion magazine, in any part of the world, on any day of any week. Franny was really sensational in that sense, but for a personality? She was given the personality of the devil. Her voice and attitude could make Scarface look and sound like Mother Theresa! She was a total bitch.

She had run away from the soccer player and into the world of massage and 'five finger boogie' which was another term we girls used for wanking or jerking off the guys. Five Finger Boogie became and actual song, sung to the tune of that Cuban song, Guantanamera. It used to go something like this, and we girls used to sing it together when we were in the pub getting drunk or high, or both.

"Five finger boogie

He wants a five finger boogie

Five finger boooooogie,

And when he comes he'll look stupid"

We'd repeat that song over and over, showing our disdain for those who paid our wages, but we all thought it was hilarious, and those who looked on, those innocents who were just there to enjoy a drink and a chat at their local hostelry, well, they thought we were all nuts and had no idea what we were talking about.

Franny could be cutting, divisive, unruly, off hand and disgustingly morose, while all the time, she just wanted to fuck you up or fuck up your happy life. She was a miserable woman, let loose into a society she despised.

One morning I arrived at the apartment in Camden Town. Franny lived there, after doing a deal with Justin, who I think wanted to fuck her, but decided not to cross that line when he realized she'd fuck him better than he could fuck her, and I'm not talking sexually. Franny stated that since the soccer player threw her out, she was homeless. Because of her beauty, she attracted so much business, Justin felt he needed to improvise to keep her around, so Franny ended up as Camden Town's gatekeeper. An appropriate title for the bitch from the west.

I walked in, and could not find her, but I heard water running from the bathroom, so, me being me, I decided to go in to the bathroom quietly and scare the shit out of her, just like in that Alfred Hitchcock film, Psycho.

Franny was a weirdo of the highest proportion. Her eating habits were, to say the least, strange, but boy, she could eat. Crazy foods too. Chips, burgers, chocolate and more to the point, she would gain and lose weight as if it was a fashion. Some days she's look waif like and other days, pregnant. No matter what, she was always bragging about her ability to lose whatever she put on, in days. We would laugh at her, obviously behind her back, and sometimes to her face, presuming she was just a crazy woman without the gene that makes one fat. She really was gorgeous, and it made me jealous I have to say. Anyway, I crept into the bathroom ready to scare the crap out of her, but the shower curtain was open, and there was Franny, butt naked, with the shower head lying on the floor and the exposed shower hose stuck right up her ass, singing some weird Italian melody! She was having a hot water enema! I stopped in my tracks, she looked at me, never batting an eyelid, and casually said, "it's my weight loss method darling. I read you put hot water up your ass and you lose weight"

Fuck! I didn't know what to do. I knew she was weird, and I knew she really fancied herself as a human being of the most gorgeous kind, but this was extraordinary. At that precise moment I wished I'd had a camera to take a pic. Who on this planet puts a hose pipe with hot water up their ass to lose weight?? No wonder the soccer player dumped her.

She also had this incredible routine she went through when she sat down, sat down anywhere. It was as if she'd just been fucked by the largest cock on the planet and was stretched out of shape. She had to maneuver her legs in such a way that she caused a stir wherever we went when she found a chair to plonk herself down on. Bars, restaurants, clubs, it didn't matter. Her legs would be spread over the impending seat and then she'd make sure that everyone looking could see right into her poosie,(she never wore panties), then she'd bring her legs together and drop down onto that chair, in a kind of dance motion. It was hilarious to watch, because you knew she was going to do it and quite often she'd make a point of brushing her long hair back with a sweeping hand movement as she dropped. It was poetry in motion, but without the poetry! Choreographed from beginning to end, and eye-poppingly hilarious.

It was precisely during one of Franny's extraordinary 'dance moves' that Alice and I became great friends. Funny how the smallest of things brings people together and even stranger how those moments can lead to incredible friendships.

Alice, as I mentioned before, could be aloof, standoffish and an introvert. When I started to get to know her though, she was exactly the opposite. At that point in my life, Maksim had moved to London, the gay dance instructor, and he was living with me, all at my expense of course, and trying to get his life together. This was before I knew he was sick and before he became introverted and unwilling to talk to me anymore.

I would share things with Maksim that I shared with no one else, because he posed no threat to me. Every man I met either wanted to fuck me or marry me or both. I'd never had a relationship to that point in my life where I'd believed, 'yes, this is the one, I am going to marry him' There had been one or two that were close, but really none that had met the mark of possible husband material. Maksim was so cool. He'd sit and listen to me bitch all night. We'd go for dinners and I would tell him things that no one knew, and if it wasn't for him and his efforts to get me off cocaine, I would have become addicted for sure. I'd been clean for a while now, 4 years I believe and had no worries about falling back into that kind of lifestyle. I cleaned up really nice and I did it all by myself. Rehab wasn't even on my radar. Really the only thing missing at this point in time was a man I could trust, a straight man, who wasn't going to fuck me, either in bed or in life.

Alice would start to chat with me during our days in the Camden Town apartment. It began that way. We would have little that was nice to say about anyone who worked in the agency. Julia was on her way out, she and Justin had a bust up over something, and the agency itself, now that Julia was almost out, was falling apart. Julia had gone independent, and she believed that was the way of the future, handling her own clientele and her own screening. I couldn't blame her for trying and thought that eventually I would go the same direction. Since the 'boss' was no longer around, candles and oils and towels weren't being replaced, girls were sent to the wrong apartments at the wrong times. Madds couldn't cope on her own without Julia's instruction, and to top it all off, neighbors at different locations where the agency held rented property began complaining about the ins and outs of all these men and women and some of the agency's leases were revoked. It was becoming rapidly chaotic. In the meantime, Alice and I were becoming closer and closer. We just sort of hit it off and discovered we had similar likes and dislikes. We used to trade stories of the men we were dating, massaging, fucking, and we would trade clients too. Some men would show up thinking I was her and she was me. It was all good fun. We were rampant. We just didn't care about the agency anymore. We did it our way or no way at all.

Some of the men, our massage clients, were passing us their phone numbers, no, that's a lie, all of them wanted to fuck us, and 90% of them tried to date us. Alice was a real hussy in that respect. She'd offer them hope, take the huge tip and then vanish into the mist of their cum. They would leave on cloud 9 and end up devastated when she refused all future advancement from them. There were so many men. Hundreds, maybe thousands, yes, thousands, who we saw, released, five finger boogie, and never saw again. Some would come back, many just vanished. Maybe they wanted to see other girls, maybe one time was enough, maybe their wives or girlfriends took up all their time after their visits to us, we would never know, nor did we care. Now and again a special man would show up, and we would all discuss the possibilities of fucking him, financially and physically, but more often than not it was, wank them off, give them hope and throw them out, making sure they tipped big and cleaned up nicely.

Alice was so much the opposite of that girl I'd met the first day I'd walked into Camden Town. She was the inspiration I needed to get out of my rut. Maksim was becoming more and more withdrawn and I needed life. I needed to be able to express myself to other people through conversation, parties, concerts, and Maksim didn't want any part of that, but Alice did. Alice was amazingly well connected. We would receive invitations to all kinds of events and then the two of us would sit down and decide which ones we should go to, always together as a team, but sometimes when we'd arrive we would split up and regroup to discuss our best options with men and what we would do to them if we had the chance. One night however, my life changed, and it changed for the worse. This is a tough story to tell, but I will tell it as honestly as I can.

I was decidedly lonely in my personal life. Maksim, as I said, (and remember, he was my closest friend for a long time), was not really talking to me anymore and certainly not offering me the advice I craved from him, which was advice I had become used to. I had dated guys, but nothing had come from any of those dates, and honestly, I was craving a relationship, a friend, a man, a real man, in my life. A man I could see when I wanted to, someone to love me, someone to cherish me and someone I could talk to and relate to on the same level. Maksim had replaced that desire for a while, but the poor man was no longer interested in me, and obviously I had no idea at the time why that was. Again, he was HIV positive and I didn't know. Alice gave me the outlet to meet people, and outlet I wanted but shied away from until she became insistent we party as a team. I have many fond memories of some of the crap we got up to inside the agencies apartments, with the guys we were massaging, and we'd built this amazing bond together, which lasted until the summer of 2018, but Alice also led me down a path that was extremely dark, though it was not exactly her fault, nor do I blame her for doing so.

We were in a bar in Camden Town, I think it was called the Dublin Castle, and it was a typical Friday evening, Lots of drink, lots of people, lots of music, lots of fun. I was feeling a little morose, maybe it was because I was on my period, but Alice could tell I wasn't myself. About 11 PM that night I went to the bathroom and Alice followed me in.

"What's wrong sweetie, you don't look or sound like yourself?" she asked me.

"I'm just tired, lonely and probably upset because Maksim isn't talking to me like he used to and I miss that."

We chatted for about a minute and then it happened. She pulled out a small poly bag from her purse, placing the white powder contents on the counter top where two sinks lined up.

"You should take some of this" she offered.

I knew what it was, I'm no saint as you know, but I'd stayed away from cocaine for the past 4 years and was determined never to go back. I knew what it would do to me and I also knew that I'd managed to get off it with ease that first time, but I also recognized it would be very difficult, should I start up using again, to get off it so easily a second time. I was tempted, so tempted. I wanted to feel good, cocaine made me feel good I recalled, but no, I wasn't going to budge.

Alice was insistent.

"Come on girl, give it a go. Just a ball, not a line. You'll be OK"

A line, for those of you who don't know, is just what it states. It's a line of white powder about 4 inches long that you snort up your nose using a straw, a rolled up 5- or 10-pound note or any other kind of tubular device. A ball, is just a little cocaine shamed like half a sphere, that you put on the end of your index finger and snort. Both have similar effects, although a line will give you far more of a buzz in the short term. Alice kept pushing, I kept my distance. I had all sorts of memories floating in my head, memories that were good, bad and forgettable. All memories, all right there, all confronting me as my demons took me into submission. I recall being adamant with Alice that destroying 4 years of sobriety was not on the cards, and then I remember she placed a ball on my finger and coaxed me into snorting it. Within seconds I felt so good, so relaxed, so at ease, so amazing and so happy. My worries all vanished. My past disappeared. Maksim wasn't even in my head. I was free, I was alive, I was spaced out, I was so high. It had been 4 years, and this little drop, this ball, had reacted inside me as much as a full line would have done. I realized immediately that I'd made a mistake, but I just didn't care. My loneliness vanished and my bravado, that modeling trait I'd learned so well, took over. I was now ready to conquer the world again and ready to do it there and then. That night placed me in a position I never thought I would be in after 4 years of being clean, but boy, was I happy. So happy in fact, I recall going straight back out into the bar, Alice was following me, and finding the first good looking guy I could, and asking him to fuck me. I don't remember too much after that though. This was the beginning of a three-month period of pure debauchery in my life. I was addicted again, no way out, and Alice had been the perpetrator, although to be frank, it was my choice, she was just the pusher.

Over the next 12 weeks, I went from party to party, man to man, line to line of cocaine. I spent money like it was going out of fashion, and so did Alice. We were living a life that we couldn't control. Maksim had left for Estonia, and I had no one but Alice. She was my friend, confidant, and much more, but cocaine was my life and I couldn't get off the merry-go-round. So stupid, but so true, and all because I was lonely. I wanted a man, not any man, but a man, the man of my dreams, to come and save me, but he just didn't exist. So many men would fuck me and promise me the heavens and the earth, but all of them, every one of them, just left me to rot. Or so it seemed. I know I was my own worst enemy, I know I was stubborn and stupid, and I know that only I could stop what I had started, but I didn't want to, well, not at first.

Three months of pure ecstasy, which led to a rude awakening one afternoon while I was in the middle of a massage.

I had this good-looking guy in the apartment, we'd gone through all the preliminaries, and he was naked and ready to receive his hand job, after I'd massaged his back. I had my hands on him, I was covered in oil, and he was asking me questions, all of which I was ignoring. I remember my hand going round and round in circles and nothing seemed to be moving. I remember his words, but I couldn't hear a thing. I remember the smell of the candles, but I just couldn't see their flames. And then I realized, I had a problem, a serious problem.

I stopped, made an excuse, gave him his money back, threw him out, went into the bathroom and sobbed. I sobbed until my heart ached. I wanted to talk to Maksim, but he was no longer around. I needed to talk, and then I screamed. I screamed until my voice was quiet, and my body went limp and I fell asleep on the bathroom floor. I was a total mess. I was so sad, so alone, so lost.

It took me a few days, after I left the apartment that evening, to come to terms with my addiction. My mind going back 4 years to when I last had the same problem and step by step it took me through the process I had followed to become sober. I had to do it all again, and I had to begin now. Alice was shocked at the transformation in my body and mind after I became addicted. Even she had difficulty keeping up with me. I was just out of control.

Alice came to see me, and I told her I was going off the drugs and sex for a year to sober up. She thought I was nuts, all the while telling me I wasn't addicted and my issues were minor in comparison to others. But I knew. Only I knew. No one could tell me what to do. This was my problem, not hers or anyone else's. I had to fix it, and fix it I did.

It took me a long time to come to terms with my inability to confront my addiction, but when I finally did, it was in the nick of time. If I'd left it another 3 weeks or month, I would probably not be telling this story today. I think I would be dead, but somehow, I woke up to my issues and found a way to conquer all addiction for, what I thought, would be the last time, and hoped to do so successfully without professional assistance. Quite how I did it was a miracle, but my mind has always been my strongest asset, even though most of the men I have been with will tell you it's my tits, not my mind. Life over that 3-month period was so much fun, until it became so dangerous, I almost never recovered. I was sucked in, turned around and spat out. I came out with a smile, eventually, and a brand-new attitude. I also came out with that pledge, no sex for a year, and no drugs ever again.

A year without sex, well. I thought, that's easy, but a life without drugs, that would be hard. Determination kept me afloat, and my pledge to stay celibate lasted 6 moths.

The Hobby

Why are those who use Escorts or the services of FBSM called "Hobbyists" and indeed, why is FBSM called, "The Hobby"?

This was a question I posed to Tiana, and one that had been on my mind since we'd met. Having done some research before writing this book, I found out that a lot of Urban dictionary vernacular is used in these services, as it is in all porn.

"Where did "the Hobby" form its origins?" I asked

"Well, 'the Hobby' or 'Hobbyists" come from men who see me or other FBSM providers on a regular basis and leave us reviews, as they also do with Escorts. Some of my clients come to see me on a regular basis, even today. It's just like a hobby for them. Some men play golf, others like to go to the pub, so the ones who see me, or any of the other girls, class this as their hobby. Hence the term hobbyist. It's all quite simple really. I have been making money from FBSM for 7 years. It's a business for me, but in that time, I have met many nice people, some not so nice and some that have given me enough ammunition to write this book. FBSM is really quite innocent" she smiles, "when you think about it, it's two consenting adults in a room, hotel or private residence, naked, with me, or any other provider, massaging that body and well, you know, at the end, making that client happy and relieved to have joined me for that particular hour. There's not really a lot wrong with that, is there?" Tiana looked at me again and pouted her boobs, as she's prone to doing when looking for affirmation of any kind.

"There's no sex involved, at least there's not supposed to be, and I know I veer from that rule now and again, but that's my choice and I don't get paid any extra for it. I am not a whore, a prostitute, an Escort, although

I must admit I have been tempted to try Escorting in the past. More money and richer guys, but we can discuss that later or in another book"

"So you HAVE done escorting, or you haven't?" I asked.

"Let's move on" she said, in a kind of embarrassed fashion," we will talk about that another time."

She was certainly hiding something from me, and although I knew exactly what that was, she obviously didn't want to discuss it any more. I moved on.

"Tiana, what's the biggest thrill you've had from practicing FBSM over the years?" I had a funny feeling I knew what was coming.

"Meeting people, exploring their bodies, in a sexual and non-sexual manner"

"How can it be non-sexual?" I asked," after all, you're naked and so it he and you're touching him all over, no place to hide, so limitations, why is that non-sexual?"

"Listen, men come to me with all their problems. They talk, and they talk rapidly and about subjects they feel that are taboo with their wives, girlfriends and male friends. I am a listening post for all of that. I listen and touch, they talk and then cum. No harm done and sexuality is not a factor. They love my body for sure, but I love some of their bodies too. They don't turn me on, well, most of them don't, at least 99.9% don't, but there's more to this than just a quick wank and ejaculation. There's a psychology too."

"Explain that please"

"I know that when I am on top of them, they will tell me anything I want them to tell me or anything they want to tell. I never have to force it out of them. I have a sexy voice and body, they have all got secrets and a past history that they need to blurt out. I don't know why that is, but it's a fact. The men that come for FBSM are desperate, most of the time, to fuck me, so they'll try anything. They'll try chatting to me, offering me financial incentives, buying me gifts, and lots of other things too, but at the end of the day, when they begin to talk, they rarely stop and within one hour, their deepest darkest secrets or desires are divulged right in front of my tits and poosie, all of which they will never get more than a quick glimpse or feel of, but I on the other hand, am their mother, their confident, their outlet for seeking solace and pleasure, at the same time of course. Do you understand?"

I thought I did, but something didn't sit right with me. And so I asked another question, "how much do you typically charge if someone wants to go further than massage"

"Alan" she said, and I could see she was getting annoyed, "I told you already, I do not do that. I am not a whore"

Her anger was there for all to see, so I decided to let it go and went in another direction.

"Tiana, what happened once you kicked the cocaine habit with Alice? Was that it or did you ever get back on the drugs?" She was agitated again, I knew I'd hit a sensitive spot but wasn't aware how or why? She's told me previously that cocaine ended after her 3-month binge with Alice, but I wasn't sure if, at all, she'd picked it up again at some point in the future. Not that it meant too much, but how many times can a person rehab themselves before professional help is required? And if she's rehabbed alone, what were the chances that habit would come back in the future? Probably good, I presumed?

Tiana continued,

"After Alice, I was strong, and focused. I was back to the 'wheel them in, toss them off, kick them out routine' with little or no intention to spend my cash on anything but things I needed or wanted, but not drugs. My pledge was to stay away from both sex and drugs for a year. That was my desire, that was what I would aim for. There was nothing or no one who would make me deviate. I am totally committed when I make an internal pledge and on this occasion, I had awoken with a shock, deciding that if I didn't change my whole life, I would end up dead, something I didn't want because I wasn't washed up or depressed or in need of an intervention. I was still young, vibrant, pretty and looking for 'THE ONE' someday so I could marry and have kids. Celibacy was my only option. Detox was my only option. Saying NO was my only option. And I did all three. I never thought twice about doing it too. Once I'd made up my mind, it was a done deal. I told you more than once, I am strong, and when I decide on something in my own life, it generally happens."

"How many 'Hobbyists' do you think you've seen in the 7 years you have been working in FBSM?" I asked her. I was expecting an answer in the thousands and I wasn't wrong.

"About 10 to 20 per week minimum, 45 weeks a year for 7 years. You do the math" she smiled.

I did the math, and I was shocked.

"That's about 6500 men in total?"

"No", she said, the math is wrong. I think maybe double that"

"So you made a mistake with the numbers?" I asked

"Yes, and on top of that there have been days and often weeks where I would sit around doing nothing. We had a streak in London once when for 3 moths I say only 3 to 4 men a week. Things went dead. I don't know why this happened, but it did and at that time I seriously considered quitting the agency and just like Julia had done, I would go independent. It never happened, well, not until I got to LA."

"What did you do with no money coming in over those 3 months?"

"I had a sugar daddy, but that's another story." Again, that wry smile and those rolled back eyes.

"OK let's discuss what happened after Alice. You mentioned your desire for celibacy, did you get through the whole year?"

"Well" she laughs, "not exactly. I lasted 6 months. But that was a lot for me."

"OK this I need to hear about. What happened after 6 months?"

"I met THE one"

"You did?"

"Yes, I met him and I thought that this was it."
"What happened?"
And with that question, Tiana started off on another set of stories that would blow my mind.

Tres Amigos

Tiana breaks down, right in front of me, first time ever. Then as suddenly as she'd started to cry, she stops, and laughs.

"I was so angry, I was hurt, I was lonely, I was feeling used and I was just really tired. 3 months of celibacy, no sex, no drugs, no alcohol, had taken their toll. I felt like a cripple. I know that sounds stupid, but that's how it felt. I would get on trains and into taxis, I would go out to dinners, and to pubs and bars to listen to music and everyone was having such a great time, eating, drinking, kissing and hugging, and then there was me. I know my celibacy was self-imposed, and it was my decision and mine alone to make it happen, but I really felt isolated, often depressed and sometimes even cried for no reason at all. I realize now that this was all part of my depression and the sadness really hit home to me at that point. Now, even talking to you about all of this, makes me look at my life from a different perspective and I can see that some of what I've done and been through, although my choice, has led me to lead a kind of fucked up life in many ways. My inability to cope with my depression became horrendous. My anger occasionally boiled over, I was continually crabby, nothing was good enough, and practicing FBSM was a nightmare. Having to be nice to men who just wanted a release, or to fuck me, well, I just got tired of the BS. I hated the one-liners, and each client had their own, even though they were all the same in the end. "How long have you been doing this?" "What do you do for fun?" "Would you consider coming for a drink with me after"

FUCK OFF, was all I could think of. I couldn't stand it any longer. I was teetering on the brink, but I didn't know what the brink actually was, until one afternoon, Alice came in and told me I had a client coming in to the Camden

Town apartment at 6 PM and I had to be done by 7 because he was going to a gig.

I wasn't in the mood. I asked Alice if she'd be prepared to make him 'happy', but she had other plans. I was stuck, with no way out. Everyone around me was enjoying life, but I was hating it. I tried to think of where I should go next, back to Estonia, over to America, up to Scotland, but my mind was broken, and for me to decide anything at that point in time would have made no sense at all.

The doorbell rang at 6 PM and my life's perspective suddenly changed. It was such a meaningful moment, and yet such an innocent one too.

Dave stood there, all 6'2" of one of the most gorgeous men I have ever met. We looked at one another for what seemed like an eternity, but yet it was only 20 seconds at the most. Dave was James Dean reincarnated. He was so handsome, ruggedly so, perfect features, chiseled chin, great eyes, steely blue, hair that was to die for, and a body that was lean and muscular, and then, and then he spoke. He was American! I went weak at the knees. "My dream man" I thought to myself, as I showed him into the apartment.

Our conversation began and there seemed to be electricity between us. It was magical. I asked him to shower, and he did so, and then he came back in and lay on the table. Before he did this I took a quick look at his cock. It was perfect in all ways.

Have I told you about Jewish cocks?"

"No" I replied

"They are perfect. More perfect than any other cock. I don't know what it is about them, and by the way, I didn't know at the time that Dave was Jewish, well, not quite yet, but I guessed from the size and shape of his cock, that he was. I was right of course, but let me give you a 'cock' run down.

Cocks come in all shapes and sizes and it's a complete fallacy to say, 'his feet are huge so his cock must be' or, 'he's black, so he must be well hung'. Total nonsense. It matters not the shape and size of the man, he's either got a decent sized cock or he hasn't. Trust me, I have seen thousands of them, and I AM an expert. I know a great cock from a bad cock. I know who will fit perfectly inside me and who I will never feel inside me. I know who is too big, and too thick and I also know that Jewish cocks are the most perfect on the planet. Jewish cocks are superb in shape, head size, girth and they have NO foreskin, which, as I've told you, is not only my preference, but the preference of most of the girls in this business.

I've had thin men with huge cocks and tall men with small cocks, both very surprising at the time. I have massaged over 10,000 cocks, some long, some short and some too funny to talk about. I have seen cocks that bend to the right, bend to the left, that are concaved, convexed and all shapes in between. Some cocks have spots, some have shinny heads, some cocks are just plain ugly, too ugly to even look at, but at the end of the day, I massage them, often with vigor, just to get it over and done with, but on occasion I like to ogle for a few minutes at the wonder of a man's genitalia, especially if that man is hot, which Dave certainly was. He had the most perfect beautiful penis I had ever seen and that, along with the sexual electricity and chemistry floating unquestionably between us, made for the best time I'd had in many months. My celibacy was nagging inside my brain. Good cop, bad cop. One side said, go for it, the other said, no way, you're on sabbatical. I was tormented. So tormented, that I needed to wipe my poosie several times with lotion, to make it look like the lotion was the wetness coming from between my legs, and not Dave's charisma. That's something else I haven't told you, when the client is underneath me, he wants to finger my poosie while I stroke his cock, and to avoid any disappointment on his part, and to ensure he believes he's turning me on, during the massage, when he's on his front, I gently rub massage oil on my poosie to make it seem wet, so that when he is turned around, he feels enlightened and happy when he fingers me and I am 'wet' Or maybe I did tell you that already, in any event, that's a trick of the trade and a turn on for the client because he believes, quite wrongly, that it's him that's making me wet, when it's actually lotion.

"I understand" I said, but really, I didn't

She continued

"Dave was rock hard from the moment he showered, until the moment I decided, 'to hell with celibacy'. I rolled him over, gazing amiably at his fat Jewish cock, and I blew him. I rolled my tongue up and down his member, I put it in my mouth, I caressed it, I made it my own. His explosion was tumultuous, all over the sheets and the floor and into my hair.

"Not had a release in a while Dave?" I asked him. It was so evident. He came buckets, gallons, tons, all over everything that surrounded us and as he did so, his climax shook the building like a 6.8 earthquake. Dave was a happy bunny. I sat with him for a while and our conversation continued. He asked me to come to the bar where he was and his band were playing that evening, not sure if I told you he played lead guitar for an up and coming band in the USA, one that's quite famous today, but he appealed to all of my sexual wanton, from his mannerisms, to his speech to his body, to that amazing cock. My celibacy wasn't really over, just sort of on hiatus, but my mind was wandering towards fucking this guy forever.

I went to see him play, and we had a great night. He pleaded with me to go on the UK tour with him for two weeks, but I refused. That night ended with a kiss goodbye and no fucking. I kept my promise on the sex front and drank diet Coke all night. I was depressed beyond belief when I woke up that next morning, my mind still in turmoil, but my celibacy still intact.

And before I had a chance to ask another question, Tiana continued her solo conversation, commenting quickly that her non-affair with Dave had prompted her to recall a story about another client who came into Camden Town regularly. This guy was called Gordo. I let her carry on while she sipped on yet another coffee.

"You know there's nothing that pisses me off more than a man who cannot ask for what he wants, and tries to get what he wants in a roundabout manner. If you want something, ask me. If you want me to suck you off, ask, if you want to lick my poosie, ask. I am not a lottery ticket. It's not one scratch and you win! "
I laughed, and I wondered where she was going with this.

"I see men every day, some who I know are good in bed, and some who I know are crap. I can tell by their first touch whether they would fuck me into submission and that I would enjoy it, or I can tell that it would be one squirt and done, wham bam thankyou ma'am. It's not rocket science with me or with any of the other girls I've met in the 7 years I've been doing this. Some of the other's I know will fuck their clients and moan and groan and pretend to orgasm, throw them out and then come in and bitch to me that the guy was crap and had no idea what he was doing. 99% of men don't know how to satisfy a woman. It's a fact. Porn has a lot to answer for. You sit and watch these women getting fucked up the ass, fucked in their throats, fucked in their poosie by men with giant dicks, a non-stop festival of pure unadulterated fucking, all for the purpose of getting the viewer, mainly men, hard and jacked off so they will come back the very next night and buy something else and repeat the process. What you see though on TV or in those movies, is all stage managed and crude and NO woman on this earth, unless they are a nymphomaniac, wants to be treated that way. We should do a chapter on Nympho's Alan, I know a few and it would be fun to read about how they react when they see a cock. Anyway, I digress. So when guys come to see me and the other girls and ask me to fuck them or vice versa, I am always blown away by how little they know or care about to please me. Gordo was that perfect example. Gordo was a regular, for all the years I was in London, he'd visit me once a month, like clockwork. He was chubby, not fat, but certainly overweight, and he'd come in, so posh and so pleasant and always apologetic. I would describe Gordo as 'very British', from the way he dressed to all of his mannerisms." And with that, Tiana sat up and started her British accent as she adjusts her sports bra, underneath her leather jacket and blouse, and moves into full acting mode with a very posh English accent. It reminded me of the way Margret Thatcher used to talk.

"Well hello T, I am so sorry that I'm 2 minutes late today. Please forgive me". Or, when he came, it would be, 'Oh golly gosh, that was spiffing T"

Used to drive me nuts. So fucking English, just snobby, without emotion or feeling, as if he was being worked like a puppet from behind. Over the first two years, Gordo went on a diet, a diet that helped him lose over 40lbs. During that time, he'd come to see me, and by the way, Gordo had a huge cock, huge! Oh my goodness, was that thing large, but he took ages to cum. I'll get to that shortly. His diet made him grumpy and sad and each time he came in to visit, while the weight loss was going on, he would just remind me of a man who was suffering with no one to talk to except me. He was so reserved, so upset and so willing to suffer, just to lose this 40lbs, that it became detrimental to the way he lived his everyday life. He hated everything he did, from work, to dating, to his football team, Arsenal, who he did nothing but insult as I massaged him and prayed that this time I could make him ejaculate in a timely manner. Gordo was unique in many ways, but Gordo just didn't have the balls to ask for what he really wanted.

My phone rang one afternoon, it was Madds, and she got right into it. Remember, Madds had no filter, so she blurted it out.

"Babes, Gordo is coming today, and he wants to go down on you"

Let me give you a brief history of what my Ad says and even today it says the same.

I state quite clearly that I offer B2B,(body to body), nude massage with mutual touch and that I also offer face sitting, and foot fetish. I also state, quite categorically, that I DO NOT offer F/S, 'full sex". Any man who wants to partake in any of the items I list on my Ad, just has to ask and I will accommodate.

"Madds is he being serious?" I asked. I was so annoyed. I had known Gordo for quite a while and I couldn't believe that he would not have the courage to ask me this himself.

"Quite serious Babes, and he wanted me to ask you on his behalf"

"Well" I told her," don't' say anything to him, I am going to see what happens when he arrives."

Gordo walked in later that afternoon. We exchanged the usual pleasantries, and he showered and got on the massage table. From the moment he entered until he left, he never said a word, not a single word. He was his usual polite self, and we chatted, but he never asked to go down on me and he never tried. Not only did it not happen on that occasion, but for the next two years of meetings once a month, he never asked, never suggested and never tried. I cannot stand a man who is too frightened to confront his own fetish and hides behind politeness and fear, but Gordo was that man. And, as I mentioned, his huge cock, which I believe he had no idea how to use, took forever to ejaculate. I would get blisters on my hands just from trying to wank him off. Sometimes, when I knew I had back to back clients, I would massage Gordo for only 15 minutes, flip him over and begin jerking his huge penis. Often it would take more than a half hour for him to cum. No joke. I wondered every time we did it what his issue was, and to this day, I am not sure, but I think he had mental problems from his past, which we never discussed, and he couldn't relax. Even when he did finally cum, there were just dribbles of sperm and not the fountains I was used to from men his age. Gordo was nice, he was a friend of sorts, but he was someone who I could never imagine living with let alone sleeping with. During my period of celibacy, when Gordo arrived and told me about his diet, he reminded me how difficult it was to remain sex and drug free, if only for a year and when I saw how miserable he was from dieting, that only enforced my opinion that I should just go out and begin fucking again. I was horny, I am always horny, but I just had to find the right guy. My depression, although I didn't realize it was depression back then, was enhanced by the girls who surrounded me every day, the men who came on to me and the alcohol that was free flowing around me. I was in a continual quandary over how to behave, how to react and how to get out of my funk. Life has never been easy for me, although it's never been too difficult either. It's been what I've made it. Yes, I know some of you reading this book will think I am a slut, some might think I'm a whore and a druggie, and some might just relate to what I have been through, although nothing I have been through has been that bad. My life has been what I've made it, and when I was trying to be celibate, no drink, no sex, no drugs, my depression was inevitable without proper counseling. Counseling is something I have never sought, believing firmly in my own ability to control my destiny and my inner self, along with my habits and my addictions. But when I am in control, what surrounds me and the positions I place myself in, are out of my control and make it hard to see the light and stay on the straight and narrow path I am forging to recovery. I hope that makes sense? So when that door opened once again, and Oz, marched in, long haired Oz, sexy dreamy Oz, well, my libido again skyrocketed and my ability to control my sexual desire was tested to its limits.

Mads had warned me that this Australian guy was on his way and that his voice sounded 'just amazing babes' and when the door opened and Oz entered the apartment, I was instantly wet between my legs. Dripping wet!

It was the same old story. He was a turn on and my mind was trying to turn him off. I wanted him, and I wanted him badly. His dick was huge, much larger than Dave's and Dave had really been well hung. I just stared at it, and stared again, as he walked from the shower to the table and lay face down. We hit it off, we hit it off so nicely that I thought I was going to cum before I'd even touched him. His voice was soothing, sweet and erotic, his mannerisms were just tantalizing and his familiarity with my likes and dislikes, uncanny. I flipped him and I wanted to just fuck that big wonderful cock, but I resisted, knowing that I would regret it, and tossed him off in just moments. It was wonderful and yet it was surreal. He knew I wanted more, I knew he wanted more. He knew I was dripping wet, and I knew he wanted to just enter me and make me cum and cum again, but nothing more happened. He dressed, and then just before he left, he asked me out. We both loved the band Temple Fortune, and they were playing at the Hammersmith Odeon the following night. He had tickets, I had time, so we agreed on a date. I was so so excited. I knew with Oz I was in real trouble and celibacy was really on the line with this man. I didn't care, and I agreed to meet him, knowing that if I did, I'd fuck him. But, who cares, right? I needed sex, he needed sex, what could be wrong with that? Too much! That's what was wrong with that.

The concert was at 8 PM. I arrived at 7.45 and by 8.30 there was no sign of Oz. His phone was off, I'd tried calling him, my texts were going unanswered, and I was standing outside the Odeon, all alone, grumpy, willing him to show up. People were all around me, having fun, getting drunk, kissing, but I was all alone. I felt so small and so alone and so vulnerable, wondering exactly what it was I had done.

At 8.45 my phone rang, it was Oz. I was relieved.

"Where are you?" I asked, kind of shouting as I did so, but also excited that at last, he'd surfaced.

"Got stuck underground on the tube. Some kind of incident, I will be there in less that 20 minutes"

His phone went dead. I waited and waited, all the time just thinking about how the evening would end, knowing deep down, we would fuck.

20 minutes passed so slowly and my mind told me to run. I had been standing for an hour just waiting and with Oz now a no show, I bolted.

I took the first train back to my apartment and was underground for about 30 minutes. When I resurfaced I had 4 messages from Oz asking where I was. I never saw him again, I never talked to him again and I never thought about him after that. I was so close to getting 'back in the saddle' so to speak, but something inside me drove me to leave and to continue being celibate.

I would have regressed into sex and drugs with Oz, or with Dave, but I didn't and at that time I sincerely believed I was on the straight and narrow again and that I could beat anything, on my own, without help from trained professionals. How wrong was I?

The 3rd Amigo

My demise began when I went back to modeling. I was forced into this change by my own self admission that by keeping my job in FBSM would not see me through my 1 year of self-sustained celibacy. There were too many distractions, and too many ways to fall back into a lifestyle I really didn't want and a lifestyle that I'd had enough of. Too many close calls, as you now know, and I really wished to see out my whole year. It had been 6 months, or perhaps just a little more and I was doing so well. I was happy with my efforts but so unhappy inside, and needing to push myself even more to get to that finish line, which I could see, but I just couldn't touch.

Modeling, or a return to my old career, offered me an outlet that I believed would keep me on the straight and narrow for the remainder of my celibacy, though just why I believed that is almost beyond thinking about. I'd had such a hard time staying celibate in that career too, but perhaps it was the thought of change that gave me the impetus to try. I found a new agent, Mike, nice guy, and well connected, and he'd managed to get me into London fashion week. This was around October 2013 I think? London fashion week was huge, lots of work, lots of exposure and lots of partying, which was something I wanted to stay clear of. My first gig was at a YSL show, and I made the runway with ease, again, without the cocaine and alcohol, something I hadn't been comfortable doing in the past. I breezed through that day with such grace and confidence. The event finished and as is always the case, everyone, models, designers and all the hangers on, retreated to the after party. I was still sober and of course stood out like a sore thumb as everyone got drunk or high or both and I just hung around drinking water on my own. I felt totally miserable, but knew what

I had to do and why I had to do it, pretending in my own mind that my glass was filled with gin and not water, and reaching out pleasantly to anyone who cared to chat to me.

I was facing the front of the hall when suddenly I felt a presence behind me and then a tap on my left shoulder. At that time in my life, just like the other 100 million other people on earth, I was reading Fifty Shades Of Grey, desperate to meet my Christian Grey. Pure fantasy I know, but seriously, who wouldn't want to meet a man like that? Anyway, I turned round and this hunk of a man was staring me down, right between my eyes, and he was so close to me, we felt like we were already making out with one another.

"Can I buy you a drink?" he offered. Stupid question really because at the party all the drinks were free, so I just laughed.

Buster, as he came to be known, briefly introduced himself to me and asked if we could go somewhere else where he could really buy me a drink. I told him I was sober for the past 6 months and he apologized profusely, but said he'd be delighted to buy me a coke at a place of my choosing. Buster was dreamy and fitted all my criteria for a possible romantic encounter. He was in the music business, had apartments in London and New York, and other than his looks, which were Christian Grey-esque, he just had this aura about him that made my legs buckle and my poosie wet, yet again. My first thoughts were 'oh fuck, another opportunity to get laid and ruin my plans' but with some willpower and determination, I thought again and decided to go out with him and sip a coke that evening. No harm done. Right?

We were a perfect match from the first moment we spoke, and within days, we were dating. It was just magical. We'd go for dinners, to the theatre, to movies, and honestly, after telling Buster about my yearlong celibacy plans, he respected my choices without question. We both knew though that fucking was just around that proverbial corner, it was only a matter of time.

My modeling was talking me all over London again, and his back and forth to New York and beyond meant that we'd see each other on occasion when he was passing through London, and therefore the urge to sleep with one another got stronger as we grew closer and time and distance kept us apart. Each time we spoke and every time we met, I just wanted to fuck his brains out, as he did mine, but I kept my promise and never crossed that line, until one fatal evening, when the best laid plans of mice and men, went south, but south for a very good reason.

My inabilities to stay off drugs in the past and also in the future, and alcohol too, stem from my fear of loneliness. I more certain of this the older I get. I hate being lonely. I've had an inability to be alone and a desire to find Mr. Perfect since I was 13 years old. It just doesn't go away. I seem to attract men who are always unavailable, my fault of course, but that vicious cycle is never ending. With Buster, yet again, I believed I'd found a winner, and that feeling grew intensely the more we dated and the more we were apart. My celibacy, I thought, was going to come to a premature end, and that day was almost upon me. I couldn't remain celibate with the feelings I was gaining from my relationship with Buster and one evening, with only the intention of having sex with him, we were out to dinner and I relented and drank a glass of red wine. My sobriety ended at that moment. I had to have the wine because I knew I was going to fuck him after dinner. It was now or never. I couldn't have sex without alcohol or drugs, my preference of course and something I'd always done, so I agreed to wine and then I agreed to fuck him. The sex itself started of nicely and then descended into rough fucking and bondage, just like Fifty Shades. My fantasies of meeting Mr. Christian grey were being played out live and in person. I was ecstatic and I was also buzzed from my one glass of wine. Our sex was truly amazing, and when it was over and done with, 7 months and 14 days into my yearlong celibacy, I was not unhappy or sad, indeed, just the opposite, I was so happy and I thought, perhaps and just maybe, in love with Buster. Yes, in love, what a great feeling. It was a complete release for me. I felt free as a bird again and fulfilled, more satisfied than I had in a very long time and relaxed. All the tension of the past 7 months drained out of me in an instant, and normality, my normality and that feeling of belonging just exploded in my bosom. I was home and back to where I never thought I would belong ever again. Amazing, was the only word I could conjure up as I lay in bed having cum many times in many different positions. This was bliss and I was looking forward to spending as much time with Buster as was humanly possible in the coming months. My agent was his friend, I don't know if I'd mentioned that previously, and the first time we'd met, that night at London Fashion week, Buster had been challenged by Melvin, my agent, to come over and ask me out, a task which he'd obviously performed quite successfully. I didn't know it at the time, but it was a kind of bet the two of them had, a bet which my agent lost. I was so pleased that Buster was now in my life, relieved that my efforts with celibacy had gone on for over

7 months, but delighted to be back in the saddle getting regular sex, having alcohol again and hopefully staying away from the cocaine, which honestly was just an extension of the booze.

Buster and I became close, very close. His prowess under the sheets was amazing, I practiced massage on his body regularly, and on his cock, more often that that! We became inseparable. Then one afternoon Mel, my agent, called me and asked me to go to a music video audition in Bristol, which is in the west of England. I agreed to do it because the money was great and if I got the job, it would only be two days' work and compensation for what would normally be a week's worth of modeling. A no brainer. I was given a paid first-class ticket to Bristol for the day and off I went. Buster was in New York at the time and although I hadn't seen him for weeks, he was due back later that month and we had a lot planned for his two weeks stay in London. I'd been dreaming about him daily and nightly. I had all these fantasies screaming inside me about what I was going to do to him when he arrived, and more importantly, what he would do to me. He made me so wet, and so secure all at the same time. Another guy who just did it all and treated me like the woman I wanted to be. I never had to worry about anything. He really took care of me.

I got to Bristol and the audition was not what I was expecting. The director, insinuating that Mel, my agent, had suggested I fucked anyone and everyone, had tried it on with me by coming over and hugging me while trying to grope my breasts at the same time. He was disgusting, he was seedy and he was just not someone I wanted to be around, so I walked out and took the first train back to Paddington Station London. On the train I was fuming. Why would Mel have suggested I was such an easy lay and that this man could do what he wanted with me? I decided to call and confront him. I dialed his number and got right into it immediately, shouting and screaming at Mel even though the carriage I was in was full of people. I must have looked like a real bitch. Mel couldn't get a word in as my rant grew louder and louder. I was accusing him of treating me like a whore and trying to Pimp me out and then I made a comment that changed everything. I remember it word for word like it was yesterday.

"You even tried to pimp me out as a bet to Buster!" I shouted. People were looking or they were trying to look away.

Mel replied, "well I'm glad you brought that up, did you know he was married?"

I felt that I had been shot through the heart. There was total silence and I hung up on Mel. Married??

I'd been with married men, you know that by now, but all of them had been up front with me, every one of them, but this one, Buster, had hidden that very important fact. He was married??? I wanted to jump off the moving train, I wanted to scream, I wanted to kill someone, but most of all, I just wanted to cry.

My whole premise of celibacy was to last a year. My reason for breaking the promises I'd made to myself were because of Buster, one of the best people I'd ever met, my Christian grey, my savior, my rock. Now, all destroyed over a stupid bet? My life had turned to turmoil instantly, and on a moving train no less. All my efforts, ruined, and my relationship with Buster? Well, as soon as the train arrived at Paddington, I called him to New York and told him to get fucked. I was inconsolable. I then called Mel and told him I quit. I was done with modeling, done with Mel and I was headed back to FBSM, alcohol and cocaine if necessary. This life was cruel, but this last relationship had done irreparable damage. I was aware of my feelings, even though I knew I'd get over them, but I was unaware of the spiral and strain that this sudden ending would put on my psyche. I would go into freefall for a while, but that was to come. Right there and then, all I wanted was a drink and a line of cocaine. And with that in mind, I called Alice. It was time to party and to forget about the idiot I'd just wasted the last two months with. I was ready to get high and get back into massage and ready to carry on where celibacy left me off.

Life with Mr. P

We had discussed Tiana's tumultuous affair with Mr. P earlier on in one of our previous meetings, but at the time she'd told me there was so much more to come, so we decided to dedicate a whole chapter to him. His job, a member of Parliament in the UK, was high profile, and although I have pressed Tiana often for his real name, her loyalty towards him has remained intact and to this day she has never revealed to me exactly who this MP might be. I have no reason to press her any further because all the stories she's told me are so perverted and so real and I don't wish to inquire further in order that I save myself from finding out who really runs the country where I was born. Mr.P is a pervert, a gentleman and a cad as you are about to find out.

Tiana continued

"We were great together. He would come in for bi-weekly massages, and then it turned to weekly and then we started to go out together. He is married, I still talk to him, even today, and he has kids and is still married, but as I told you earlier, we only ever had sex once, in all the 6 years I have known him, just that one time, and it wasn't even good. It was amazing!" Tiana pouts her perky breasts in my direction yet again as she remembers in her own mind what exactly happened when she fucked Mr. P. I can tell in her eyes, and in the way she speaks, that she loves this man, no matter how long ago it was since she slept with him, her feelings are there for me to see.

"We were like conjoined twins. After he decided he was going to be my 'sugar daddy', and I accepted graciously of course, we would jet off to all these European cities. We went to Copenhagen, Brussels, Paris, Rome, together, as a couple, no hiding, no incognito, no worries."

"You would hold hands, sit with one another, eat together and no one recognized him?" I was skeptical.

"Yes, he wasn't afraid of being recognized and often people would come up and chat with him about his life in politics, his career, his current position, and I would be right there. No one ever questioned me. I assumed they knew he was married, but who knows. He was such a gentleman, but he was also kind of perverted. What I really loved about him was that he took care of everything. He was really a mentor to me. He would pay for everything, he would arrange all our trips, he would even make sure I was up to date on my rent. I loved him for that. He was so organized and caring and I never ever had to worry. I like that in a man. It means I can be the woman I am supposed to be while he, the man, takes his rightful position in taking care of me. Call me stupid or old fashioned, or call me whatever else you want. This is the way I was brought up by my mother and it's what I believe in. Mr. P fulfilled all of my dreams and more. We just never had sex, other than that one time, but we did all sorts of other fun stuff"

"Why did you only have sex one time?" I asked.

"Well, that's another story. You want to hear it before I carry one?" "Of course" why wouldn't everyone want to hear this, I thought. He's a UK politician, was he crap in bed, or did she just fuck him and decide she didn't want him anymore, or did he have guilt after he banged her? After all he was married with kids, although that didn't seem to stop him moving forward after they fucked. I was all ears.

"So" she sighed 'massage was a regular thing with Mr.P, and after two or three visits, he asked for more, so I blew him. He loved it. I am really good at giving blow jobs, and I often use my technique to make guys cum really quickly just so I can move on to the next client. Blow jobs cost more money. Normally I got 100 UK pounds extra for doing that. Anyway, Mr. P loved his first blow job and then things started moving at a frenetic pace. We started having dinners, lunches, drinks, movies, hotel stays etc. He was so into me, and I was into him, so quite naturally, one evening after a fabulous dinner in the center of London, we went to his hotel, a hotel where he stayed regularly, where everyone knew him, and eventually they all knew me, and we had a few drinks in the bar and went to his room and we fucked. I remember lying there and while he was fucking me I realized that I had no deep sexual feelings for him"

I interrupted.

"Hang on, how can you love someone, which you just said you did, then blow them, spend time with them, travel with them and fuck them, but have no sexual feelings for them?"

"I can. I am wired that way. We were great together, but when he fucked me that one time, and remember, we still see one another and talk to one another, even today, I had no feelings for him or what he was doing to me at the time. It was just mundane sex. We made love, he came inside me and I felt nothing. Not one ounce of love or sexual desire to do it again. Trust me, I wanted to try, but I knew it would be a waste of effort, I knew I'd get nothing out of it and I told him that, told him straight to his face. And that's when our real friendship and relationship began. We were and still are, very close. I would continue to blow him regularly, but intercourse was just a no no. He was also frightened of becoming too attached to me, scared to let go, and I could sense that when we fucked. It was a cagey fuck, do you know what I mean?"

I didn't.

"He was putting in too much effort without placing any effort on me at all. Strange to hear now, but at the time, the right choice and we went on to enjoy some great times. We would have so much fun. I went to Glasgow with him. We were there for some conference he attended, and we were lucky enough to score tickets for a concert that same evening at the SEC in Glasgow. It was Foo Fighters I think. Anyway, I went out that day and I bought two sex toys, one for him and one for me and when he came back from his working day we went to bed together for a cuddle before dinner. My toy was a vibrating poosie egg, his a vibrating butt plug." At this point in time I was moving uncomfortably in my chair just thinking about what was coming next, and T could tell that I looked surprised.

"You know what they are, right?"

"Of course I do.......NOT!" I was laughing now, "What the fuck Tiana, explain more please?"

"Alan, a vibrating egg is a device that I can put inside my vagina and turn on and off as I desire by remote control. It's so much fun if it's controlled by someone else though. The butt plug is for him or her and has the same function"

Fuck me, I hadn't lived!

"I inserted the egg and he inserted the plug and we traded remote controls. Off we went to dinner and then to the concert. At dinner, he would turn the remote up and down, turning me on an off inside and making me cum again and again. I would do the same in return, except, his was a butt insert and much more uncomfortable than mine, but also much more fun for me!

Can you imagine trying to eat a bowl of soup and suddenly you're hit with this urge to climax?"

I honestly couldn't!

"I was in heaven, he was in Hell. I would watch him as he was about to chomp down on his chicken and I'd turn the vibrating plug up to full power. He'd go all red, be very uncomfortable, squirm for a moment or two and then look like he was about to puke his chicken all over the table. Then I'd turn it down and he'd relax and enjoy the next bite while we both rolled around in laughter. This was a very upscale restaurant, filled with people who were just staring, and staring at him more than me because he was well known. After dinner we went to the concert, and things got out of control a little. My vagina is a sacred place and also a place where not too much fits. I know you're laughing now, especially after all the tales of large cocks I've told you about, most of which my vagina has swallowed with ease, but honestly, even tampons have difficulty staying inside me and when we arrived at the venue, I could feel that I had vibrating egg issues. I never wore underwear with Mr. P. He didn't like it. He wanted easy access at all times. He would play with my clit in taxi's in restaurants, in movie theatres, and any other public place he chose. He also loved touching my tits. So, no underwear. We arrived and began to walk towards the entrance of the concert hall and Mr. P decided to turn up the power on the egg, quite an inopportune moment and the first time he'd done so when I was in a standing position. I was so surprised, I missed a step, opened my stride and the bloody egg fell out of my vagina, right in front of this huge crowd of people. My heart stopped, my poosie stopped, but my blood pressure went through the roof. The egg started to roll, Mr. P began to howl uncontrollably with laughter, my face turned bright red and people just stopped and watched as this egg rolled and rolled towards to curb. No one understood what happened other Mr. P and I and as the egg approached the end of its use, by rolling onto the road and underneath the wheel of an incoming cab, Mr. P suggested that he find the closest bathroom to remove his butt plug in order that we remained on level terms. I refused him this pleasure and spent the rest of the evening turning his butt on and off just to annoy the heck out of him. We had such a blast that evening and really every evening we were together.

Mr. P, and I called him that for a reason, had some perversions other than the sex toys. If I tell you this, it'll blow you away, which by the way, is the only time I will ever blow you Alan!" she laughed hysterically, as did I.

Mr. P and I were in bed one afternoon, in his hotel. I'd just massaged his cock and he'd come all over the sheets. It was a mess. I suggested we call room service, he suggested otherwise.

"I want you to stand over me and piss into my mouth"

"What?" I was dumbstruck. I'd heard about men who loved 'watersports' but I'd never met one.

"Go for it" he demanded

"I'm not doing that"

"Well go in the bathroom and piss in a glass and bring it back here."

So I did. I ventured into the hotel room bathroom, took the cover off the glass and sat and peed into it. I then returned to the bed and handed it to him. Mr. P took the glass and drank the lot, like a shot of tequila, straight down, no stopping. He looked at me with his sexy smile and said,

"I just wanted to taste you, to have part of you inside me"

Well, I wasn't sure what to say, so I just smiled and told him that was fine. Pervert! Then another time I was on my period and he went down on me. He pulled the tampon out of my vagina with his teeth and then licked it. It was covered in blood. Gross! But that was Mr. P, he was really into me and being part of me.

Our time together was special for me. It gave me an opportunity to be with someone I truly cared about. It helped me grow into a stronger woman by watching and learning from him as he worked and played, often very hard, and it became a convenient way for me to travel and to see and obtain the finer things in life for free, while taking care of Mr. P's never-ending sexual fantasies and desires. I knew he was never going to leave his wife and kids and I didn't want him to. I wanted a friend, a father figure and a real man, not some toy boy who had no direction in life. My relationship with Mr. P is as strong today as it was in 2014, only now we don't have to sleep together, I never blow him and our mutual respect for one another is just that. Respect.

He no longer represents his constituency in the UK as a MP, and he's still married and has two grown up kids, but Mr. P came to me when I was with the agency and stayed with me even when I went solo and rogue. He's a darling of a man, and one I will never forget.

Going Rogue

Julia had gone, left the agency and left under a cloud. She'd decided to go it alone. Her ambition was to be a kept woman for the rest of her life. No idea how she was going to do that, but she had her plans and we had ours. By WE I mean Alice and I.

Julia was well organized, neat and tidy and always on top of everything, a true asset to the agency with her ability to delegate. As soon as she departed, things went to Hell, and really never recovered. All of the apartments were left unattended, unclean and understandably, our clientele dropped off. Madds could not be controlled. She upset the clientele more and more with her brash and uncontrollable manner. She just didn't care. Her attitude was outrageous. I recall listening to her once on the phone, she came to London from Swindon for the day and we all went to lunch. Her phone was ringing off the hook from the moment she arrived until the moment she left, and some of the conversations she had were unbelievable.

"Come on babes, it's only 120 Pounds, you can't sit and wank off at home for that price and enjoy it"

"Babes, she's not going to fuck you, she's going to massage you and toss you off, pay up, don't be a miser"

"You want to go down on her? Then you need to do a private deal with her babes, not me, so go talk to your banker and make sure you bring enough cash to satisfy everyone"

This and so much more. She just didn't have a filter. Whatever was on her mind came out just as she'd think it, no filter. Business for a period of time was so slow that Alice and I would sit around for days on end doing nothing. No money came in, but plenty was going out. There was a period of time that we had no clients for about 3 weeks straight, and that was a killer. We didn't know what was going on. Justin seemed to have lost control of his own business and I found this hard to take. He was such a formidable character, but ever since Julia left, he'd become withdrawn, or perhaps he was just saddened by her loss, in any event, he vanished and became an owner who we felt didn't really care what was going on inside his own company. Alice and I had plans. My sobriety was over, I'd been fucked, literally by Buster, and I was ready to begin this vicious cycle of sex drugs and rock'n roll, all over again. Why not? Right?" I didn't know what to say. I was still thinking about the vibrating egg falling from her vagina at a rock concert, pondering that scene with my vivid imagination and asking myself, why would anyone do that? "Alan, are you with me?"

I wasn't, I was lost in all sorts of thoughts and I had so many questions. Tiana is a beautiful 30 year-old Estonian, she's articulate, funny, and very easy to listen to with her sexy Baltic/American accent, but honestly, and I am not one to judge, how can anyone do what she's done and come out the other side in one piece with all of her inner-self still intact? It was mind blowing to me that she'd been such a 'wild child' and survived with very few scars, physical or mental. The more I listened, the more she divulged, the more cautious I was that deep down there were scars yet to be unearthed, and not being a therapist, I wondered how I would react and what I could say should such a situation arise. I also was curious how her parents had been totally unaware of her lifestyle for all this time. Anyway, my brief was to listen and not to judge, as I mentioned before, and I wanted to get as much from her as was humanly possible while she was in the mood to chat, because who knew how long this was going to last. According to Tiana, she had enough information and stories to fill 5 more books, and that's just what we might end up doing.

"Yes, I am listening" I told her. And with that, she marched on with her diatribe.

"Alice was mental, mental in many ways. I know mental is a strong word, but it's a word that you British use as a term of endearment when you like someone and you know they are way over the top with their standards of behavior. Alice was most definitely mental and had an incredible influence on what I did as a human being. I am not really a follower, but I often followed her.

No idea why, but I did.

One evening I called her and suggested I'd make her a really nice dinner. "Dinner at my place?" I'd asked. "I will cook, and you can bring a nice bottle of wine" We were all set.

I shopped, I cooked and got everything ready. She called. "I have a new friend T, she is from Australia and is joining the agency, can I bring her?" Instead of just Alice and me, it became Alice, Sue and me. I didn't mind, after all, at one point in time I was the newbie, and so I made a little extra food to cover our newest guest.

The two of them showed up late, not unusual for Alice, but annoying all the same. I served dinner, I served wine, I served more wine and more wine and then after we'd finished the 3rd or 4th bottle, Alice had this brilliant idea to call her drug dealer, Stavros, and get some cocaine delivered. We were all in agreement, after all, none of us were sober or on hiatus from drugs, so 'fuck it', a line or two of coke, and who knew, perhaps we'd all get lucky.

Stavros sent his side-kick, Anton, who showed up with a few grams in a plastic bag. Alice paid him and then the party began. One line of coke became two which became 4 and between the 3 of us and another 2 visits from Anton, we snorted enough to sink a ship. I was so high, higher than a kite, and all the time we are snorting, Alice, our ringleader, is begging for more and more and more. It got out of hand. Alcohol had dried up, coke was finished, and we were wasted, totally wasted. It was now 6.30 AM and I was supposed to be at work by 9. By now, modeling and Mel, my agent, were history, and FBSM with the agency was my way forward, or so I thought, and that day, I believe it was a Saturday, I was working. Alice, the bitch, had already called Justin and told him she was sick. I on the other hand was too high to call and knew that one of us had to be there on time. I decided that desperate times called for desperate measures, and with that in mind, at 6.45 Am I headed to Tesco, the local supermarket, to get more wine. If I was going to suffer through until 9 PM that night, I was going to do it drunk. "Fuck the rest of the world" I thought, as I headed out to get more fuel for this fire that was already burning out of control.

Returning with three more bottles of wine, after spending the last of the cash I had in my pocket, Alice, Sue and I drank ourselves into oblivion. It was now 8.30 and I decided just to call in sick and fuck the consequences. I was the best masseuse the agency had, and they knew it. I'd come out of sobriety and I'd binged, and work was just not going to happen that day, the wine and coke had made sure of that. This was the beginning of Alice and I going rogue. Rogue was going to be a murderous and tortuous decision that neither of us would ever regret, and this is how we'd started. Cocaine was back, booze was back and now all I needed was a fuck. It wasn't too long before that happened.

I got up two days later, didn't know where I was, but I'd received a dozen calls and texts from Justin. I looked at my phone and then I searched the apartment to see if I might have any remnants of our binge episode from Friday night to munch on. There were none. My apartment was eerily quiet. The girls had obviously gone and I was all alone, left to contemplate my continued failings and desires to binge on drugs and booze. It didn't take long for the tears to come, lots of tears, so many in fact that I soon came round to the fact I was drowning in my own self-pity. I couldn't have that and after two cups of coffee and some deep thought, I sobered up to the fact that I was destitute and alone and that these were contributing factors in my surrender to drugs and alcohol. I didn't know what to do about it, other than what I'd done in the past, be aware and be strong, then conquer. But did I want to? Probably not, probably the last thing I wanted to do right there and then was to become celibate again, indeed, I just wanted to fuck someone, anyone, right then, and without caring who he would be. I was overwhelmed with lust and frustration. And then I picked up my phone and checked my messages.

Justin had called several times, and texted too. Something was up. I knew he hated the fact both Alice and I had ducked out on work the day before yesterday, but did I really care? I called him, ready and willing for the barrage of abuse that was about tom come my way.

"T, we have a problem" Justin told me, without any prior small talk.

"What's the issue?" I asked

"I need to close Camden Town immediately. It's a long story, can you get here ASAP?"

"I will need a couple of hours to get ready" I told him.

"You don't need to get ready, you just need to get here. You won't be working today, at least you won't be blowing anyone, you'll just be helping me get out of here"

"You going to tell me what happened?" I was curious, and also slightly concerned.

"Yes, when you get here"

And with that, his phone went dead. I just looked at the phone and pondered what could have possibly gone wrong so quickly, and then I decided to check my other messages.

One was from Mr. P, asking to see me that day, and five were from Alice, all they said were, 'call me"

After freshening up, cold shower time again, which is something I only do after binging. It's sort of a turn on for me. Makes my nipples erect and my poosie wet, not sure why, but it does, and it takes my mind off the night before and the mess I knew I was actually in. It's a sort of non-orgasm, orgasm. Can't really explain it other than it makes me feel good, if only for a few minutes."

I blushed. She continued.

"Alice was driving me nuts with her texts. I used to have a client who did this to me, his name was Tom. He'd text me 50 times until I relented and replied with four words, 'yes I'll blow you', and then he'd stop and call Madds to make an appointment, at which time, Madds, who was well aware of Toms texting, would tell him I was booked for at least the next two weeks. After about 3 months of back and forth, Tom disappeared, for good. Funny thing was, I saw him once, only once, and we got on really well, but he was obsessed with me after that, obsessed in the creepiest of ways. I was glad when he vanished. Alice on the other hand, wasn't going to vanish, so I texted her telling her that I was on my way to Camden Town to see Justin and asked her if she knew what was going on. Immediately I pressed SEND, my phone rang.

"Haven't you heard?" Alice asked me, her tone of voice was extremely high pitched, suggesting she really was panic stricken. Alice had this trait of elevating the pitch in her voice when she got excited. She'd do the same when she was fucking someone and enjoying it. She'd scream to the rafters. I know, I have been in the room next door to her many times while she's been engaged in great sex. It's impossible to ignore and her climaxes are like a gospel choir reaching the end of their performance, enthralling and great to listen too.

"Hear what? Justin just called and told me we are closing down Camden and I had to get there ASAP to assist."

"You know the coffee shop at the entrance to the building?"
"Of course"
"Well it turns out that all of our clients have been frequenting that place before they come up to see us, and they've been chatting to anyone and everyone about what goes on in the apartment, so the owner of the shop, the big fat guy,

Russel, you know him, right?"

"Yes"

"Well he spoke to the building manager, who talked to one or two of our clientele, who spilled the beans, and we've been given 2 days to pack up and leave. Well, Justin has, because it's his problem, not ours."

"Fuck!" was all I could say. "What do we do now?"

"Justin told me we have a new place to go to, and it seems that Julia was responsible for paying the rent in Camden and Bond St, and she's stopped doing both, so Justin is strapped for cash, which means the next place is going to be shitty, and probably not worth showing up to."

"What do you want to do?"

"I think you and I need to discuss in private. We are the two best masseuses he has, so why don't we just go it alone?"

All of this was too much for my poor head to take in. I think I was still high and drunk, Alice on the other hand, was in full flow and ready to move on, or so it seemed. Alcohol and cocaine has little effect on her. I think that's why she can go all day and all night and then show up as if nothing ever happened.

I, on the other hand, was having great difficulty taking all of this in.

"I need to shower and get dressed, and then I will go to Camden. Will you be there?"

"I am here now!" she shouted. "Get yourself in a cab" and with that, the call ended.

We moved out and into a new place near Nottinghill Gate. It was crappy. The neighborhood wasn't great but the place itself was even worse. It was unfinished, unfurnished and undecidedly dirty. Our clients didn't want to come there, even though we were close to the underground station, and we started having days where no one would show up. Madds wasn't helping either. She'd speak to prospective clients on the phone and they'd ask if there was showers available, which there wasn't, and she'd tell them, "who needs showers babes, just have a fucking bath!"

It was a mess. Our takings were down, my rent needed paying, and my cocaine habit feeding too. Alice and I decided, enough was enough. We were going rogue. No discussion, just a plan, which we sorted very quickly and efficiently, in our own minds, and then we just did it. When Alice and I do something, we don't do it half-heartedly, we do it with vigor and with intention.

Our plan? Well, sugardaddy.com, where else. And so, within days of moving to Nottinghill Gate, Alice and I were on line and in the groove to find us both men, real men, who would pay our bills.

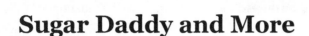

Sugar Daddy and More

Buster, remember Buster, that fucker! He kept calling, texting. He was relentless. I ignored him. I couldn't escape. It was mind boggling, he was becoming a pain.

'Fuck me, see me, dinner with me, etc…'

I got annoyed, frustrated, and upset, but still he came on to me, weekly, then it became daily. I needed to get rid of him or see him. I was horny and he had a huge dick. He was married, he'd lied to me, he'd been a thorn in my side for a few months now, but I wanted to fuck someone.

I decided to see him. I decided I was going to fuck him and when I picked up my phone to text him the good news, I knew it was a mistake, but a mistake I wanted to make. Sounds crazy, but that's how I felt. I needed something outside of cocaine and booze, and decided Buster was it. In the meantime, Alice and I had posted profiles on sugardaddy.com, and we were both determined to find a man or men for each of us to see and men who would take care of us by paying all our bills. Business at the agency had died a death. I had no income coming in but I was still spending plenty, so why not let someone else pay? Right? It's not difficult. I have the body, I have the mind and I have the will, so why not have the man too?

Our profiles went live. Mine was pretty simple. A few words about me, and some lies about what I liked, and a few sexy pics and hey, you know how it goes? Show a man your tits and they will salivate until they can touch them. My profile said I loved Yoga. A lie, but it turns men on with imagery of me stretching my legs to enable them to fuck me harder. I told them I was a model, not really true, but again, it brings a certain connection into their heads, especially their smallest and most stupid head. "Hey I need to fuck a model, the guys will love it when I tell them I am fucking a Vogue or Victoria's Secret girl" You get where I'm coming from Alan, don't you? I actually did. I could see the logic immediately. I mean, who wouldn't want to fuck a model? Well, I wouldn't, but then that's just me, but a Yoga aficionado? I smiled and she continued.

"We'd placed our Ad's and we waited. In the meantime, I called Buster and we met up. It was nice seeing him, but with Buster, although we love each other's company, after a few hours, we are both ready to kill one another. It's hard to explain, but we are both such fiery characters and when enough is enough....

Anyway, we met, I shouted at him, he shouted at me. He explained that his marriage, the one he'd never told me about, was in tatters and that his wife had caught him in bed with a Swedish model. Did I really care? He'd lied through his teeth and he deserved everything he got, as far as I was concerned. His lies had led me to drink and cocaine, well, not really, but that was my thought process as he sat and spilled the beans about his current troubles. I really didn't want to listen, but as the wine took effect, not only did I listen, I was giving him the come on to take me back to his place and to fuck me. He knew it, I knew it, and in time, about thirty minutes, we were on our way. Buster lived very close to my place and that was convenient. After I stopped off to pick up some of my clothes, I knew I would need a change for the following day and that I was going to fuck him all night, we headed to his place. We arrived and he waited less that 15 seconds to jump me. It was rough sex like I've never had before, and as you know, I have had rough sex. Even with him! He tore off my dress, he stuck his tongue into my throat, he was slapping my ass, my tits, my poosie, and my legs. He was thrusting inside me and then stopping, bringing me to climax and then withdrawing. He tossed me like a rag doll on and off his bed, his couch, his kitchen counter. We were fucking like maniacs, all over his apartment, and you know what? I loved it. It was amazing sex. Better than anything I'd had in many years. Passion and pain, a lethal combination. My high, my climax, my total pleasure. He never came until I took his cock and smacked it with a spatula and then bit him hard with my teeth. He was so vocal with his orgasm and me with mine, I thought the neighbors would run in thinking a murder had taken place. It was just fabulous. We finished up and he asked me to go again. "You on the blue pills?" I asked him, but before I had finished my sentence, he was hard and inside me, fucking the shit out of my, now red raw poosie. I loved it, and I worshiped sex like this. We fucked all night. He apologized for his indiscretions, I apologized for nothing, then we fucked some more. Buster knew nothing about my cocaine habit, and I kept it that way for many months to follow, but I didn't need cocaine with sex that was this good. I'd never liked rough sex, well, not really, but this was fantastic and I wanted more and more. Buster spent a few weeks in London before returning to New York and when he did, I was all ready to explore my connections on sugardaddy.com. It hadn't taken long. I had more than 30 responses in the first two weeks, Alice had 3. I sat down with her and explained the nuances of using a site like this and what she needed to do to increase traffic to her profile. She listened and then acted. Within hours of a few minor tweaks, and much racier pics, she had another 10 replies. I on the other hand was on to my first 'date' with a young Indian businessman, who seemed very nice and also very rich. He was going to be my guinea pig, and boy what a guinea pig he turned out to be. We made arrangements to meet near Liverpool St Station, in a public bar. He was early, but I was earlier than him, I wanted to sit and watch, just in case he wasn't who his picture suggested he'd be. He walked in, smartly dressed, polo shirt, jacket and jeans, and I recall thinking that he was fairly handsome. We hugged, sat and had a few drinks, then he gave me 100 UK pounds for my time and left. We never kissed, we never did anything, and he paid for the drinks, but nothing happened and off he went. Strange experience, but for 100 pounds, who cared? Not me. Business had been shockingly poor since Judith left and Justin had moved us to that shitty place in Nottinghill Gate. Any financial compensation was appreciated, and the Indian man gave me enough to go buy some cocaine. Yes, Buster was gone, cocaine was my substitute for his cock.

My next date from the site was also an Indian, not sure why, but this one, Sanjib, was delightful. He fucked me and gave me 500 UK pounds. I felt like a whore, but cocaine made me get over that fact very quickly, and he only lasted a minute before he came inside me, so the experience was quick and I repeated this experience with Sanjib often, just for income. Drinks, dinner and a 60 second fuck for 500 pounds was the deal of the week!

Alice was also on fire. She'd met a weirdo who just wanted her to masturbate naked in front of him nightly and he paid her 200 pounds per orgasm. What a bargain! I was looking for better, and better came along, but not before my date with this Hugh Heffner look alike. Oh my, what a story that was. I met him in a bar, he was about 75, perhaps older, although his pictures showed a man closer to 60. Anyway, I showed up and I swear this man was Heff. Exact double, even in the way he dressed. Totally freaky. We had drinks and then we went to his place near the Portobello Rd, where, after he invited me in, I realized from all the toys lying around, he was a BDSM addict. That didn't put me off, but what did make me want to vomit was when he came out of his room completely naked, obviously on Viagra, his dick was stretched and erect to its limit, I had to look at this aged wrinkly body, which was disgusting in itself, and a flagpole of a penis, ready and waiting for action. He made me strip, and gave me props, a bra with nipple holes and a short skirt and then he began working me with his toys. I hated every minute of this, which lasted over an hour. He wouldn't get soft, and he stank of cigarettes. He smoked three at a time, one in his mouth, one in his hand and one burning in an ashtray nearby. It grossed me out and even the 500 UK pounds he paid me didn't seem enough to compensate me for the disgusting experience I'd endured. He called me several times after that, he lived in New York or Cincinnati, I just can't recall, but I never saw him again.

It was the start of a strange BDSM period for me, Buster was back in town, and I wanted to fuck him before exploring more responses I'd had from sugardady.com.

"Want to go to a BDSM orgy tonight?" Buster asked me, quite nonchalantly and without breaking sweat.

"Sure" Why not, right? Never done it before so let's give it a try.

He collected me at 7 PM, and when he walked into my home, he was carrying a blindfold. I had on a mini dress, with nothing underneath it. No underwear, I was under strict instruction not to wear panties or a bra, and it had to be that way or the date was off. Excited and also apprehensive, Buster threw the blindfold around my eyes and marched me out to a waiting cab. My heart was racing, but Buster played with my naked clit as the cab drove for over an hour to this secret destination. When we arrived, Buster paid the cabbie and removed my blindfold. We were outside one of the largest homes I'd ever seen, and there were over 40 Rolls Royce cars and Ferrari's parked right in front of me.

"What the fuck is this Buster?" I asked him. I was panicking, honestly, I'd never seen such wealth.

We entered the home and were welcomed with glasses of champagne and some canapes, the veggie ones were excellent. There must have been 50 to 70 people, male and female, stunningly beautiful people, bar one or two, and all dressed to thrill. I didn't look or feel out of place, I just felt naked, but I was still fully dressed. Hanging on the walls of this mansion and set up inside glass fronted cabinets, was a plethora with BDSM shit. Handcuffs, whips, nipple hooks and all sorts of other crazy paraphernalia. It was scary yet intriguing, and it made Christian Grey look like the Bishop of Durham, a total innocent.

Buster spoke.

"I am going to blindfold you and take you into another room. Please trust me." On went the blindfold and we walked slowly into another area of the house and then into a room, where I was greeted by total silence. I felt like we were alone, but my 6th sense told me there was someone else there, someone I didn't know. Buster told me to keep the blindfold on and remove my dress. I complied. I was now completely naked. I then felt my arms being tied and my legs bound. My heart was now racing. I had hands, 4 hands, all over me, and I was sweating, nervous and decidedly anxious. And then, out of nowhere, I was whipped, and whipped hard. There was no conversation, just the noise of the whip hitting my naked flesh and the wind it created on its downward swing into my buttocks. It was so painful and yet so erotic. I was taken aback by the ferocity of the blow to my backside, but that was nothing in comparison of what was about to happen. The blows got harder and harder and my pain got more unbearable by the stroke, but yet, I was turned on, turned on like never before. I was on the verge of crying, yet I was also close to orgasm. It was amazing, and frightening at the same time. My beating continued for a few minutes, and then 4 hands became two and two hands became one penis and then it started. Buster, I presumed it was him, although I was still blindfolded, I sort of knew how his cock felt inside me, began to fuck me. Hard and then harder, slow then faster, deep then deeper and I came and I came and I came. I think I even squirted, for the first time in many years. I was in heaven, I was in pain, I was overcome with submission to this man's great cock. What a feeling. What an experience, what a night.

When he eventually came inside me, I felt him cock throb as it ejaculated deeper than any cock before him, and his warm cum just spread inside my ovaries, only do be defeated at that last hurdle by woman's best friend, LUCK! I was not using any contraceptive devices, shocking, I know, but I relied on men to use condoms and or withdrawal. Buster did neither.

I had never felt like that, ever. Buster took off the blindfold, we got dressed and then left. No words were needed, no gestures, nothing, we just left, and we got back into that cab, who was still waiting outside, and drove all the way to his apartment, again, about an hour's drive, where we fucked all night and into the morning. Sensational, and very satisfying. Mr. Cocaine was rendered obsolete once again.

Buster and I were like brother and sister, plus the sex. We just fought all the time, and then made out the rest of the time. It was such a weird relationship, but the best sex I'd had to that point in my life. I knew he was fucking other women, he made no secret of that, and I was fucking other men, which he knew about, but together, we were magical, animalistic and a complete anomaly. Out affair lasted only a few months more. I got sick and tired of feeling sick and tired as he lied his way through many events he denied, yet I had access to real proof he was cheating and lying to me. I got fed up and eventually we parted and I went back to cocaine, not part time, when I was missing his huge cock, but full time, when he was completely gone. I realize now, that he was by far the biggest high I had at the time and that cocaine was just a poor substitute for what I couldn't get from him. I still chat to him now and again, even today, but I know that deep down, he misses me more than I miss him.

I also realized that sugardaddy.com was my future and not Buster. He's asked me to move in with him after that orgy, but I decided we'd never be a match and declined. At sugardaddy.com, at least I could pick and choose who I wanted to fuck, and I got paid for it. I got paid even if I didn't fuck, but with Buster, it was all take from his part, and I got nothing in return other than his cock.

Alice and I were truly on a path to destruction. After I'd adjusted her profile on the sugardaddy.com web site, her love life and financial situation took off into the stratosphere. She was meeting the right kind of guys with the right kind of cash. We didn't need to do FMSM any more, or so we thought, we just needed rich horny guys to keep us in the lifestyle we were accustomed to and to assist in facilitating cash for cocaine. It wasn't difficult, at least not in the beginning, and we both thrived. I had several guys on the go, some who I fucked and others who I just took cash or clothes, or trips abroad from. It was easy. It seemed that my life was changing, and changing, I hoped, for the better. Alice and I would compare wild stories each day and night, when we'd get together, which was about once a week, travel schedule permitting, and we discussed opening our own agency and web site, but it never happened. We were too engrossed in taking cash and gifts from the guys we were meeting. It was all so simple, or was it?

Home

Tiana seems always to be calm when we chat. Nothing seems to fluster her and her lack of mood swings seem to confirm that her addictions are now condemned to her past. Today I decide to confront her directly about the addiction issues in her past and how exactly she pulled herself from the brink, not once, but several times. With utmost composure and absolute calm, she begins.

"I firmly believe that we all control our own bodies and that addiction is a state of mind that our bodies agree to because our minds tell it that excess will be fine, and then our minds say, enough, and that addiction can end. I realize that I am wired differently in this way and that so many addicts cannot do this, in fact the majority of addicts are incapable of stopping on their own. I however am special and have the will and the internal power to cease and desist from any addiction as and when I want to."

"What about sex?" I ask. I knew she might not be doing cocaine, but I also knew she was having lots of sex, sex that she'd admitted wasn't great, but sex nonetheless.

"Sex is different. I want to meet the love of my life. You know from what I've told you that I have been close many times, but, wrong place, wrong situation," her voice tapers off and she looks upwards towards the heavens for her next sentence.

"Sex with Buster was fabulous. Sex with other men has been great too, all those men were completely unavailable to me, even though I dreamed that something might change, it never did. And then, on sugardaddy.com, I met Darren, from Texas."

"Who was Darren?"

"Darren is this dreamy blond Texan guy who found my profile to be interesting, but was quite clear from his initial communication that he was married and had kids. He happened to be in London and wanted company. I couldn't really see his face on the shots he'd posted, but he looked OK and indeed, when I met him, he was more than just OK.

Darren was just amazingly attractive, sensational actually. One of the most handsome guys I had ever met. We had an amazing time together that evening."

"Just one evening?" I asked, interrupting her in full flow.

"Yes, just one, but boy, was it amazing. Darren was a distraction from the dreary surroundings at Nottinghill Gate. That apartment will live in my memory as one of the worst places I'd ever been. Bond St was also shabby, but Nottinghill? Gosh, it was a basement, and had no light. It was dull, dingy, dreary and downright disgusting. I hated it, hated it with vengeance. I was given whole days on my own in that place because it was only a studio and there was no room for anyone else to do massage. I would get three days a week, and one of the other girls would get the same. I drove myself insane on down time. Business went from bad to worse, and with date like Darren, when I was actually out and about and being appreciated and also earning, it was just so pleasurable. I loved my sugerdaddy dates. I was still fucking the 'cum in two seconds' Indian guy at 500 UK pounds a pop, but Darren made it easy to want to give it all up and find my true soul mate. His looks, were just wow! We chatted, we drank, we had dinner, and then we fucked. Our deal was 500, but at the end of the night, in fact, it was around 7AM that following morning, when I woke to find him cooking breakfast and making me coffee, I decided that charging him would be a mistake. He'd taken his time to make love to me, make love properly, not just fuck me. He'd licked me from head to toe and back again. He'd entered me with care, thrusting gently and then more vigorously, as I guided him to my pleasure points, one at a time. Then, without asking, he'd fucked me doggie style, one of my favorite positions, pulling out before coming all over my ass. It was so erotic and so mind-blowingly exciting, I just decided he was going to have a freebie. He couldn't believe it when I told him to keep his money and suggested we meet again in three weeks when he came back to the UK. I told him that would be great, but I knew he had two kids and a wife that he loved and I also knew, because he'd told me, that he fucked other women regularly, so in my mind, this was a one off. There would be no more Darren. I also had booked a trip to

LA, city of my dreams, for that following week. I had enrolled in a dance/acting class, hoping to pursue my dreams of ending up in Hollywood" Tiana stops and raises her eye brows as if to say, "I know, more fool me" and then continues.

"The trip was for one week, one week on my own, enough to see LA and do some of the classes I'd dreamed about and I'd also picked up some modeling work. I purchased a ticket on BA several months prior and was so excited to have this opportunity to be where I thought I belonged, Los Angeles. I'd never been there and the dread in my mind was that I would be disappointed and all of my dreams would be shattered. I was so nervous when I purchased that ticket.

As I counted down the days, one by one, then hour by hour, I found that the excitement was greater than that of having sex with Buster, and believe me, sex with Buster was always a thrill. My libido and my job had taken a back seat to expectation. I had even made some sugardaddy dates for LA, which in the end, I never kept."

I stopped her right there in her stride.

"Are you still on that web site even today?"

"Oh yes, I get lots of messages, but I never answer them" Tiana picks up her phone and shows it to me. "Look" she says," over 40 messages, all unanswered, and that's just this week."

I take a look, and sure enough, there are messages from Rickthedick, 'what you looking for baby, come to dinner with me' and men just like him, who are all looking for young ladies to entertain them and to pay them for that privilege.

"You're very aware of why I don't do sugardaddy now, so let's talk about that another time. OK?"

I agreed, I did know why, something I haven't written about in this book, but maybe the next, and Tiana started up again, without giving too much though to anything but her LA story.

"We landed, it was around 8 PM and when the plane was descending, my window seat gave me the perfect view of all of LA and it's electrical show, which was a sprawl that went on into infinity."

Having landed at LAX many times myself, I fully understood what she was describing. LA just goes on and on and on and seems to never end. When you land at night, it's so impressive and it looks like a trillion stars have been placed on the ground.

"When the wheels of that airplane actually touched down, my heart skipped a beat and then I cried, tears of joy, tears that I will never forget. It was as if I knew I was home. This was it. I had landed in the place I was meant to live, and I just knew it. I had an overwhelming feeling of comfort, satisfaction, and relief. I was here and I wanted to jump out of my seat and scream to the heavens. These feelings continued from the minute I got off the plane until I reluctantly re boarded that very same plane one week later.

The smell in the air, that warm air, that still air, that exciting air, it just took over every sense I had in my body. I was staying in Sherman Oaks, a suburb of LA, situated in the San Fernando Valley. My hotel was nice, a Hilton I believe, and I hired a car. Suddenly my life took on a new meaning. All thoughts of FBSM, sugardaddy, the Indian, Buster and everyone else, just vanished. I was solely concentrated on the present and not the past or the future. My life, at long last, seemed to have meaning. I knew I had to be here, right here, (she was using present tense because we were in LA conducting this interview, and LA is where she lives today), and I was going to do everything in my power to get here, which as you now know, I did. That week was the catalyst, the catalyst for my entire being." She was shedding small tears of joy as she related this story, and I could see what this had meant to her and just how genuine she was at this point.

"LA, yes LA, city of my dreams and now my home, and all because of some, not so silly, childhood fantasy. It's amazing to think that this one week which I spent here 4 years ago, propelled my being into living here full time. That week was the best week of my entire life and if it wasn't the best, it certainly was the most important.

I spent the whole week looking around and becoming acclimatized to the city and its culture, reaffirming in my own mind that yes, this was my city, the place where my life would explode and then blossom into what I always imagined it to be. I just cannot explain how important that week was, even though it was fairly uneventful, (I truly loved just being a tourist), it was the most eventful week I had ever lived. Nothing happened, yet everything happened.

When it was time to leave, I was distraught. I thought of a million reasons not to go back to London, all of which were completely irrational, but at the time, made sense, then no sense at all. I had the bug, I was addicted, and I needed to return as soon as I could to live out the rest of my life and my dreams."

I Just Want To Go Back

"Mr.P, behind the wheel of his shiny new Jaguar, came to collect me at London Heathrow airport. Because of his status as a politician, he received so many benefits, such as free parking, expedited immigration privileges, and so on. When I landed, he was there and I was whisked through by an entourage of his choosing, right past all the long immigration lines, right through customs and right into his arms. I was sad to be back and he was happy to see me. I'd sat at my window seat on the jumbo jet from LAX, for 10 hours and 40 minutes, dreaming of my time in LA and how I would return and live there, and now, as I was frog marched into Heathrow Terminal 5's main lobby, to be greeted by Mr.P's happy face, I just wanted to turn around and go all the way back to the USA, or puke. I had no choice at that point and although Mr. P wanted to give me a huge hug, I made a B-line for the ladies room, where I found a vacant cubicle, sat down and cried. I must have been in there for 5 minutes, sobbing uncontrollably, when there was a knock on the door and a strangers voice asking if I was OK. I pulled myself together and left to find Mr.P, who by now was pacing up and down with worry. I hugged him and asked him to take me to his car, where, within 60 seconds of sitting down in the passenger seat, I broke down in tears again and told him that I wanted to leave the UK as soon as I could and move to America, and not just any place in America, but LA. He sat and listened, tried to console me, and then decided that this wasn't the time or the place to talk me out of my dreams, so he started the engine and we left for London. He was staying the night in his usual hotel, and after dropping me off to get some clothes and to help me unpack, I went with him to his room for the night, where he ordered food and we spoke. I told him all about my trip, how I'd felt right at home from the moment I'd arrived in Los Angeles, and how London and my life in the sex industry meant nothing to me anymore. Mr.P knew me better than most, and he just let me talk. He never said much, but he knew I was deadly serious about leaving the UK and he knew when I made my mind up to do something, I always did it. We ate, and we lay together all night. Nothing happened. He didn't want sex, he didn't want FBSM, he just wanted to hug me and let me sleep. When I woke up the next morning, we ate breakfast and I left, as did he. Before I departed, Mr.P grabbed me and suggested I take a week or two to think about my life and what direction I was going and not to rush into anything I might regret. I could tell from his facial expression that he was more frightened of losing me than I was of moving to Los Angeles. He probably believed that if I left, he'd never see me again. I always knew he loved me, even though he never told me and I also knew that if it wasn't for his wife, kids and career, we would have had a chance at making our relationship permanent, but that was not to be, and we kissed one another on the cheek and left.

On my way home, a term I now used very flippantly, knowing that home for me was going to be LA, Buster texted me.

"ARE YOU BACK IN LONDON?"

Alice was calling me too, and the office wanted to know when I would be back doing massage. My Indian sugar daddy had plans to see me, plans which we'd made before I'd left, and all I could think of was Santa Monica pier, Hollywood, and that warm scented air running up and through my nostrils. Oh, boy, was I a mess.

My mother, who I called to let know I had returned, told me in no uncertain terms that I was foolish to even think about going to live in the United States. She kept on and on about how everything in America isn't like the movies, but I knew it was. From the week, a very short time I know, that I'd spent there, LA was exactly how it was portrayed in the movies, every cliché was correct, and I just loved it. My mother pleaded caution, but she too knew that once my mind was made up, that was it, I was so stubborn and would never be shifted into any other direction. She said, 'you're impossible', so many times, I began to realize that I actually was, but I was proud of that fact. My mother suggested I come back to Estonia for a few days to talk to her. I suggested she pack her bags and come visit me in LA when I moved there. Our call ended abruptly.

The next couple of days were a blur. Madds had arranged a few FBSM sessions with some regulars, all of which I did, but all of which I cannot remember. Even though Alice and I had gone rogue and decided not to work with Julian any longer, as a favor to him, I used to get Madds to send me clients when I needed money. I liked it that way, and Julian was grateful that I was still willing to help out now and again. I was on a different planet at that point. I'd fucked the Indian, again, he came in less than a minute and paid me double what I normally received because he'd missed me, and Alice and I went out a couple of times to have some drinks and shoot a few lines of cocaine. I was just about getting back into all my old habits, something I'd sworn on the plane home from LA I would not do, when Buster, who'd become rather persistent, called me. I didn't answer at first, but, as in the movies, he called, and called and called, until I gave in and answered with a very severe "WHAT?"

"Hi Sweets" he said," How are you, how was LA?"

"Why?" I answered brashly, and I could tell from his silence he knew something was up. As I mentioned before, my relationship with Buster was tumultuous, and often brutally frank. I still, to this day, believe that if you placed the two of us on a desert island for a week, one of us would kill the other before that week was over. We got on so well, to a point, in fact we had a great admiration for one another, but we were cut from the same cloth with regards our stubbornness, and neither of us knew how to compromise in an argument. I was always right, but he was always more right.

"Fancy a trip to Moscow with me for 4 days, leaving on Sunday?" he asked.

"Nope" came my reply.

"Come on, it'll be fun. We are staying at the Four Seasons, I already booked it, and I bought you a return ticket. I know you're dying to spend time with me, so please don't say no"

I just didn't want to go. I was tired, grumpy, sad, lonely, frustrated, all at the same time. Buster could be persuasive at times, but then, during that particular call, I wasn't interested in any of his proposals, I just wanted LA and I wanted nothing else.

He continued, because I'd not said a word since he'd made the offer or traveling to Moscow, and he became sympathetically eerie with his choice of words.

"We can explore the city, at least you can, and I'll let you spend what you want on my credit card, and maybe, just maybe, we will meet a gorgeous

Muscovite and have a threesome!" he laughed. I didn't.

"Fuck you Buster"

"Babe, listen to me. Whatever is wrong, maybe 4 days away will resolve your issue."

"You're my issue Buster, so fuck off, I am busy"

I was about to put the phone down when he said,

"OK no threesome, let's try for a foursome!"

I laughed for the first time during that whole conversation and thought to myself, 'what would be wrong with four days in Moscow?' It was August, so the weather would be good. I had no expense to worry about, so that would be good, and then there was sleeping with Buster! Well, I think that might be good too.

"Buster" I said, "When do we leave?"

I could hear his beaming smile through the phone. I'd made his day.

We left on the following Sunday. I'd seen 'Cumquick' my new nickname for the Indian, twice in the past few days, so I'd made plenty cash. Fortunately, Alice was off with some guy from New Zealand, another sugardaddy.com disaster in the making, so I'd not had the opportunity to blow all that cash up my cocaine addicted nostrils, and decided Moscow would be the shopping trip of all shopping trips. Buster was so excited to see me when he picked me up that morning, I could see his erection bulging through his jeans as he approached me for a hug.

"Missed you babe" he said, as we embraced. I'd not seen him for several months, but it felt good to be next to him, at least for a short while. I knew a short while was all both of us could take and I also knew he was a lying cunt, not a term I use too often, but for Buster, it seemed increasingly appropriate.

"Did you bring your whips and handcuffs?" I asked sarcastically.

"Of course darling, and when they lock you up in Lefortovo, they'll come in handy"

I'd been to Moscow before and knew that Lefortovo was the home of the KGB and FSB. It's a place I walked past once and decided never to pass again. Creepy.

We landed in Moscow some six hours later. I was ready to get drunk, he was ready to fuck. We did both. The hotel was wonderful, the sex was good, not great, and the food, ample and satisfying for the first night.

Buster had 4 days of meetings, I had 4 days of doing nothing. Buster handed me his credit card, which I took with grace and embarrassment, and while he worked, I shopped, only I didn't buy anything. The only thing on my mind was LA, and why I wasn't there spending his money instead of here, where there's not too much to buy. I like Moscow, it's interesting and it's also filled with the strange and exotic, but they are miles behind the rest of the planet when it comes to buying luxury goods, although that's changing rapidly.

Buster would come back around 7 each night and after we fucked, or I'd given him a massage, blow job, or BDSM sessions, we would go out to eat. On our last night there, with Buster sick and tired of me talking about my wanting to move to LA on a permanent basis, we went to this very upmarket restaurant in Moscow called the White Rabbit. Google it, you'll be surprised that in a country where half the populous is starving or living on the bread line, that such a place of opulence exists. All the socialites in Moscow go there to eat, and when we arrived, I was dressed to impress. My tits were perky and nipples hard and showing through this sheer dress that I'd bought in LA. I looked like a porn star, but a porn star who knew how to dress. I could see many men ogling me as Buster and I walked into that place, and I loved that feeling. For the first time in weeks, I felt kind of normal and any thoughts of LA had vanished, if only for a while.

We sat down and had a few drinks at the bar. The bartender was a slim, sexy, blonde Russian lady, about the same age as me, but much prettier. In fact, stunningly beautiful. She had perfect breasts, perfect legs and a perfect smile. Buster was into her from the get-go. Their banter back and forth was infectious and I knew immediately where this was all going.

I never told you, Buster and I had threesomes on occasion, once with my agent and him, remember Mel, the guy who introduced us? I will tell you about that another time, but that night, there, in front of many people, Buster was in his element, and so was I.

If you've never had a threesome before, I need to tell you something. There has to be attraction on all sides and not just between two out of the three. It's important that everyone is into everyone else, otherwise it just becomes mundane and boring, and I can tell you stories where that has happened too. In this case, we were all attracted. I wanted to lick this lady, Christina, from top to bottom, from the moment I set eyes on her, to the moment we all ended up in bed. She was delicious.

Buster, with all his charm, set it up. The deal was simple. She'd finish work, we would finish dinner and he told her to come to the Four Seasons, giving her a key car to the room after the deal was done. We had two key cards, and Buster was happy to pass one to Christina. Setting this up was simple for Buster, he'd done it many times before and Christina was smitten and ready and willing to fuck both of us for the 200 UK pounds Buster had offered her. We couldn't wait, but first, we ate.

When we were done, Buster and I headed back to the Four Seasons. We showered, had sex, and settled down for the night. About 2 AM, the door opened, and in sauntered our new friend. I was out of it, Buster was erect and ready. She came into the room, casually walking towards the bed, undressed, and placed herself under the bedsheets in between Buster and I. It began with some soft pecking and licking and what followed was a slow and deliberate build up, led by Buster, into full blown sucking and fucking session that lasted the whole night and into the early hours of the new day. I think we were done by 8 Am or thereabouts, but no matter what time it was, it had been incredible from start to finish. Christina was amazing. Her smell, her touch and her ability to turn Buster and I on for hours on end, sensational. We were fucked from head to toe and back again, both of us, and we fucked the shit out of Christina. In the morning, when all was said and done, she told us in no uncertain terms that she was sore and felt like she'd just come off a horse after 4 days riding nonstop in the desert. I felt the same, and Buster? Well Buster was drained.

We kicked Christina out, after paying her, and packed up our things, ready to catch the evening flight back to London. As we left the hotel, the dread of living in London hit me once again and my state of sexual satisfaction turned slowly and then rapidly into deep depression, which Buster could tell, was evident just from my facial expressions.

I'd tried had to compress my feelings for 4 days, but as suddenly as they'd vanished, while I was walking Moscow's scenic streets, they'd returned and my only wish now was to get to the UK, pack up and leave for LA. Buster could not understand any of this and while we'd been happy together for most of our time in Russia, probably helped by the fact he worked all day and we only met up at night, we were now at another crossroads.

"I'm going to move to Tokyo" he said, rather casually actually, "and I want you to come with me"

"What?" His words had come from nowhere. No prior discussion, not a word of a hint, nothing.

" Why Tokyo?" I asked.

"New opportunity"

"I'm not moving there Buster, and if I ever did, it would not be with you!"

He was slightly taken aback by this statement, and as we settled down into the limo that would shuttle us back to Moscow's international airport, our conversation ceased and we never uttered another word to one another until we landed in London and said our goodbye's, which I thought, yet again, would be forever.

I told you, many times, Buster is great, but only in small doses. I had my dose and wanted no more. We were done, done for good. He could go to Tokyo, he could go anywhere he wanted, but I was only interested in LA, and I think I'd made that clear to Buster on more than one occasion since I'd returned from my week over there. Between my mother, Buster, Cumquick and Alice, no one, although they'd tried, was going to talk me out of my future. My future was in LA, and nowhere else. I was on a mission and a mission that I knew would be hard to accomplish, but accomplish it I would.

Birth Control

Birth control never existed in my life. Yes, I sometimes asked guys to use condoms, but more often than not, I didn't. I never took the pill, it disagreed with me, as did condoms, they made me itch, but in general, I never used anything, and I survived. My thoughts were, perhaps I was unable to conceive as I'd never had an 'oopsie'. Probably a stupid decision on my part, but I get regular checkups and I'm disease free. My whole life revolves around sex, it still does, but I am very choosey when it comes to who I sleep with, I know, I have heard it a million times, you have no control over who has what disease. I've been lucky I suppose, or maybe luck played no part in it. Who knows! Buster and I went to one more BDSM party before he split for Tokyo. As far as brining any extra excitement into my life or our love lives, it was really a non-event. There were many people who attended, half of who were on the end of a leash. Do you know what that means?"

I didn't

"It means they were the subservient. If they wanted something, they needed to ask their masters, the men, or women at the other end of the leash. If they needed fucking they had to plead. If they wanted a drink, same thing applied. Anyway, we arrived, I wore the usual see through dress without underwear, and Buster had a leash around my neck. We partied, we drank, we had fun, but no one else in the room made any attempt to fuck me, which was unusual at these parties. Someone always wanted to touch me, kiss me, finger me, or more. I didn't recognize anyone from previous events and we had a good time, left and went back to Buster's place and fucked. It was a standard evening for the two of us, the only difference? Buster packed his bags the following morning and went to live in Japan. No goodbyes, no tears, no last-minute regrets, just a kiss, hug and 'see you later', as he drove off into his future. I wasn't sad, I wasn't anything but calm and contented. I decided to call Alice, to see if she'd meet for lunch. At that time, she and Sue had joined a new site. Live-inGirlfriends.com. This site was strange, but effective. Rich guys, single, with huge homes, looking for a live-in sex partner to fuck now and again and to talk to occasionally, but not to marry or date. I know, the world is a crazy place. Both Alice and Sue were all set up in homes comfortable homes, putting out for men who had more money than sense and who got less sex than most. They were happy, and I wasn't. Maybe I should join that site too, I thought. Maybe not. After several tries, I couldn't get hold of her and I remember I received a direct message from the sugardaddy site.

Adrian was from San Francisco, he looked like an OK kind of guy, and as Buster was now officially gone, and I had nothing to do that evening, I decided to meet Adrian for a couple of drinks near Baker St.

A couple of drinks? Right, not on my watch. He was in his 40's, kind of good looking, very Alpha male and ready for action, my kind of action. We drank, had dinner, fucked like bunnies and then in the morning, he left, leaving the cash on my side of the bed, and I thought I'd never see him again.

I don't want to sound blaze about sex, but unless you're an exceptional lay, I don't really want to see you again. I am very particular when it comes to bedding men. Some I love, as you well know, some are there to be taken advantage of financially, well, I suppose they all are in the end, and some are just 'one and done'

Sex is a game to me. I want money, they want me, and my body, and we compromise with payment. I don't have an issue with that. It's the same with massage. I want paid and they want to be rubbed and released. No problem. They pay, I perform. The difference between me and a prostitute is I talk to them and have dinner with them and spend the night. I don't just get fucked and then leave to fuck again. My rates are higher, and I believe my morals and conscience too." She looked at me smiling and says, "don't laugh, it's the way I feel"

I stopped smiling.

"Adrian was cool, he was also good in bed, we had unprotected sex. I don't know or recall why it was unprotected, but it was. I make no excuses. I am responsible when I want to be, but that night I wasn't.

He vanished into the ethernet and I went back to massage at the agency, the occasional date with 'Cumquick' and back to trying to figure out how I got myself back LA to live. My goal, my dream, my ambition, it all lay in Los Angeles.

About 6 weeks passed, all pretty mundane and uneventful. I woke up one morning and I felt unusually sick."
She stares at me again, and says," you know where this is going, don't you?"
I did.

"Funny how the body can tell you something, something you don't want to hear, but something that you know is going to change your life. There's no sound, no words, just feelings. Feelings that can be strange at first, especially if you've never experienced those feelings before. I wasn't sure, but yet I was certain. I'd missed my period, but only by a few days. My nipples were all tingly, and the strangest thing is, I felt that I had company. Sounds crazy, but I did. I believed that someone was with me. I just couldn't figure it out until I realized that I was probably pregnant and at that point, I was truly sad, and also excited, though why I was excited, I will never know. I didn't need a pregnancy test, I didn't need to go to a gynecologist, I just knew, and I knew it was Adrian's. What to do and who to tell? My dilemma, my problem, my decision.

Alice was back and available, her live in situation didn't work out. Apparently the guy she was co-habiting with was a total freak, demanding all sorts of weird sexual favors from her in lieu of rent. I knew that she'd been pregnant before, she was 15 at the time, so I decided to ask her opinion. I also knew I couldn't keep the baby, because I'd never see the dad again. Adrian was definitely never coming back, at least I thought that at the time, and although I'd had sex with Buster the day before Adrian, I was pretty certain the baby was his and not Buster's. I just had this feeling.

Alice was so calming and also very understanding. We met, discussed my situation and she told me that the only way forward as to abort the pregnancy. I knew she was right and even though I would have loved to have kept the baby, there was no way on earth I could have brought it up on my own and no way I wanted to even try. The clinic was in the west of London, private of course, there's no way I could let the State pay for any termination that was purely down to my irresponsible behavior, and I had the money to cover it. Alice was helpful in arranging everything for me but when it came down to attending the procedure, I took the bus, alone. I wanted to do this myself, no help, no one to talk to and no one to try and talk me out of it. It just had to be done, sad, but true. My fault, my blame and my stupid mistake. I told myself I would never let this happen again.

As the bus wound its way across London, it took more than an hour to get to the clinic, my mind was racing as I sat alone in my seat. I had been so careful, yet so irresponsible, all my life. Surprisingly I'd never been pregnant before, as I sat totting up the number of times I'd had sex without protection. I'd been fortunate beyond words. But now, well, I was a mess. I was a drug addict, of sorts, I was drinking heavily, now and again, and I was having gratuitous sex with men I would never see again. I asked myself many times, what this was all about, and many times I came back with the same answer, I am doing this to get to where I belong. Los Angeles.

As the bus pulled up close to the front door of the clinic, I walked the few yards to the door and went inside. I checked in. It was, as described, a sanctuary for single mother's to be. The reception area was filled with women, old and young, heads down, silenced by a mistake of which they were only half to blame. There were no men. Strange, because you'd think that support would be forthcoming for at least the lucky few. One girl had her mother with her, the rest of us were all alone.

I was in and out in 3 hours. I wasn't sad, I was relieved. I was in pain, and I was so many other things at that time, but I cannot remember exactly how my other feelings were stacked. All I know is that I was alone again and ready to take that same bus, this time one and a half hours, back to my home. That journey was the most painful I'd ever taken. I didn't have the luxury of a car ride, my friends were given a self-imposed ban from attending, so the bus was my only option. I was in so much pain, and thought that journey would never end. No regrets, but plenty of time to think back on my past, as we drove back to the east end of London. Boy, was I a mess.

Two days straight in bed, most of which were spent asleep, and I was my normal self again. It was as if I just brushed the whole experience off my shoulders and carried on. Probably my only way of coping with such a loss and mistake.

I decided to get back into FBSM for a while and stay away from the sugardaddy experience. I called Justin and Madds and set up some kind of work schedule, but honestly, that period is a kind of blur for me, perhaps understandably so.

I went through a lot when I terminated that pregnancy, but didn't realize it until weeks later. It sort of hit me one afternoon, and although I's sort of breezed through my delayed pain and remorse, it was still a terribly bitter experience for me, which left a huge scar, clearly visible to this day.

About a month later, my phone vibrated with a sugardaddy message. It was Adrian. I deleted it.

6 weeks passed and again he tried to contact me. He was back in London. I hesitated, and didn't delete it. I decided to tell him what happened. I never thought I would see him again, but since he was being persistent, contacting me regularly, something I never thought would happen when I found out I was with child, I thought it would only be right to inform him of out complete foolishness, in person. I didn't know how he would take it, I didn't want anything from him, I just wanted him to know. Probably a bad choice, but a choice nonetheless.

We set up a time and place to meet. I showed up for drinks, nothing else. I wasn't going to sleep with him again.

I dressed down, not even washing my hair, putting on jeans and a shabby looking shirt and showed up looking like I'd just come from the gym, all hot and bothered. I never wasted any time. I got straight to the point.

"Adrian, when you left me last time, about 4 weeks later I found out I was pregnant, and the baby, which was yours, was terminated. I just wanted you to know. I also wanted to tell you in person and show you the respect that this mistake deserved. We made that baby together, and I made the decision to terminate. I am sorry."

He looked at me and was silent for a few minutes. Maybe it was only a few seconds, but it seemed like minutes.

"Tiana," he muttered, "I cannot have any kids, I had a vasectomy 4 years ago"

I slumped in my chair, my diet coke spilling out over the carpet as I realized with much regret that the baby had been Busters' and not Adrian's! Fucking buster had been great, at times, and now all I could think of was FUCKING BUSTER, although not in the sexual sense.

Oh dear, what a mistake.

Sex, Drugs and ......

No matter how you look at Tiana's life, from a societal standpoint, her honesty is refreshing. At first when I sat and listened, I was shocked, then surprised, then just amazed at the way she's led her life to date. I never pass judgement on any human being, there's just no point. Everyone on the planet who is free to choose, can choose their direction and live with the consequences. After all, who am I to tell anyone what's right and what's wrong. After reading this book, and again, you need to remember that Tiana is alive and well and thriving, you may very well think that she, as a woman, has overstepped her sexual boundaries in order to gain self-advancement, and really, there's nothing wrong with that, as long as it was her choice and no one else's. In the end though, as I sit contemplating what kind of life she must have had, and I'm sure there's so much more than she's even told me, Tiana does not appear to be a woman who is easily manipulated, but rather one who is willing to experiment, one who is particularly keep to see life from all angles, and one who certainly enjoys her sexuality. There are tens of thousands of other Tiana's out there. Some get out of the business and lead normal lives, but other's stay stuck in the quagmire of sex and debauchery they grew up in. Tiana is different, I think, in that she admits what she's done and has little or no regret about any of it. Massage, FBSM, which gave her the entry into this life of sex and drugs, seems innocent enough, but she's dug deeper and deeper into this debaucherously fascinating industry, trying more than just her patience and curiosity, and she's come out the other end, although maybe just not completely, into a world that she feels she controls and not one that controls her. Things though have not always been this way.

"Alan" she begins, "remember Mel and Buster were great friends?"

"Yes, you told me that"

"Well, one afternoon, not long after Buster and I began seeing one another, the three of us decided to go out for a drink. We ended up in a well-known pub in the center of London. It seemed innocent enough at the time, but now that I think back, I believe they contrived together to make this happen in order that the 2 of them might try to fuck me together that same evening. Remember Buster's love for threesomes?

I'd had threesomes before, several times, but always woman, man, woman, and honestly, I rarely, if ever enjoyed them. The issue I have is that I like one cock inside me and I don't like to share it. Maybe it's jealousy, maybe I just like to be one on one, but when another woman is involved and we are sharing the man, I feel threatened and sometimes manipulated, depending on who the other two performers are. Some threesomes are lovely, don't get me wrong, I do enjoy parts of what we do, especially when the man is inside me and I have the woman sitting on my face at the same moment. It can be erotic, but more recently, when this scenario has occurred, I have shied away from the enjoyment aspect in favor of just performing to the completion of the task at hand. Sounds callous and calculated, I know, but that's what threesomes have become to me. We're at the bar and Buster and Mel and I are having a jolly old time when suddenly Buster turned round and asked if we'd all like to go back to his place for a bite to eat, and some more drinks. Again, I thought nothing of it and of course, agreed.

Mel is a handsome kind of man, and frankly, if he'd not been my manager, I would have fucked him before that evening. He was however married, I know, it's never stopped me before" she rolled her eyes upwards feigning the look of a woman who knew just what she knew she'd become, horny around most good looking tall me.

"I was staying at Buster's house most nights then anyway, so it seemed natural for us all to congregate there after the pub. We were sort of half-drunk by that time, as we piled into a taxi and headed to Shoreditch. I was feeling great and Buster was feeling me, right under Mel's gaze. Buster fingered me as the taxi made its way towards Busters home. It was kind of erotic in a way, and kind of sleazy in another. Mel sat and glared at me. I could see his erection under his pants. It was growing by the minute. He was so turned on and that in its own way, was making me wetter and wetter. I began to realize that a threesome was on the cards when Mel, sitting opposite me in the London Cab, blurted out, "if you carry on doing that to her Buster, I will need to insist on having my turn too." His words, his voice and his erection turned me on even more and as soon as the taxi stopped outside Buster's apartment, we all got out in a hurry, entered the apartment and immediately began fucking. It was amazing sex, and it went on for more than 2 hours. I was DP'd for the very first time. Double penetrated, for those who don't know what that is. Buster was in my poosie, Mel in my ass, all at the same time. Amazing!" They fucked me so hard and for so long that the next day I could hardly walk. We all slept in the same bed that night, I was the possie sandwich I'd always wanted to be. We fucked some more the next morning and when it was all over, I realized that two cocks were indeed better than one. The only thing I thought could be better would be two cocks, a line of cocaine. I thought to myself that would be my next adventure.

We never did that again, Buster, Mel and I, but the whole episode was truly gratifying from a sexual standpoint.

I was kind of elated, deflated and decimated, knowing afterwards that the two of them had planned the whole thing, Buster admitted that much when he was drunk one night not long after, but really, I was sort of honored in a way that they'd chosen to do it with me. Maybe that's a silly way of thinking about it now, but that's how I felt at the time. These guys could get into bed with almost any women they wanted, any day of the week they wanted, and yet they'd chosen me. I never felt used, I never felt violated, I only felt satisfaction.

Drugs has that effect on me too.

When I look back on the past 7 years, and I realize that I am still a young lady, I know now that loneliness has played a huge part in my past life and that addiction, stems from that feeling of anxiety that has come from being lonely. My upbringing in Estonia obviously played a huge part in my addiction to sex and then drugs and alcohol, although even now, I really don't believe I am a true addict. Seems crazy, now that I am spilling the beans on my entire life to date to expect anyone to believe that my addictions are anything other than self-serving and continuous, but honestly, I can stop when I want, and I can start when I need to. I know this to be true. I am sure that some of the 'experts' out there will tell you that this is normal addiction behavior, but Alan, I am honestly clean right now, cleaned up all by myself, and I have no intention of going back. I know I have said that in the past, but each time, it's been easy to cease and clean up my act. My age is now catching up with me and I realize that I need to be clean moving forward, but drugs, any drug, have little influence on my daily well-being. I don't care if I have them or I don't. That being said, after Buster and Mel fucked me, in fact, after Buster went to Japan, I remember one night I was out with Alice and her boyfriend. He was not a nice guy, indeed, he was a total prick, and I didn't like him. A few drinks in the pub and then the cocaine arrived, courtesy of Alice and her dealer, the one we already discussed. It was a Friday night and I wasn't working the next day, so I thought one or two lines would be fine and then I could sleep soundly right through until Sunday morning, when I would be working again. Total addict behavior, right? I know it was, but let me finish this story"

Tiana has a small tear dropping from her right eye onto her cheek as she thinks back to the night she's about to discuss, and as I sit there waiting for the 'bombshell' that's about to come, I realize that this one might be a real 'biggie' because it's not often that Tiana tears up like this.

"The cocaine arrived and the alcohol kept flowing and the night wore on and one line became 4 lines and 4 became 6 and so on and so forth. I was wasted, I was drunk and I was about to collapse. We'd done some partying in our pasts, but this was excessive, even by our standards. For some reason, and I can't quite recall how, I was at home, and Alice and I were still snorting coke in my living room. I don't even remember what time we left the pub or indeed how we got to my place and I also don't remember how much coke we did before we left the pub and how much we did after we got to my place. I do remember that suddenly I felt very sick, I felt overcome with grief and emotion and I felt that I was about to die. Alice, and she told me this two or three days later, put me to bed. I lay in bed realizing I was about to die. I knew this was it, I just knew, and believe me, it was the most wonderful feeling. It was a beautiful experience from the minute I lay down, until the realization hit that this was it. I was OK with everything too. My life was suddenly calm and peaceful and most of the things I'd done in my life to that moment, seemed trivial as my body and my mind crossed over into another dimension. I was having a complete out of body experience, and this was going to be the last few minutes I would spend as an earthly being, and honestly, I was OK with it, I truly was.

Life was meaningless, and death was meaningful. I could see my future, the calmness and serenity of it all. I could feel something pulling me towards another world, though I don't know where that world was, it looked inviting. I was completely gone."

Tiana was crying now and I could tell this was a very painful yet very sincere account of what I presumed she was going to tell me was an overdose on cocaine. There seemed no doubt in my mind from her mental state at that moment, this was a story she'd never repeated to anyone, so I sat back and watched the tears flow as she continued.

"I had to accept that my body was no longer mine. It belonged to someone else, like a spirit, I was floating, dreaming and certainly quite serene. I didn't care what was about to happen, because I knew it was better than what I had on this earth. I accepted it, I even embraced it, and then….

And then, as if nothing had happened, there was this incessant banging noise in my head, bang bang bang. I woke up, I had no idea what was going on other than I was back, back in the real world, the world that had left me lonely and afraid, the world I was used to and one that I would continue my journey, knowing how close I was to leaving it and my legacy behind. I'd gone to sleep, I'd thought for good, alone, with all my past surrounding my demise, and had woken up, revived and groggy, with no idea where I was or what had happened. It was my birthday that day, did I tell you that?" No you didn't" I replied

Perhaps I was lucky, perhaps I was stupid, perhaps my life was supposed to be like this, but no matter how it was supposed to be, I now knew with little doubt that whatever was waiting for me after this life was both beautiful and meaningful and it took the fear of dying completely out of my psyche for the rest of my days. And the banging noise was still going. I was dazed and confused, so I picked up my phone, I had over 100 text messages and most were birthday wishes. I couldn't understand where this noise was coming from, and then I realized, it was the front door. It seemed impossible, but there I was, lying awake in my bed, alone and with nothing but memories and the door was being kicked in. I struggled to get up, it was around 6 AM, and I made my way to the front of the apartment. I opened the door and Mr. P was standing there. He looked and me, and I collapsed into his arms. I was shaking uncontrollably, shivering wildly and throwing up all over his shoes. He panicked, and he picked me up and carried me into the lounge area. He lay me down on the couch, and tried to figure out what had happened to me. He kept asking me questions, but I didn't understand what he was saying. I knew I was in trouble and he knew it too. I think he offered to call 999, (that's the emergency number in the UK), and get an ambulance, but then he changed his mind, stripped me naked, dressed me in my sweats and bundled me in his car. Honestly, I have no idea what he said to me, or what he did to me or even how he did it. I was on a different planet, but he took me to a coffee shop around the corner from my house and ploughed cup after cup into my system and he forced me to eat something, no idea what it was, but I remember he forced it down me, only to see it come shooting back up as puke, green and solid.

As he spoke to me, I realized that I had OD'd and so did he. He explained he had to be with his wife that morning and had only come to my place to surprise me with a gift, all of which I found out at a later date once I'd sobered up, and that he needed to take me back and leave me, to ensure he wouldn't be late to pick up his kids. After dropping me off, making sure he tucked me into bed, he left, and I was alone, alone and scared. Unable to get up, I just lay there, counting my fears and my good fortune that I was still alive, although at the time, good fortune didn't seem to be the appropriate, only because I had done this to myself and felt I didn't deserve to be alive. I spent the rest of that day alone. Buster tried calling me several times, Alice, who to this day does not believe I OD'd, avoided me like the plague, not only that day, but for weeks after. I was so saddened by my inability to overcome my fears and my desperation for continual acknowledgement and companionship, that I really and truly believed my life wasn't worth living. But then, as the day grew old and the night arrived, I began to peck up a little and I began to appreciate what I had again and that this could be a second chance, a chance to get stronger, a chance to learn.

You see Alan, I know my addictions are self-inflicted and my recoveries are self-induced, but I also know that whatever happens to me, there's a better world ahead. A world where I will be peaceful and happy and never alone again. When it comes to sex, massage, or threesomes or BDSM or whatever it is I decide to do, it is meaningless, other than to have a little fun and to entertain other's as well as myself. I believe that we are given our bodies for fun. We all enjoy one another, so if I have slept with one man or 100 men, it's not important. If I have done one line of coke or 100 lines, it's not important. What's important is to have fun when you are here, and then when you're done with your body on this earth, to enjoy the peace you get for all eternity.

The OD was a wakeup call, a wakeup call for the rest of my life, or so you'd have thought, right?

Wrong.

I was close to OD-ing on occasion after that and came back from the brink of at least 2 more occasions. The first time though, the time I just described to you, was by far the closest I ever came to dying. I sincerely hope I never get that close again because I still have much to achieve, as you will find out when I continue my story.

Crippled Men, Erectile Disfunction, and More

"The doorbell rang, I knew the client was due at 7 PM and it was already 7.15. As per usual, I had back to back massage appointments, courtesy of Madds inefficient booking methods, and I was already in a panic, knowing this first guy was a new client. I hate to rush people who are new. It's best that we get off on the right foot and then when and hopefully they come back, I can be a little stingier with the time I spend on them. The training was simple, as I have told you before. Get them in, get them out, and spend as little time as you can making them cum. First timer's were now my life's blood as far as money goes, the old clients seemed to be dwindling into thin air. I relied on new blood, and new blood it was, as I gazed into the eyes of a reasonably handsome American guy. We hugged and he came inside. He looked quite excited and also a little nervous. I told him to shower and get undressed and then to come back into the room for his massage. He came out of the bathroom, after taking a shower, and I was looking the other way, not noticing that he'd already found his way to the table. I spun round to begin taking my own clothes off and as I did so, he was taking off his right leg! Yes, his leg. It happened in the blink of an eye, kind of, pardon the pun, but the leg was history and now it was lying on the floor next to the table. I had never massaged a man who had any missing limbs, so this was a first, and it made me nervous and I must admit, a little squeamish too. I didn't know what to say or to do. Part of me was curious and the other part was kind of frightened. He lay there naked, I was still fully clothed, and he didn't bat an eyelid. He never spoke and he never looked at me. It was as if everything was 100% normal, and honestly, now that I think about this situation, why wouldn't it have ever been anything else but normal? I asked him to lie on his tummy, which he did, and I began to massage his back. By now, I am running about 35 mins late and need to find a way to catch up and catch up quickly. I get done with his back and move south towards his legs. "Oh fuck!" I thought, "what do I do now?" So I closed my eyes, and moved around the stump part of his amputation, massaging gently as he lay in complete silence. When I thought I was done, I flipped him over, still, he never spoke, he just closed his eyes and went to sleep, until I touched his cock, which jumped to attention and saluted me in only the way any cock can, full on hard. I decided, with time so short, to move in for the kill, of cum, as we in the business refer to it, and I tossed him into submission. The funny thing is, and I know this probably sounds gross, but when he came, his stump side, the remaining part of that right leg, kind of shivered into orgasm at the same time his penis ejaculated. It jumped a little as he moaned and groaned, and then it went limp, sorry for the pun again, but it did, it died at the same time his cock died, and then, as I wiped up the mess he'd made, he just sat up and screwed the prosthetic back into its socket, got dressed and left. At no time did I get a single word out of him, not even a thank you when he was done, which is kind of the norm for any many I masturbate. I was so curious, so incredibly wound up, and so incapable of asking him what had actually happened to his leg, and for weeks after, I regretted my inabilities to confront my demons. But, all stories have an ending, and this one didn't end on that particular night. About 3 weeks later, Alice received a call from Madds, and guess who was coming back in for a massage, yes, Stumpy. This time he'd asked for a new girl, I must have been terrible when I massaged him because he certainly didn't want me again. I told Madds to let Alice know that he was on one leg and had one that had been amputated, which she did, but Alice being Alice, just didn't care. She was direct and, in your face, and when Stumpy arrived, and she told me all of this after she'd finished with him, she just looked him right in the face and said something along the lines of "Tiana told me you only have one leg, what happened?" He'd been in a car crash, lost his leg and his will to date and so he found these massage sessions a welcome alternative. He didn't like the fact that I never spoke to him, it goes both ways buddy, and so he wanted a change. Alice then took over from me and he became a regular with her. I was pleased for both of them, because even though I think I am a very caring human being and masseuse, which we will talk more about in a moment, that man really grossed me out. He was my first handicap massage, and he wouldn't be my last, I never discriminate, but at that time it just bothered me when his leg came off, I don't know why, but it did. Which leads me to my next story, the man in the wheelchair.

ED, quite common now, but not too common a few years ago. I can tell when someone I'm massaging or having sex with has taken a blue pill, It's very evident in my opinion, because after 42 or 43 years of age, a man's penis isn't rock hard in the sense that it looks and feels like a tree trunk, it sort of withers and softens as the years go by, but when a client arrives and is in his 50's or 60's and he's erect before I have even shown him one nipple, well, that's a sure fire sign that he's taking Viagra or Cialis or whatever other ED pills are out on the market. I wish they'd invent a pill to keep women wet longer. I'd call it Niagara, and it would keep me wet for a week!"

I laugh, she laughs and we contemplate the future, just for the briefest of moments.

"Anyway, I am very careful with every one of my clients and especially the regulars. If they have ED I will make them cum, guaranteed. I can tell you that I have had men who have Prostate cancer and when they walk in the door they tell me that they cannot ejaculate, but by the time they leave, they are smiling from here to the cancer unit at John's Hopkins with their middle finger raised in defiance of every surgeon and doctor who has ever told them they would never ejaculate again. My caring touch and my soothing voice and also my great tits, are a complete testament that cancer can be cured by gently caressing a man's member and his ego jointly and subtly until they pass semen.

The doors of the apartments I worked at were often adorned by men just looking to attempt ejaculation. Something they couldn't do because of mental issues or physical issues, but something I was able to achieve for them by taking my time and performing the miracle of patience and coaxing. More often than not it's worked well, but sometimes, well, sometimes it just worked, barley, but successfully.

The appointment I had one afternoon was quite interesting. The man at the door was in a wheelchair, accompanied by his father, who was pushing the chair inside the apartment. I presumed, rightly or wrongly, the man in the chair was paralyzed from the waist downwards. By now, I was a little bit more comfortable doing massage on handicap clients. The father, and I am using that term because

I am not sure what else he could have been, wheeled in my client and then left, without any word of what he wanted me to do or when he'd return. The client, James, was a little more vocal. After I explained what our normal process was, James basically asked me to lift him onto the massage table and undress him and he seemed to think that this would all happen quite easily. I looked at him, and he wasn't that small, and said "How do you expect me to get you on there?" as I pointed to the table. "Your caregiver should have thought of that" James was rather perturbed, but insisted it would not be a problem and that I should just try. So I did, actually, we did. He was great, trying all the way to be as light as he could possibly be and as helpful as he could be.

I undressed him, again, presuming he had no feeling from the waist down, and began massaging him and chatting to him. Before I knew it, he was slightly hard, not hard, but moving in that direction.

"You seem to be enjoying this" I said.

"Yes, I think it's very nice."

"So you have feeling in your lower extremities?" I pointed to his dick.

"Sometimes. Want to suck it?" he asked, as a wry smile appeared on his unshaven face.

"I don't do that." I told him, lying of course.

"Well what do you do?"

I moved my hands onto his prick and began to massage it slowly. He started to moan, and he was enjoying everything I was doing to him. Suddenly he erupted, only a few spots of a yellow liquid, but he moaned out loud, kind of shouting at the same time, and I knew right there and then that this had been as close to a normal ejaculation as he was capable of, but an ejaculation all the same. He lay back and relaxed, I was still holding his penis.

"Was that enjoyable?" I asked him.

He just smiled and closed his eyes. I felt that had been his first ejaculation in years, but I didn't want to ask.

"Would you like to try again?" I offered.

"Nah, I am done"

He asked me to dress him, which I did, and then then, just as we completed that task, his 'father' or caregiver arrived and helped him into his wheelchair.

"Have fun?" the father couldn't wait to find out what had happened. I was embarrassed for the two of them.

Without comment, they left, leaving me to clean up, although there wasn't too much to put away on this occasion. He'd paid me a little extra, just because..... well, just because. I was so delighted to have helped that man out, but also ashamed in a way I cannot explain. How sad that one has to spend one's life in a wheelchair with little hope of any kind of normality.

But in truth, it was this experience that taught me to take care of all my clients with extreme patience and with gentle touch. I was a different woman after James, different in many ways, but mostly compassionate and understanding to all of my client's needs. If you read the Ad's, even today, by the other women out there practicing FBSM, some of them are like me, but a lot are very uncaring and callous. They will rob you, cheat you, con you under all sorts of scenarios, and very few of them see the long-term picture. It's sort of, get them in, get them out, and don't worry or don't care if they ever come back. My attitude is very different. My Ad never says, "NO BLACK MEN< NO INDIAN MEN< NO HANDICAPED"

My Ad welcomes all. I do not discriminate. I urge you to read other providers comments on their web sites and Ad's spaces. You'll soon see how they shy away from anything but rich white dudes, known as the safe bet, who are over 40, will cum in a jiffy and pay full price. It's unfortunate, but it's all part of this game. I will never do this. As you will see when we talk about my career in the latter years, I have clients who have been coming back for years. No one ever leaves me, unless I tell them to.

Massage is a service business, and service means leaving someone, anyone, begging for more and happy that they came to see me. I am always leaning towards that goal, even if the guy is black, and or crippled, or is just looking for a quickie to get something his wife won't give him. Service, that's the name of any game, and service with a smile, and of course a happy ending. But often there are issues that sometimes lead me to ponder, "why the fuck am I doing this right now?"

Foreskins, remember them?"

As I sat, subconsciously holding my own dick while she spoke, unintentionally of course, and keep it extremely discreet, I nodded. I had some feint recollection of a prior foreskin conversation, but I knew that at any moment now, It would be re-visited, and this time with a vengeance.

"I hate foreskins. In the UK there are so many men who have not been circumcised. There's no excuse for it. It's not just something that Jews do, it's 2019, and EVERYONE or at least every male, should have it done, in the interests of hygiene and saving the day for every masseuse who wants to practice happy ending massage. Let me tell you, the foreskin is God's gift to the medical industry, and they know it. Most men, obviously they have no choice at birth and it's up to the parents to sort it, are unaware they have a foreskin until they reach puberty and are standing next to someone naked in the shower asking them why their penis is so clean and lovely. The answer is, simple, MY PARENTS KNEW I WANTED TO PLEASE! Did I tell you I hate foreskins?" She repeats once again. "You did" I replied.

"Alan, I had a client in London who I named Fish Cock, not Hitchcock, but FISH cock. Want to know why?"
"Yes, I can't wait for this one" I said, anxiously grabbing my balls to ensure they were still attached. I had a feeling this was going to be a doozy.

"Men with foreskins are often unaware of the dirt and grime that manifests itself underneath that skin. If not washed properly and regularly, that 'mess' can create havoc when unleashed inside a woman's vagina. It's like, foreskin-agedon, only worse. Fish Cock was an East London builder. Typical annoying cockney accent with very little to say for himself. He was by no means crippled and certainly never suffered from ED, BUT, when I met him and began massaging him while he lay face down, I knew there was going to be a hygiene issue from the get go. He stank, his arse stank and his cock too."

She stopped and had a think to herself, then continued.

"I did a thing called, Tiana's Revenge. Want to hear about it?"
Sure, carry on" I said

"Well, when the guy was on his stomach, and his arse was honking, really smelly and vile odors were escaping towards my bloodhound like nostrils, I would massage their backs, then body slide them with my tits, making sure my tits went right inside their arse crack. Then I would flip them, and what's the first thing they would do? Now, bear in mind, my tits are now stinking of their arse odor, often so badly that I couldn't help but mentally vomit as I tried to block that odor from my mind."
I was now cringing and on the verge of puking myself.

"First thing they do, is grab my tits, it happens all the time, there are no exceptions. They can't wait to grab my perfect tits, and then, and then they suck my nipples, ingesting all their own arsy smell and germs. It's disgusting and vile and I pray that each and every one of them learns how to bathe after tasting their germy cocktail of oil and arse bacteria. But they never do, and often the same guys return, smelly as before and ready to repeat"

This was really TMI, I thought, but hey, it was all part of her days work I suppose, and I could only imagine the residue these guys left on her bedsheets. I shook with disgust that that thought.

'So, back to Fish Cock", she continued, "Well, when I turned him over, the very first time I met him, boy was it large, very large, but as I peeled back the foreskin to make his day a lot happier, I could smell the great unwashed before I could even see it. He had a yellowish-white coating of gunk hidden between his foreskin and his cock head. It was disgusting. I almost puked, but within two seconds of me rubbing his head, he came, making it almost impossible to see the residue of his bacterially laden cock, through the mist of his stinky spunk. A real treat if he's your last appointment before dinner. I used to hate guys who refused to shower before they came to see me, and hated even more, those who were dirty and had a foreskin. Some guys had foreskins that were kind of stuck to their cock heads, making it impossible to roll them back and expose their heads for stimulation. Some had foreskins that rolled all the way back to their balls and some, well, some were just the epitome of God playing a joke on them, with foreskins that were uglier and smellier that a Japanese wrestlers jock strap, and I apologize in advance to any Sumo wrestlers who are reading this and are offended. I mean no ill will to any of you guys.

Goodness, foreskins killed me, but Fish Cock's was the worst I have ever encountered. Alice used to fuck him as well as massage him, because he asked me to fuck him and I refused, she was desperate for the cash and he would throw her 1000 UK pounds every time she bent over and took it doggie style, which was often in his garage at his house in the east end. After the first time I massaged him, I ran in the opposite direction. I think I had him as a client twice more, but each time I was looking the opposite way when he flipped to expose his ugly smelly foreskin. I disliked that man intensely. Thank goodness Alice wasn't fussy. To this day I have no idea how she fucked him or indeed why, other than for the cash, but there's no way I could have done that. I had a relationship with a man once, a man who had a huge, but clean, foreskin. I just didn't enjoy the sex. I think it was phycological, but who knows. I would never marry a man with a foreskin..." I interrupted.

"Why did you say that the foreskin was a gift to the medical industry?

"Oh, you didn't know??"

"Know what?" I asked

Baby foreskins carry some incredible human growth factors that make them ideal for curing wrinkles on woman's faces. The cosmetic industry uses them to produce creams and lotions that can slow down the ageing process."

"You're bloody joking" I quipped, but then I pulled out my phone and Googled this fact, and yes, low and behold, it's true! "So why not just cut them all off and help old ladies?" Tiana was serious. "There should be "Cut it short and help a Masseuse' sticker. She laughed. I laughed and I also decided to bring this chapter to a close.

"Do me a favor" I asked, "Can you tell the difference between a cock that's been circumcised by a Moyle, compared to one that's been done in hospital by a surgeon?"

"You mean there's a difference?" she replied.

I just rolled my eyes and decided very quickly that this subject matter wasn't going to get any seedier, so with that in mind, I said to Tiana.

"Next time you get a close look at one, a circumcised one, ask the guy..." and I suddenly stopped dead in my tracks. It wasn't worth perusing. I had learned enough for one day and she'd been keen to move on the talk about her next trip to LA and her next life's love, John Paul.

Back to LA, Back to Buster

"I'd been back in the UK about 6 months and was really miss-managing my time. I hated London now, and I knew that LA was going to be my home. Everyone, and I mean everyone in my life was trying to talk me out of moving to the USA. They all believed I was nuts, or often just high. The reality was, I was neither. I wanted to live in Los Angeles. I loved Los Angeles, but I had no way of getting into the USA due to visa issues. I wasn't a student, and I wasn't from a country that claimed amnesty for visa purposes, and my friends, and also my mother, kept telling me to appreciate what I had in the UK and just make my life there. I was having none of it. The FBSM job had its moments, and of course I was often making good money, then great money, then no money. Cumquick was still around, though not as often as he used to be, but still in the picture nonetheless. I'd taken down my Ad on suggerdaddy.com, I had sort of stopped the cocaine habit, although I have to admit I still liked a line now and again, especially when I felt lonely, and that feeling of loneliness really tore me apart on occasions. In general though, I was plodding along, waiting for the chance to go to LA again. I had a few UK pounds saved up for a rainy day, and one Saturday afternoon, while perusing my modeling magazines, I saw an Ad for a photo shoot in, guess where? LA! I had to apply, and I remember as I did, I was shaking with excitement of the possibility I might actually get to return there after all. I sent the email, and prayed. In the meantime, I had arranged a date with Cumquick to meet at our usual hotel for drinks, snacks and sex. Another 500 UK pounds would be in the bank and that could go towards my LA air fare. I showed up early, again, and Cumquick, who was never late, was already at the bar with my drink poured and sitting on the table waiting to be consumed.

With Cumquick, things were always the same. Conversation was limited to a few lines, drinks and snacks to a few minutes and then sex, well, as you know, sex was in and out and over in moments, hence his name, Cumquick. That evening however, we were sitting chatting away about nothing in particular, when Cumquick, almost spat his drink across the room.

The reaction was so sudden and so surprising, it caught me completely off guard and for a moment I thought he was having a convulsion, or that indeed, he'd cum in his pants and my 500 pounds was gone in a flash. I asked him what the problem was and without further prompting, he bowed his head, ducking aimlessly to his right and whispered in my ear that his business partner had just walked into the bar, hand in hand, with a woman who wasn't his wife.

Cumquick was so obviously shocked, and I'd never seen him like this before. He tried to hide, but couldn't, and so he tried to make more conversation with me than usual, but he couldn't and with me getting quite tipsy on champagne, I held no qualms just approaching the man and saying to him, 'hey, Cumquick and I are about to fuck, wanna join us?'

So I did just that. Cumquick shit his pants and the woman who accompanied Mr. A, my acronym for Cumquick's partner, was so shocked, she just dropped her G and T on the carpet, right in front of the crowded bar and stood in silence with her jaw wide open ready to say something that just wouldn't come out!

"Babe" she said, "who the fuck do you think you are"

"Babe" I replied, "I am the woman who fucks your date's business partner, and they often share, so why not get used to it and open your legs for both of them, right now."

"I was so drunk, and I was so bold and I just didn't care. She took exception to my brashness, surprise, surprise, and after a brief discussion with Mr. A, she stormed off and left the 3 of us, Cumquick, me and Mr. A, to go to Cumquick's room and have a threesome. Only it never happened. I got into the room, they followed, and as soon as I took my shoes off and jumped on the bed, I felt really sick and puked all over the clean sheets, not just once, but many times. Mr. A, who had gone from being dumped by his bitch, to being very excited about sharing me with his business partner, ended up leaving the room hurriedly to try and recoup the loss that his bitch had cost him, and avoid puking himself because of the incredible stench from my vomit, and Cumquick did pretty much the same. That, quite unfortunately, was the last time I ever saw Cumquick, and when I woke up the next morning, lying on the very same sheets I had so violently soiled, I found an envelope by the bedside with more than double my normal rate in cash and a brief note from Cumquick telling me enough was enough. I couldn't blame him, but I will be eternally grateful to him for paying in full for what was going to be my next trip to LA, a trip that I went out and booked within one hour of waking up that morning. London had finally died on me and I one her. It was time to leave, and time to leave for good. I just had to figure out a way to make it happen. And, with a little luck and a lot of common sense, I would do that very thing.

The flight I booked this time landed during the early part of LA's afternoon. The sun was out, as per usual and it was a lovely springtime breeze that greeted me as I got into my rental car in the Avis lot at LAX. I had enough cash to splash out, and with that in mind, I treated myself to a week at the Ritz Carlton in Marina del Rey, an excellent up-market, on the water suburb, about 25 minutes west of LA downtown. I was home, I knew I was home. I immediately relaxed. I calmed down. I became who I knew I was and not who I was supposed to be. I was just me. From the moment I touched down, I felt like a different person. This was it, I was where I was supposed to be. Second time there and second time feeling that way. They, my friends, could shout at me all they wanted. They could tell me not to come, they could try to talk me out of this dream, but I was more determined than ever to make this my home. I was LA bound, my heart knew it, my brain knew it and my body knew it. I just had to make it happen. My week was pretty non-eventful, but oh so enjoyable. I met a couple of guys in the bars I went to and completed my modeling assignment and was paid handsomely for the work that I did. I loved the hotel I stayed in, and I toured a little, worked a little and played some too. It was so much fun, and when it was all over and time to go home, I was dreading that flight back to London. I contemplated missing it, I contemplated all sorts of other scenarios to keep me in LA, and I even contemplated finding a man to marry on the spot, in Vegas, so I could stay. Nothing I thought of made any sense. I packed my bags and went to dinner at the Cheesecake Factory, alone, to drown my sorrows and just as I entered the restaurant, my phone rang. I used to use this service called Viber, it gave me free internet calling to anywhere in the world, but it only worked when I was connected to WiFi. As I entered the Cheesecake factory, my phone must have picked up a signal and it began chirping. It was Buster!!

"How are you darling?"

Fucking Buster!!! He was in New York, where he'd just purchased a new apartment after returning from Japan, and he was now divorced. I was in LA, and after a brief summation of his last 6 months of travel he said 'come on out to NY, I will buy you a seat tomorrow on any flight you like, just don't go back to London' I couldn't refuse, could I?"

"At 7 am the very next morning, I boarded an American Airlines flight to New York, in first class of course, and I discarded my BA return to London from LA. I had no idea why I was doing this, but something inside me told me that I needed to be in NY. At this point in time, any animosity that remained from carrying Busters, now terminated child, did not exist. My focus on that flight was New York and quality time with one of the greatest fucks of my life, Buster, but long term, LA was where I had to be. I just knew it.

When I landed and made my way into Manhattan, my desire to get laid was huge and compelling. Buster and I hadn't seen one another in over a year, and I felt it would be a great opportunity to just fuck each other's brains out while I explored NY and discussed my future with him at leisure. It was going to be a tip to remember and I was as horny as heck when I knocked on his new apartment door in Chelsea. I just wanted love, to be loved, to be recognized for who I was and to be fucked, yes fucked, from his bedroom to his kitchen and back, and I wanted it there and then, no waiting.

When Buster opened the front door, I knew immediately that something had changed. He was aloof, he was high, he was weird, he was not the Buster I had known all these years, and he was just very strange. He was divorced now, a bonus, although it didn't seem that way at first and his interest in having sex with me was limited. We never fucked for two days and when we did, it was crap. In fact, I lived in his apartment a whole week and we only had sex twice. It was awful. There was a moment when I believed that Busted might have decided he was gay, that's how strained our intimacy had become. One evening a blonde Russian lady appeared at his front door, armed and ready in her see-through mini dress, no bra and holding a bottle of champagne in between her fake tits. At first I was shocked, because it was me who'd opened the door to expose this 'vision' of a woman, probably 5 years younger than me and perhaps ten times more attractive, but after taking a step back and realizing that Buster could be fucking anyone he wanted without my permission, I relaxed and when

Kate introduced herself as Buster's neighbor, we all enjoyed an hour or two chatting before she made some piss poor excuse to leave and I woke up to the fact that yes, indeed they were fucking. That experience kind of ended my week in New York with a subtle hint that Buster and I were done and that LA was my next port of call after all. Buster made no apologies, bought me a one-way ticket to London, in coach for goodness sake, and we parted, friends, but certainly not lovers any more. I had no qualms about leaving, and neither did he. We knew it was over and I knew he'd moved on. I just couldn't understand why he'd invited me to come to NY in the first place, but after some thought, I believed he needed to see me to confirm with his inner-self that I was no longer going to be part of his life. To me, that seemed the most logical explanation, although I would never really find out.

Back in London, it was back to the grind and back to my shitty job with the agency and that shitty apartment in Nottinghill. I did decide to move to a nicer home in Canary Wharf, a part of London that fascinated me, and a part of London I grew to love, but I just hated my working environment in Nottinghill. It was dark and dingy and sleazy and all the things that I hate about life. But with Alice having regular sex and a strong relationship with her new boyfriend, and my other friends all doing their own thing, I knew I had to make some cash and make it quickly to enable me to return to LA. FBSM it was, and FBSM it would be, for the foreseeable future.

Madds had arranged a massage with this new client who she decided had the sexiest voice on the planet, John Paul, a French dude from Paris. She'd gone 'ape' when she'd called to tell me about this dreamy guy who was on his way over to be 'satisfied', believing that just by listening to his voice, she'd determined he would be stunningly handsome and a wonderful catch, for her!

JP arrived, and yes, he was cute, but not as 'dreamy' as Madds had believed. He showered, he lay on the table and my usual massage routine began. I'd only been back in London a week, and I was still kind of jet lagged and really hadn't found my rhythm, opting for irregular sleep patterns and too much thought of a return to LA, so when JP flipped over and I began to massage his chest and then his cock, and he suddenly stuck two fingers into my possie, he caught me completely off guard and without words! He then flipped me on to my back, before I had a chance to object, and he went right down on me, sucking my clit and sticking his tongue and his fingers inside me.

"Hey, you can't do that" I told him, but not with too much conviction, because honestly, I was really enjoying it. He didn't listen and just continued, ready and willing with his erection, to enter me and fuck me.

I pushed him off, "STOP!" I shouted, and he was rather surprised by the volume and tone in my voice.

"I just don't do that"

"Why not?"

"Because you paid for massage, I am not full service"

"How much for full service?" he asked.

"I told you, I just don't do that" I insisted.

"Let me take you out then. I will buy you dinner" he offered.

We were both naked, and I was wet, really wet, so I knew there was some kind of attraction there.

"OK" I agreed, "let's do that, but first I will finish you off, because you already paid for it"

He told me not to bother, got up, got dressed and paid. He gave me his number, taking mine in the process, and he left.

'Wow', I thought to myself, 'that was just weird, weird but nice' I think I'd like some more of that.

Within 12 hours, JP called me and we went to dinner. We had a great time, no sex, but he was very affectionate. I was extremely relaxed around him, something I'd never experienced before and I felt no pressure to fuck him or do anything else that seemed expected of me in other past relationships. JP was fun to talk to, fun to kiss and fun to be around. We went out a couple of times over the next few days and then we fucked. We fucked and we fucked and we fucked some more. It was fabulous relaxed comfortable sex. JP was all over me. Everywhere we went, even public places, he would be kissing me, touching me, fingering me, rubbing my tits, and so much more, and I was loving every minute. He obviously knew what I did for a living, and he didn't seem to care. One afternoon we went to Hyde park, a glorious summer's afternoon in London, and we took a pic-nick and bottle of wine to enjoy on the grass. We never ate, we just fooled around, creating quite a show for those who were watching and then receiving a round of applause when, in broad daylight, I took out JP's cock and blew him in front of many onlookers, who found us just amusing and fascinating to watch. To this day, I think they were all just jealous. Our relationship blossomed over the next three months and I found myself falling for this quirky handsome Frenchman. I still had ambitions to go back to LA and JP knew that. He didn't care, all he wanted was for he and I to be together, even if it was only for a short time. He understood and appreciated that we live for today and not tomorrow and he accepted me for who I was and appreciated everything we had together. I never cheated on him once, I stopped doing drugs and I concentrated on making money, totally focused now on the next step in my life, LA. I just had to be there, he knew it, I knew it and the stars were aligning, so they knew it too.

Turning Point and Marilyn Monroe

"Back in the UK, JP and I were so happy to reunite after my latest USA trip. We had fun together. I was beginning to appreciate what a find he really was. He did everything for me and he couldn't care less what I did for a living. We rarely, if ever, discussed it. All he wanted to do was fuck me. He loved the challenge of public displays of affection, only he often went too far and would finger me in taxi cabs, on busses and in plain sight of the public when we went to the park for a walk. He didn't care, and frankly neither did I. We were a real item, and Alice was jealous, because her new beau was really substandard in comparison to JP. My entire world sort of revolved around him for that period of time in London and even though LA was my final and ultimate landing point, and he knew that, we had so much fun and such great sex, it was tempting to just say, 'forget it', I'll stay in the UK and see what happens. But, as is normal in my life, I either fuck things up, or someone else does it to me and I allow them to do it so it hurts. In this instance, it was of my own doing.

We, me and JP were invited to a party, somewhere close to the West end of London as I recall, where his friends were gathered to celebrate a birthday and an upcoming trip to Greece. A group of them went there every year, and they had this party every year and when we showed up, the first thing that I noticed were this group of stunningly beautiful women standing in one corner of the room, which immediately put my radar at full blast. I have this internal self-esteem issue and although I realize that I am not the prettiest woman who ever walked this earth, I also know that I am fairly attractive and when I meet other women who are beautiful or who I feel might be on the same cosmetically appealing lever as me, my instincts, not the good one the jealous one, go into unnecessary overdrive. I hate it, but I cannot stop it. And that's just what happened. We marched in, all bravado as a couple, and when JP saw his friends and then these women came over to begin conversation, (they obviously all knew one another), I was left sitting like a dried-up wallflower in the corner of the room, drink in hand, with no one to chat to. I was so annoyed and I was planning there and then to get out and go somewhere else. It was really the first time since I'd been with JP that I'd felt this way and honestly, I had no reason to because he'd not done anything wrong. All he was doing was having fun.

My phone started to ring.

"Hello?"

"It's me" said the voice from the strange number.

"WTF, where are you?" It was Buster. He was in the Dorchester hotel.

"I'm here for a few days. What are you doing tonight?" he asked

I looked around and all my jealous side saw was JP chatting with his buddies and these other women. I took quick stock of the situation and said to Buster, "hang on, I'll be there in 25 mins" and put the phone down. I went to JP and told him I needed fresh air and that Alice and her boyfriend were just around the corner, so would he mind if I took off for an hour to have a drink with them because I hadn't seen them for months, which was true.

JP said no problem, and with that, I left. I went outside, got in a cab, went to the Dorchester, got right in an elevator, up to the 6th floor, turned left, knocked on the door room 611, Buster's room, went inside, stripped naked and fucked him senseless. We fucked so hard and so fast and in every corner of his suite. It was good, but not great and when Buster came, which was after about 45 mins of fucking, I kind of felt guilty, got dressed quickly, bidding him farewell, and knowing I would never see him again. It was over. I went outside, got in a cab, went back to the party and spent the rest of the evening with JP and his friends and never gave the whole episode a second thought until…

JP exploded inside me about three hours later. Two fucks in 4 hours, one good and one great. I was a mess. I knew there and then I had screwed up the relationship with JP, even though he had no idea about Buster and I also knew Buster was history. We would chat on the phone again, but I would never see him, ever again. At the time of writing this, that still holds true. JP on the other hand, was a different matter. I was the one who'd ruined the relationship and although he'd no clue what I'd done, I did, and I couldn't believe I had blown it. All I did know was that I was unable to be faithful to a man who adored me and who I thought I adored. I couldn't do this anymore. I was so screwed up mentally, and now, listening to myself tell these stories, can you blame me?

I decided a few days later to book another trip to LA, to go there and have a serious think about my life. I set up meetings with agencies and with agents too, not telling JP that I had done this. JP could wait, he knew I wanted to be in LA, so he'd be there in London when I got back, and I didn't see any point in upsetting the apple cart just yet but dumping him. Certain that LA was going to help me out, I wound up booking a flight for the following week, and when I did, relief set in, relief that suggested I was getting away from the chaos surrounding me, chaos that no one but me had created, but chaos all the same. Getting on that flight 8 days later was the best thing I could have done. It relaxed me, it aided my inability to live a normal life in London and it gave me another opportunity to explore the place I would hopefully, one day live. As I sat by the window and the plane took off, my whole persona relaxed and a huge sigh of relief overcame me. I began to cry and the lady in the seat next to me asked me if I was OK (this seemed to be a regular emotional roller coaster with me). I told her not to worry, and I fell asleep. I never ate the food or had anything to drink the whole way there, but when we landed, wow, it was an amazing feeling once again. If I can explain it in any way that makes sense it would be like this. When you have a headache and nothing works to relieve that headache, not even pain killers, you are at your wits end what to do to relieve that pain, then suddenly and for no reason, it stops and you feel like a new person. That's exactly how I felt from the very second the wheels on that plane touched the ground in LA. I was re-born, instantly. Nothing in London, either past or present mattered any more. I was focused on LA and LA only. I saw LA as my future, my only future and to Hell with who I upset in the process. My whole life to date had been a replica of what I'd imagined it when I was a mere child. I had the looks and I had the brains, but no one in my life cared about the brains. My looks took me anywhere I wanted to go, and as we know, not always the right places. My refection in the mirror, whenever I cared to look, was Marilyn Monroe. She was my hero. I grew up idolizing that woman, I don't know why and I don't really recall when my obsession with her began, but I think I was around 5 or 6 years of age. I watched movies with her in the staring roll and couldn't take my eyes of her blonde hair and stunning legs. I think she became my dream from a very early age indeed and her life was then my life from about 13 years old. We are so similar, at least I think we are, but having never met her, and obviously I will never meet her, it's hard to know whether my fantasy was indeed her reality. No matter what, she had this saying, and it's a saying I think belongs in my life too. It goes something like, "when someone goes to bed with Marilyn, they wake up with Norma-Jean." I too feel like that. Since my looks have driven my career, good and bad, since I was 13, most of the men I have slept with have gone to be with someone they believe is their fantasy and have woken up with just plain old me. My looks have been my calling card and my real life has been my nemesis.

On the plane I'd had time to rest, but when I disembarked, my feet just ran towards what was waiting for me in LA that week. I was ready for whatever life threw at me and excited to be back in the city that was going to be my new home, although not quite yet.

Staying at the Ritz in Marina del Rey, my sort of home from home, was financially out of my reach this trip, and I'd settled for a Holiday Inn close by the Ritz, just to ensure I could afford to do other things outside of work. In America, it's impossible to get work that pays anything but cash, unless you are a citizen, or indeed an illegal with a confirmed or fake social security number. I was neither and the interviews that I attended that week bore little chance of gaining any work. One or two of the agencies promised that they would consider using me where cash was the form of payment they received for each job, but I held little hope of every hearing back from any of them. It was a little disheartening, but also it made me more determined to find a way to get into the country. I'd heard so many stories of women who had married for Green cards and then citizenship, and more stories about illegals who just stay and work for cash only. Neither of these situations appealed to me. If I was going to do it, I was going to do it the correct way, I just had to find out what the correct way was.

While staying at the Marina, I always walked from Santa Monica to Venice beach. I did it daily. I loved that walk, and indeed still do. It holds great fascination for me personally. Santa Monica has a great pier, some wonderful shops and restaurants and certainly some very interesting people, most of whom seem belong to the 'beautiful' crowd. You know the types I am talking about? Fake boobs, fake lips, fake butts, etc. Huge diamond rings, or a desire to hook one from one of the rich guys driving past constantly in their Ferrari's, Lamborghini's, Mercedes etc, muscles at the ready, but cocks always coming first. They all have this 'small penis syndrome', well some of them do, driving a replacement for a part of their anatomy that seems inefficient. You have to watch these guys, they all make me laugh. Pull them out of their cars, grab them by the balls and offer them the best fuck they've ever had, and I guarantee they will run a country mile. They are all talk, but they all really entertain me. And as I walk south to Venice Beach, home to the original Muscle Man Gym and Arnold Schwarzenegger too, my smile gets larger and larger as the muscles get bigger and bigger but the penis's get smaller and smaller. I can tell you from experience, without lifting up one single piece of clothing, what man would be well endowed and who would not. I get picked up all the time on that walk, even today, but at that time, I was hit on at least every 200 yards, of every day I walked that route, either way, back and forwards to my car. It was amazing.

Some examples.

"Hey Sexy, want to go for a ride?"

"Honey, want to go to bed with me to make babies?"

"You have better legs than my kitchen table"

"Great tits, and headlamps too!"

And so it goes on. Nothing every phased me, but as I crave attention, that part of my daily walking was lovely and well deserved, in my humble opinion. The more attention I received, the more inclined I was to walk, even if it meant going back and forth several times. I loved it!

On this particular trip I had two days left before I needed to be back in London. I didn't really need to go back, but JP was there and so was my current career, and without any guarantee of getting into the USA other than by being illegal, I just couldn't miss that flight back. Walking down the beachside path from Santa Monica, admiring the golden sands and the calm Pacific Ocean, with pelicans flying above me, a cool breeze melting away my stress, I decided to stop at a beachside store to buy some cold water. The temperature that day was well into the 70's and I was parched. I walked up to the Mexican guy serving outside the store. He was in attendance of the quick stop fridge which had drinks and ice cream. I bought a bottle of water and received a tap on the shoulder. I turned round and came face to face with this African American guy, in his 40's and quite good looking. He asked me what I was doing in Venice, I had almost walked all the way there from my original starting point in Santa Monica, and we struck up a conversation. He walked with me the rest of the way to Venice Beach and then as I was about to bid him farewell, he quite unexpectedly asked me out to dinner. I had nothing planned for the evening and so I agreed. His name was John.

We met, had drinks, had dinner, and had no sex. It was great. I like him and he liked me. He knew I had a boyfriend and after our dinner he knew I needed to live in LA. He was divorced and had a 15-year-old kid. His wife had moved away, and he understood what it was like to want something and not be able to get it, his kid living in Colorado, being the perfect example. I spent a few hours telling John about my life and my fascination about Marilyn and how my life had been built, rightly or wrongly, around the premise that I wanted to be like her. John sat and listened and listened intently. At the end of the evening he didn't even try to kiss me, which was in my opinion, a bonus. We hugged and he suggested that the following afternoon, when my interviews were over, that he'd take me to see Marilyn Monroe's grave in Westwood. I couldn't hide my excitement and of course, I agreed immediately.

It's one thing idolizing someone, it's another thing trying to be like them, but it's something completely different to sit in front of a memorial to that person, knowing you want to talk to them, knowing you think you can feel them inside you, but knowing also, that they are dead and there's nothing either of you can say to one another that will assist in making an emotional situation any less emotional than it really is. That's exactly what happened when John and I arrived at Marilyn's graveside the following afternoon. I just burst into tears, uncontrollable and seemingly never-ending. John, the perfect gentleman, took a few steps backwards and let me bawl. I did this for over ten minutes, at which time he come back towards me and took my hand, clenching it in the most reassuring manner. "you see John, my whole life has been lived around her ambition and insecurities" I told him. I think he understood, but I will never know. He was so kind and understanding. John really helped me through that afternoon, something quite unexpected, to say the least, and then he took me to dinner and dropped me off at the Holiday Inn, offering to put me up the next time I came back to LA. What a great find he turned out to be, such a gentle personality and a great listener. I'm not sure that John thought I was anything other than a fruit and nutcase, but in the end, it mattered not and we parted friends with me thanking him for all he'd done for me over those last two days in LA.

Back on the plane, back to my window seat and back to all the trepidation that was London. The moment I got on that plane, the moment my worries of JP and Alice and everything surrounding my crappy existence over there came flooding back. LA was my release, London was my imprisonment. The thought of going back to JP, even though I think to this day he's the nicest guy I ever met, was daunting. I didn't want to go back, let alone go back to him. London seemed like my past, right there and then, as I sat patiently waiting for the cabin crew to go through their safety demo, and my future? Well, I had to get to America, come Hell or highwater. As we took off over the Pacific once again, my mind was racing. I couldn't sleep and all I could think of was Marilyn and her legacy, whatever that was and this made me even more determined to finish the job that she'd started. I felt it my duty to do so, don't ask me why, I just did. If it wasn't for her, perhaps I would still be a virgin living in Estonia, instead I'd become this play-thing for men, this toy, and object of sexual desire and fantasy, sad, I know, but that's what I'd let myself do, fall into the same trap as Marilyn had, knowingly. I loved Marilyn, again, even though I only know her as in icon, and as I said, I felt that our lives had paralleled, but then it hit me, did I really want to be her? Was I going to become her? The answer, sitting in that seat was a definite NO! I don't want to be used and abused by men or by anyone for that matter. I want to be me. Wow! Now that I am telling you all of this, I realize that it's all true and that something needs to change rapidly, because although these stories were from a few years ago, perhaps I am still living the same way, and nothing has actually changed?"

Tiana stops and looks the other way, as I watch tears roll down from a face covered in stark realization that nothing has actually changed. I weep in compassion with her own inability to change, but my tears, unlike hers, are dry.

London, Final Curtain

"That landing, oh yes, I remember it well. Wet, windy and full of remorse. I was back and I hated every minute of that fact. My sixth sense told me to go home, pack and get back to Heathrow for a return flight to LA, but my common sense, and there wasn't much of that left, told me not to be so hasty and to take it one step at a time. There was one thing that I knew instantly, the moment we landed, the very second I got off that plane. JP meant very little to me. It was such a shame because he'd been everything I'd looked for in a man but yet he was nothing like the man I needed. It made no sense to me because JP had given me all that I needed, but I knew I needed even more and I needed it in America, not in the UK. I had toyed with the thought of offering JP the chance to join me in LA, kind of runaway together, but again, my common sense told me that this made for trouble down the road and I didn't need the baggage if I was set to make a new life for myself in a different country. I arrived home, and within minutes JP was at my front door. Poor guy, he was so excited to see me and wanted only to hug and kiss me and have sex with me. I, on the other hand, wanted very little to so with him and indeed, when he hugged me that first time, after walking in my front door, I cringed, horribly so. It was such a weird feeling. Here was the man I thought I could nurture and spend more time with than any other man I'd ever met in my life, and yet, I was rejecting him out of hand. I made up a poor excuse to be by myself and told him to leave. Before doing so, and while sort of making his way back to the front door kind of dejected from my rejection, he told me that Alice was pregnant and that John was the father. "Fuck" I thought, no wonder she'd been so aloof all these past weeks. I knew something was up, but not that! It was also going to be her birthday the very next day and she'd arranged a get together for all of the friends we had. JP asked if I would go and of course, I agreed. It would be nice to see everyone after my 'triumphant return' from LA, but also I hoped that by taking JP to the party, I might feel differently than I did at that precise moment and take him back into my bosom, where he thought he belonged. Sleep, I needed sleep.

"You're preggars?" I shouted down the phone at Alice when I awoke the next day, "oh, and happy birthday to you"

She was 3 months gone and sort of happy that she was going to become a mother, something I couldn't figure out, only because John, the dad, was a complete dickhead. 'Why on earth wouldn't she terminate?' I thought. In any event, we spoke for about an hour and we were both looking forward to her party that evening. JP on the other hand, was now become a pain in my arse. Continual phone calls had led to a conversation in person just before we entered the bar for Alice's party. "Are you seeing someone else?" he asked

"No" I was blunt and to the point.

"Then what's the issue? Why won't you come near me, kiss me or fuck me?"

He was totally on the money, and he knew it, only his premise that I'd found someone else didn't sit well with me, it just made me mad. Why does every man on earth believe that because you won't fuck them after dating them for a few months, it must be that you're fucking someone else? It just wasn't the case with JP. My mind was in LA and so was my body, but I just couldn't explain that to him at that moment in time. It was hard enough just rejecting him, knowing that the past 5 months had been fantastic, but I didn't want to lose him, not just yet and not at Alice's party. The funny thing is, Alice had become a kind of recluse for the last few months, no drugs, no alcohol, no partying, and no one could figure out why. With the news breaking that she was 'up the stick' and pregnant, we all now figured out why she'd been MIA, but no one really knew why she'd decided to have a birthday party when she couldn't participate in our usual debauchery.

We all gathered around this huge table in a restaurant in London. Alice had her family and some of our friends there. I think there must have been 20 of us in total. During the meal, JP and I were chatting, but slowly I began feeling awful. We'd smoked some weed, but weed hadn't really done anything to me in the past, so this feeling was more intense and more drug related. It felt like someone had spiked my wine. My whole body went numb and JP could see I was in real trouble. We left immediately and took a bus, because we couldn't get a taxi, back to his place, which was close by. On the way home, I thought I was going to die and indeed, when we walked into his apartment, I collapsed on the floor, never thinking I would wake up again. It was the worst feeling ever. I honestly thought I was dead. JP obviously looked after me and put me to bed and when I awoke the next morning, he had left for work and it took me an hour to reclaim my full body feeling and my bearings. It was the second to last time I would see JP, the last time being at his own birthday the following week, which turned out to be yet another farce and something I should never have gone to. We hardly spoke that night, after which, our relationship ended. My loss, not his.

Christmas came, and I never went to see my mother in Estonia, the first time I hadn't done that in many years. My mind was so lost, lost in thoughts of LA and my future, and I knew that I had to make moves now, or forever hold my peace and become a could've would've. Someone who says I could have done that and I could've done this. If you could have you would have! Right? I was stronger and more willing to achieve my goal than most and Christmas, that Christmas, was my turning point. And then my phone rang. It was JP with one last attempt at reconciliation. Now remember, in all the relationships I'd ever had in my past, not one person, one single man, had ever invited me to meet his parents, not one!

JP, "would you like to come with me to Paris for Christmas to meet my mother and father?"

Me, "ummmm, no thanks"

End of conversation. What had I done? I didn't know, but I never heard from him again, and honestly, although I have some regrets, that conversation pushed me onwards to America and greater things.

Christmas was a total bore, as was New Year. Not flying home to Estonia was the catalyst to throw me back into my work, FBSM, and honestly, over that holiday period, I was worked off my little feet. I had been given a new apartment by the agency, this one was in Earls Court, and it had character, so unlike Nottinghill Gate. I was happy to see people there, as opposed to grinding though one massage at a time in the other place. My life was kind of free again, no ties, no plans, not ideal for me, but a change none the less, and a change I embraced. With my head floating all the way to LA, I would sit at the end of the massage table, gently, or sometimes not so gently, rubbing strangers' cocks, often between 10 and 12 a day, counting the cash as they ejaculated all over my hands. I didn't want sex anymore, I was celibate once again, and I didn't want any drugs or alcohol, I just wanted cash. I was done fooling around, I was done splashing out or non-essentials. LA was going to be my new home and LA was my sole focus. Alice was heavily pregnant now and I only saw her on occasion. She no longer worked, but we would catch up here and there just to shoot the shit. I couldn't understand why on earth she would want to go through with having her baby, but she seemed happy, and really that was all that counted.

One cock after another, the cash started mounting, so much so, I knew that by March I would not only have enough to buy a ticket back to LA, but I would have enough saved to stay longer and in any hotel of my choosing. John, remember him, the dude I met on my last trip over there? He had been in touch, nothing other but a friendly call here and there to check up on my and he'd also been kind enough to offer his place as a stop gap lodging should I return. I was going to take him up on that, but firstly, one cock at a time, I needed to achieve the goal I'd set, my monitory goal.

Facebook was about the only way I kept in touch with friends and family, and indeed, it still is. I was invited to go on a modeling trip to St Petersburg, the pay was great, the weather was crap, I think it was around -22C, if I remember correctly. Anyway, just before I was leaving, I received a message on Facebook from Estonia that Maximus had died. The message, from my friend Katrina, was short and to the point and it completely devastated me. I was all packed and ready to go, I was geared up for a week in Russia and then to receive this news, felt like a sledgehammer hitting me between my eyes. I cried and cried and cried. Maximus, even though I'd not seen him for some time, had been one of the most influential people in my life to date, and suddenly he was gone. I didn't ask why or when, I just replied with one word, funeral? Deciding on whether I should make the Russian trip depended on when Maximus would be buried, and thankfully, Katarina responded in minutes telling me that it was all set up for 2 weeks from that date of her initial communication to me. That would give me time to go to St Petersburg and then fly straight to Estonia to bid farewell to a true friend.

Maximus had meant the world to me, for many years now, and he'd treated me like his daughter. The least I could do was attend his funeral, even though I realized his soul had already departed this earth, my belief, not anyone else's. To go would be very hard for me, I knew his religion and his family would want an open casket funeral, something I would dread seeing until I actually got there, but Maximus would have wanted me by his side when they buried him, and so with that in mind, I planned my Russia trip and then a follow on flight to Tallinn, where I would stay with my mother and pay my last respects to Maximus.

It was around that time, maybe a day later, bet certainly before I left for Russia, that I received another Facebook message from someone I'd never heard of. She was called Estrella and was from Colombia and she'd insisted that Max had told her to contact me should anything happen to him. It was all very strange. Estrella lived in LA, how weird was that, and was adamant that she and Max were going to be married and that her loss, she was very specific that this had been HER loss, was far greater than anyone else's loss. I recall reading this and throwing up. I knew Max was ay and that there was no way that he would ever have planned to marry, and I also knew that HER loss was not as great as my own. I replied to Estrella thanking her for the message and explaining that I was off to Max's funeral and when I returned I would be back in LA and it would be lovely to meet up with her. Not sure why I wanted to meet her, but Max must have been close to her to tell her about me, so, why not.

Open caskets are not something I tend to appreciate, in fact, I do not see the point. Max did not look like Max, and I was not myself, as they transported him slowly towards his final resting place. I dislike funerals, I dislike anything to do with death, but this was very personal for me, and so, with a heavy heart, I tolerated the experience with the glow of LA's warm sunshine and sandy beaches emblazoned in my mind every time someone bent over to kiss dead Max's head. It was disconcerting, sad, humbling, frightening, and very tearful to say goodbye to Max, and I didn't really need all these other people surrounding me, all with their own memories and personal griefs, spoiling my last moments with him. But they were present, and I made the most of a somber occasion by chatting to Max through my memories, all good, of him, one at a time as I contemplated our time together, which for the most part, had been wonderful. At that funeral, I was told in private he'd died of AIDS, which had made the Facebook conversation with Estrella even stranger. Why would Max want to marry anyone, let alone a woman in LA, if he was gay and had AIDS. Just didn't add up.

We laid Max to rest and I jetted back to London. My assignment in St Pete was over and so was my patience with the UK. I booked my ticket to LA to arrive the day before my 27th birthday, something my grandmother, God rest her soul, had predicted would happen. She'd told me on my 21st birthday that by the time I was 27, I would have found my passion and my calling and that I would be at peace. There's more to that story that I don't want to go into in greater detail right now, but the first part of her prediction was about to become reality. My bags were packed. No more London cocks, no more sugardaddy dates, the past was the past and the future was were my life lay. LA here I come. Quite how I was going to stay there, well, I was about to find and figure that all out. In the meantime, I was giddy with LA excitement as I boarded my flight to my new life."

London to LA and Back to London.

"My flight to LA was non-eventful but when I landed, that same sigh of relief engulfed my whole being. It's just knowing you are where you want to be that makes the body relax, take a deep breath and say thank you for brining me here. Hard to explain, but that's how I felt. John was at LAX to collect me, and I have to tell you, it was so nice to see him. I had arranged a hotel in the Marina again, John and I were not sexually involved and I didn't see that happening so his offer of accommodation was gracious but unnecessary, and the Ritz sufficed nicely. I liked John, don't get me wrong, but nothing had happened between us and I thought it would remain that way, even though I could sense he wanted more. We hugged in the arrivals area of LAX and made our way to his car. During the 20-minute drive I filled John in on the funeral, Max's meaning in my life and also told him that JP and I were no longer an item. I told him about Estrella and I also told him I was done with London and needed to find a way to get to LA full time. He just sat and listened and took it all in. I don't think I shut up from the moment I arrived until his car pulled into the hotel at the Marina. I was so happy to be 'home' once again. John helped me into my room, carrying my small bag and my backpack, asked me if I wanted to go to dinner, and told me to take my time and freshen up while he waited downstairs in the bar. I kept thinking that John was one of the nicest gentlemen I had ever met, kind, caring, not really after anything other than my friendship, yet on the other hand, there was something in his kindness that just spelt sex, I just hadn't come to terms with that yet. After I showered and changed, we hit the road down to the beach, ate dinner and chatter and during that time, I expressed to John my anxieties over moving to America. It was such a difficult task to get a Green card, and probably the only way through the minefield of bureaucracy the US government laid down, was to marry an American citizen, and stay married until the authorities handed down their OK to proceed to that next stage. John and I discussed this at length over dinner, coming back again and again to that one definite answer for all my immigration issues, marriage. At no time did he offer to marry me by the way, and at no time was this discussion anything other than a chat, there were no offers made, no promises and certainly no efforts by me or by John to make this happen, we were just two friends chatting. After dinner, John walked me back to the Ritz and as we approached the hotel, that's when everything suddenly changed. It was so unexpected, so out of left field, but yet, so welcoming, as he spun me round and grabbed me by the waist, right in the middle of a busy street, and kissed me, full on. Tongues were darting in and out of mouths, hands were everywhere and sexual juices were rapidly flowing. John went from 0 to 7 inches in 1.3 seconds and my vagina did her best impersonation of Victoria Falls in less time than it took to say 'fuck me please.' We raced up to my room, John was touching me all over, in public! I was excited, I was tired, I was ready to sleep, but I was horny. I opened my bedroom door and before I knew what was going on, John was inside me and his cock was huge. As we both lay half-clothed on my king-sized bed. He tried to fuck me for an hour, but even though his penis was enormous, he just didn't know how to use it. He eventually gave up trying, stopped, and while looking at me straight in the eyes, he said, and I will never forget this, 'maybe there's a way for me to help you get into this country?' I was lying with my legs open and his spent cock limp and dying, right next to my left leg, and when he said this, I was rather surprised at first. Then, as he continued fingering my throbbing poosie, (she was desperate to orgasm at this point), he said it again, only this time it was slightly muted and under his panting breath, as he decided to walk slowly to the bathroom to clean up. Had I heard him correctly? It didn't matter, because at that precise moment, the attempted sex with John had released all my tension which had been gathering and storing itself since for 5 months. JP, his parents, the funeral, so many cocks, not enough hope that London was for me and so on and so forth. I needed that release, and John had given it to me, even if it hadn't been that fulfilling. His words, not his attempt at fucking me, his offer, if that's what it was, really went in one ear and out the other. John wasn't going to help, or was he?

We spent that night at opposite sides of his king-sized bed. I slept soundly, only to be woken by the ring on my cell phone, which I'd forgotten to turn off before falling asleep. It was 8 Am and Estrella has sent a text message asking to meet for lunch. I was so curious as to who this woman really was, as was John, so without hesitation, I responded, yes, and then fell back to sleep again for another hour as John lay and fondled my tits, bringing a real sense of security and calm into my early morning nap.

After we parted company that morning, John asked me if I wanted to check out the hotel and move in with him. Made sense to me, after all, we were now very familiar with one another, so why waste the money. I agreed immediately, and we made plans to meet up later that day after my lunch with Estrella. I checked out the hotel a couple of hours later and left my bags there for John to collect when he came back to pick me up that afternoon. I took and Uber to Westwood to meet Estrella and during the short ride to the restaurant she'd picked, my heart was beating at 100MPH in anticipation of this strange situation in which I found myself. John had sort of hinted he would assist in my quest to come to live in America, but what did that mean? Estella was insisting she was about to marry Max, before he'd suddenly died, but that seemed truly impossible. There were so many unanswered questions in my life and so much I needed to do to get my life on the track that I truly wanted and desired.

She sat there, waiting for me, a half empty glass of something that looked alcoholic, unfinished and right in front of her hands, both clasped together nervously in anticipation of my arrival. She was older than me, probably by 15 years, but pretty. Estrella looked like someone I knew or had known in my past, but in the split second it takes to walk into a room and introduce oneself, I had no time to recollect why or even if I knew her.

Estrella turned out to be an amazing woman. She was a singer, short, blonde and chubby, although not too chubby. Perhaps I am being overly critical here, but in general, she looked like someone who just never made it in her chosen profession, singing. We had a wonderful lunch together, catching up on all our memories of Max. She'd known him for a few short years, and yes, he'd wanted to marry her, and yes, they were in love, but NO, she hadn't known he had AIDS. It was still all very strange, and I believed she was after Max for his money, but as she was buying me that lunch, I decided to keep what I knew about Max to myself and I changed the subject to my plight of moving to America. Estrella was completely understanding and very 'on board' when it came to finding a solution. I told her about my new friend John and how I thought he would assist my plight by marrying me. She did everything she could to agree with that as a permanent solution, everything except book the venue for the wedding! Her life in LA was quite interesting. She said knew a lot of people in the film industry and the music business, suggesting I would be welcome to join her at a party in downtown LA that she'd was attending later that week and that John was also welcome to come. "You never know" she said, "you may meet people who can help you get here darling. You have the looks!" and as she winked at me reaffirming her last statement, I had the impression that Max told her more about me that Estrella was letting on and that also deep down, Estrella would be my biggest advocate moving forward. My suspicions would be proven right, but first, and foremost, I had other meetings to go to, modeling possibilities, and meetings I didn't want to miss. Without being too rude, I promised Estrella that I would attend the party, without John, and that I would be in touch later in the week.

My week in LA was pure bliss. It was amazing to me how relaxed I was when I didn't have to jerk off one guy after another in some seedy apartment in London. I didn't miss the smelly builders, the off handed business men, the guys who thought they were all God's gift to humanity and just wanted to fuck me. No, I just didn't miss any of it, other than the money of course. But during that week, even the money didn't matter. I was wrapped up in LA's culture, it's sense of being. It's as if the city itself had been built just to take care of me and my ambitions. I loved that sense of freedom, where I could go anywhere I wanted as a complete unknown but at the same time I could feel my long-term ambition being met, if only in my mind and not yet in person. LA was my place, I owned it, I loved it, and I wanted as much of it as my body could swallow. I wanted it so badly it consumed me, night and day. My mind was preoccupied from the second I awoke until the minute I fell asleep, trying to figure out how to make this dream a reality. I had to do it. There was no option. Going to bed each night I dreamt of my life so far. I wasn't ashamed of anything I'd done, well, almost anything, but at the same time, my life wasn't yet where I knew it was supposed to be, although I could feel myself getting closer and closer to that dream. Waking up each day in Los Angeles, brought happiness and new adventures, something I only felt when I was there, and nowhere else on this planet, and believe me, I had travelled a lot over the past few years. What was it that kept brining me back here I wondered? And then my mind would reflect on my childhood, Marilyn Munroe and American culture. It was all ingrained in me from such an early age and now it was bang in front of me and well within my grasp.

My meetings that week went well, and I received offers of work for cash payment, something I loved to hear and would sign up for immediately. John and I had become really good friends, and although we'd had sex a couple of times, I knew deep down that friendship was where our relationship was headed and that our romantic connection was only a fleeting opportunity we both needed, which was short-lived, not too enjoyable and now over. I had 2 nights left in LA and the party was something I was quite looking forward to. My mind again was drifting back and forth between my friendships in London and my time there in America. It was such a push me pull me situation. My friends in London were great, my one friend, John, in LA was also nice, but although strangely enough I only really had John as my one friend, the task of making new friends in LA didn't seem daunting at all, and the challenge of beginning a new life there, well that just seemed to be necessary, not difficult. The party was to be the start of that challenge and with that taking place only 2 days before I was due to leave, I had to work fast.

Parties are always an opportunity for me to show my curves. My legs are spectacular, even if I say so myself, and on this occasion, I put on my micro mini dress with no underwear, seriously, that makes a superb impression with ALL men. I can walk the walk, and talk the talk, but my tits and legs were born to impress. John was blown away when he saw my attire, in fact his erection was bulging through his pants before he even opened his mouth. He wanted to join me, but the general rule is, models go alone, and I'd made it clear he wasn't welcome. I arrived, along with many others at this building in downtown LA. Weird setting, but nicely decorated. Estrella was already there, and as we entered, she come right up and hugged me. I was offered a glass of champagne and began to mingle, with Estrella by my side as my 'wing lady'. No sooner had I taken my first sip of alcohol, when I was introduced to this ugly guy called Timothy, who claimed to be a famous movie producer, and who had the weirdest voice I'd even heard in my entire life. He sounded like Funkhouser from Curb Your Enthusiasm, only worse. He had weird hair and spots, yellow spots, all over his face. Unfortunately for me, he wouldn't let me go. He went on and on about his own career and his ability to make beautiful women famous, when all the time I knew he just wanted to fuck me. Estrella was 'egging' me on, and out of the corner of her eye, she was suggesting I made more of an effort with Timothy, for what reason, I didn't know? Eventually she pulled me to one side, relieving the boredom that Timothy had become, and told me in no uncertain terms that the guy was rich, single and in love with me, or should I say my body. He'd only known me 30 minutes and he was in love? Forget that. I wanted to move on, and having collected other business cards from various men and women I'd been introduced to, I ended up back in Timothy's grasp.

"I hear you want to move to LA?" he asked me

"It's my dream" I replied.

"Maybe I can help?" he suggested

"And how are you going to do that?" I inquired.

He wanted to marry me, really! Yes, he even said that. What a weirdo this guy was, but hey, it was an offer, right? Onwards, I thought, as I marched away, kind of flattered but also kind of disgusted. If Timothy was up for it, then other men would be up for it too, but other men who looked the part, not some ugly trumped up producer I'd never heard of. Estrella on the other hand was full of joy when I told her what happened. "Do it!' she shouted. "why wait. You have an offer you cannot refuse"

But I could refuse it, and I did.

At the end of that night I had a plan. I would return to LA to live and I would figure everything out during the 3 months my Visa allowed me to stay as a tourist. Every trip I made to America allowed me 3 months. I was sure that I was clever enough to make that 3-month period productive and secure my long-term future, even if it meant marrying Funkhouser!

On the way home to London, I made my plan. I sat up all night on that flight and when I arrived home, I was ready. Before I'd even unpacked, my plan was unhatched, my first task, call the agency and hand in my notice, and my second task, call Alice to see how she was doing and to arrange my 27th birthday party.

On My Way- At Last!

My birthday is so important to me. Everyone in my life knows that. I even celebrate half birthdays, and that makes it twice the fun, annually! My 27th would be fancy dress. Come dressed up as someone who died at 27, or don't come at all. A fun night for everyone, but little did everyone know it would be the last time we would all gather together for such an event. I had called Madds and handed my notice in. I gave them 4 months to find someone. In turn, I had told Alice, who was still in shock when she arrived to celebrate my birthday, with her now, huge bump, protruding in front of her. The baby was due any day now and we were giddy with excitement because she knew it was a boy and we all wanted to name him. The party was a success, followed by a lull in all the excitement for me. I went back to work, tossing off guys in endless sessions in my Earls Court Apartment. It was so boring, my mind on LA at all times, but it was a living, and one that would remain with me for the foreseeable future. Practicing FBSM had its advantages, other than the cash of course, enhanced by the prospect of meeting new people all the time, and seeing them stark naked before you've even introduced yourself. Life's great leveler. They walk in, take their clothes off and then begin conversation. How many jobs on the planet can boast that kind of social interaction? None! Without shame, I was grateful to every single one of the guys who I had jerked off over the past 5 to 6 years, and grateful for every single penny they'd paid me. Big cocks, small cocks, clean cocks, smelly cocks, cocks filled to brimming with sperm and those who were nearly on empty, it didn't matter. All that mattered so far was the experience and the payout. The money had been my catalyst in the beginning, and now, as I moved towards the conclusion of my time in London, yet again, the money had become my incentive. I needed to make and make and make, in order to survive when I finally made my home in LA. I was again in beast mode. One guy came in, one went out. I was up to 15 guys a day, 6 days a week and often 7 days. The cash was coming in fast and furious, to be saved and not to be spent. Alcohol was allowed, but I never went back to cocaine. My bank account flourished and my wrist got a massive daily work out.

Alice gave birth 10 days after my 27th birthday. Both she and the baby were fine and we, as her loyal friends, threw a party in her absence to celebrate. We called him 'baby Jesus' because she would always tell us it had been the immaculate conception, and the name stuck, at least for a while, until she named him David, after her grandfather. To me it was all so alien. Alice was an enigma. She'd gone from sucking and fucking, to motherhood, all in the space of one untimely ejaculation. She was happy, and so was the dad, but I was livid. Don't ask me why, I just was. My friend had left me to care for a son, and one who couldn't talk back, just yet. Here I was, the other half of our duo, the half she'd got hooked on drugs, sugar daddies and so much more, now abandoned for diapers! It was just unforgivable, and although we kept in touch for two more years, our relationship was never the same.

John in LA kept talking to me on Skype, a twice weekly occurrence that became an institution. Every Tuesday and Saturday we would talk for an hour. He was such a good guy. I had my plan and he knew what that plan entailed and he encouraged me on every call we had, to make it happen. And then, and then it just did, it just happened.

The call went like this, and I believe it was around the end of August that year, so about 4 months after my birthday.

John "Look T, you've been talking about this for over a year, and probably longer if you count the time before I met you."

Me "I know, but it's hard to get it done."

John "Just come over and make the effort. I will look after you"

Me "How are you going to do that?"

John "Just come, move in and let's see how it goes. I will help you find a job and get you settled"

Me "I can't get a job until I get a green card."

John "Let me worry about that. Come over. Just do it!"

And I did it, I did it there and then. I disconnected Skype, knowing that he hadn't offered to marry me, but he'd offered to help with everything else, and I got on line and booked my ticket, to LA. I would leave on my half birthday, the middle of October, and I would never come back.

But before all of that could happen, I had to start saying my goodbye's, and there would be plenty of them to go around. I had so many regulars, so many ex's, most of whom I still spoke to, and so many good friends and of course so many who were not such good friends. All of them, I thought, deserved to know I was leaving and all of them needed a chance to say goodbye and I wanted to say goodbye to them too. I didn't believe for one moment that all or indeed any of them would give a flying fuck if I left or not, but some might and with that in mind, I began planning, not only how I would let everyone know, but how I would tell them all in person. Some of my regulars had spent thousands of pounds with me, or the agency, over the past few years, and for me to just leave without a goodbye, in my humble opinion, wasn't the righ thing to do, especially in the UK where people expect more than just a quick 'cheerio'.

I had a few weeks left before my 'disappearing act' came to fruition, and a few weeks in which to make as much cash as I possibly could. I thought it would be a great idea if I invited all my regular guys back for one last cum fiesta. Not all together, but one at a time, and offer them a discount of sorts, or maybe for the lucky few, a blow job or quickie fuck. That idea soon evaporated because I couldn't discriminate between those who I liked and those who I really liked. If I did it for one, I would need to do it for all, or for none. In the short term I just called a few who were special to me, brought them in, blew them and took their cash while saying goodbye and thank you. For those like Mr. P and Buster, who by the way, was back in the Dorchester for a few weeks, having reconciled with his wife and dumped the other women he was fucking, well, there would be special send off's for guys like that, plus Cumquick, who I would try to contact one last time. It was a madhouse for weeks, men coming, quite literally, and going, in and out of the place at Earls Court, and all the while, Justin and Madds were begging me not to leave because the cash register was in full swing and they too were making more than ever before from my best efforts. It didn't matter. I was out, out mentally, checked out, and almost cashed out. This would be it. LA was the only place for me, and the way I was working, like a woman possessed, was shear testament to my intent.

One by one, my regulars came and went. All of them, to a man, were sad to see me go. I received comments from each and every one of them, daily,

"what am I supposed to do now?"

'where else can I go"

"no one will do this like you do"

'can I please fuck you just once?"

"will you blow me, just for the memory?"

I laughed off most of them, but one or two I took seriously and went that extra mile, just to get some more cash. I had fun, they had fun, and in the end, they all became a blur. If you asked me today to name any of them, I probably couldn't get to 5, and that's out of several hundred guys. None of them were that meaningful to me, well, perhaps one or two were, but that's about it. In the end, and even today, it's all about the money, not about attraction of sexual desire, at least not for me. For them, it was different. For them it was excitement, desire, fulfillment, conquest, but for me, just money.

Mr.P was a different proposition. All along he'd been dead against me leaving the UK, probably for his own selfish reasons, but when I called him to let him know that this was it, and I was out of here, we agreed to meet for dinner. That dinner was most memorable for its silence than its conversation. The situation to Mr. P was simple, stay and don't be foolish. He was happily married, and it mattered not to me that he cared about me. I was leaving, and I didn't think twice about him or his family. What had happened between us had been great, but it was gone now. It was the past, and the past was all being laid to rest, at least by me. Our dinner finished, we hugged, kissed and said our goodbyes, and that was all that happened. No sex, no funny business, just a hug. I would see him again in America, but not for a while, and without shedding one iota of a tear, we bid farewell and I left.

Buster was next on my list. As I mentioned, he was back in the Dorchester, and back with his wife. He was a mess. When I showed up, we just fucked. Don't ask me why, we just did. He wasn't the same man. He seemed distant and preoccupied. Buster was probably my biggest regret in life so far, but when we finished making out, we fell asleep together, for the very last time. In the middle of the night I got up to walk around and moved his arm off my tits. It wasn't that dark, but I could see needle marks from his wrist right up to his elbow. It was a shocking discovery. I'd never noticed them before and now my suspicions regarding his moody behavior had been confirmed. Buster was shooting heroin.

I couldn't get back to sleep after seeing this and I just lay in silence next to him remembering all the great times we'd had, and of course, our terminated baby, which he still knew nothing about. After about two hours of tossing and turning, I woke him up.

"You're doing heroin?"

He didn't speak for a few seconds and then he said, "don't worry about my problems"

And that's when I blurted it out. No filter, straight to the point and without any care how he would take it.

"I was pregnant with your child and I aborted it"
He cried, I got out of bed, and I dressed and left. No extra conversation had been required. The look on Buster's face said it all. He was broken.

I took a taxi home and went to sleep. I hoped never to speak to Buster again. It was done. I was done. LA was my silver lining. I was so excited.

I had two weeks to go before I flew out and so much to do. It was really a time of reflection for me. My life had gone from poverty, to riches, to drugs, to poverty, to riches and back and forth from both for so long now. I was certainly better off now that I had been when I lived in Estonia, and I was more astute, mature and worldly, although quite how worldly one needed to be, I didn't really know. My life had been harsh, it had been beautiful, and it had taken so many twists and turns over the past ten years, but it always kept me positive, no matter how dull or derisive those who surrounded me had been. Yes, I had made mistakes, many of them. Yes, I had been fortunate, and I appreciated all of my good fortune, and yes, I had learned a lot, wasted a lot and demanded a lot too. My self-esteem had always been high, but my feeling of loneliness in life had often been overbearing and uncontrollable. I believed that that was the reason I did what I did and why I went through men like most women go through handbags. I had always been looking for that one special Prince, my Knight in shining armor, and of course, once or twice I thought I'd found him, only to realize that that Knight didn't suit that particular day. My hopes for success in LA were high, my abilities to entice men, either mentally or physically, were my saving grace and they would keep me on the straight and narrow in the years to come. My mother in Estonia knew from an early age where I'd end up living, but she told me I'd disappointed her when I made the decision to move. The rest of my family didn't care less. It was now down to me to pack up, leaving London as just the memory it was always going to become and to open a new chapter in my amazing life, a chapter that would go on to outshine anything I'd done in my past, a chapter filled with the most incredible times I'd ever had, but times that I was yet to experience. My passion for America would begin when I was 27 and ½ years old, and my mind told me that it would never end. But my life was about to take so many twists and turns, most of which I never saw coming, that my ambitions and dreams would be shattered and then reignited on multiple occasions, in situations that were unique, sexy, torrid and often beyond anything I'd ever experience before. You all know now what a crazy life I'd had so far, but that was nothing in comparison to what would happen to me in America. My next chapter was at times so ridiculous, if I hadn't lived it myself I would never have believed it.

Cannes: A Special Weekend

"Between the ages of 16 and 17, when I signed with my agency in London, I was invited to attend the Cannes film festival. It always took place just after my birthday, in May, and indeed, on my first trip there I'd just turned 16. The deal was simple. Major corporations, in the entertainment industry, sent their top people to the film festival and along with A and B list actors and actresses, they partied for a few days in the South of France. The first time I was offered a ticket and accommodation, it blew my mind. Why would they invite me and put me in a nice hotel and buy me dinners and drinks all for free? And then it all became so clear.

Companies who were offering me these trips, put on parties for rich and famous people who attended this festival and they needed eye candy to entice A listers into their gig in order to

A: make money from sponsors and from sales of food and drink and

B: to 'provide a service' to those who wanted to use it.

That service was me and many other beautiful women who were hand-picked to come to Cannes to flaunt their bodies. They system was simple. We were ferried between parties, displayed like cattle, told to mix with the clientele and then the rest was up to us. The first time I went there, I was overawed. It was a mind-bending experience. My hotel was magnificent, even though I shared a room with another girl from Russia, and it was so opulent. More than that, it was all so frightening. We were thrust into an atmosphere that seemed so surreal. Champagne, movie stars, caviar, and Versace, all readily available and all free. I didn't know what to think. On that first trip I was uncertain of how to behave, although I had an idea that if any of the A listers wanted to fuck me, or wanted a massage, or just wanted to talk to me, I had to do it. I had a choice, but then again, I didn't have a choice. Someone, I don't know who, paid for all my expenses, and with that in mind, I wasn't naïve enough to think this was just a vacation. I wanted to meet famous people, I was 16 for goodness sake, so what could be more glamorous than to tell my family I met Arnold, or Jennifer or Sly? I was in heaven, and it showed. I remember that very first experience as if it was yesterday. My long red hair, flowing happily behind a smile filled with both terror and happiness. My legs, which are my best asset for sure, were like sculpted pins, dressed and enhanced by high heels, attracting as much attention as an unwanted fart in a space suit. Everyone, and I mean everyone, wanted to look at them. I strutted my stuff, my tits pouting out in front of my low-cut mini dress, with my nipples on full beam, cause quite the stir. I was ogled at, I was started down, I was mentally raped, and I was happy. I wanted this, and I wanted it so badly. This was Hollywood, this was my dream, this was LA and this was happening.

I never fucked anyone on that trip, but I made a lot of friends. It was the precursor for my next 8 or 9 visits to Cannes, where as I grew older and more mature, my ability to attract those who mattered and those who wanted to pay to fuck me, became an insatiable cash machine with an appetite for sex and drugs and more of the same, no matter what it took to get it.

Over the coming years I fucked a famous Scottish actor, several times, at 1000 UK pounds per pop. "per pop" meant that each time he came, I received a grand. One night I made 5-grand, and he made off back to his hotel room unable to walk for a week. I fucked someone we all know, but who shall remain anonymous for now, who we all admire today and who is the star in many movies that we all enjoy watching. Let me just say, that there is nothing that is G rated about this actor. Total pervert and one who liked to piss all over me before he fucked me. The food and accommodations got better and fancier as the years progressed. The Cannes crowd got to know me, and my reputation got me invitations into the most delicious restaurants, the best night clubs, and the fanciest hotels and parties, all for free, while my bank balance just exploded during that three to four-day period every year. It was all so amazing, and then, just as suddenly as I'd fallen in love with all the glamor and glitz, my love turned to complete hatred of a situation which was no longer tolerable.

When I was 26, the 10th year of attending Cannes, I got really fed up with so many of the young female upstarts, (obviously that had once been me), who began flooding this festival with their tits and asses firm and flaunted in the direction of those who mattered. They were bitchy, careless, crude, and downright unlikeable, and I kind of woke up to the fact that even though I was only 26, I was regarded as OLD, for this type of gig. It sort of hit me the first day I got to Cannes that year. I looked around at these 17, 18 and 19 year old women from all over Europe, but mainly from Russia, all there to open their legs and to try to make money, just as I had done at their age, only I was now past this phase of my life and it woke me up with the velocity of a sledge hammer breaking up a china shop. Suddenly I just didn't belong and I didn't want to be there, no matter how much money I was about to make. My instincts were my guidance system, they always had been, and at that time my instincts told me to leave. So that's exactly what I did. I left. No sooner had I arrived, when I found myself back in London, just before my final trip to the USA. Cannes was dead to me. The whole scene, fake as it was, had been fun for many years, but now, it was no fun at all. I never went back. I didn't need to, I had other plans. My plans didn't include fucking movie stars, unless they were in LA and unless they were going to help me with my career and my financial situation and also my immigration issues. Cannes was the beginning, but LA was the end game."

After listening to all of Tiana's stories, which have taken some time to digest and to transform into something that makes this book such a great read, I decide to ask T some questions.

"When you first get in contact with a client, how do you decide if you want to see him or not?

She responds

"I see virtually everyone. I don't discriminate. Some girls won't see African American men, some won't see Indian men, some won't see white men, it all depends on the provider and her preferences. I, on the other hand, will see most men. I have had a few experiences in the past where I've found dubious discrepancies in some men's ID or some of the stories they've told me when I screen them, but in general, I don't care who they are or what they are, as long as they pay."

I continue

"In Cannes, with the A listers, as you describe them, or with just some of the other guys you slept with, can you describe how that happens? I mean, can you tell me why a famous actor would want to pay you to have sex with them knowing they are under 24 hour scrutiny from the general public and knowing that one slip up could ruin their careers?"

"Honey" she begins," men are men. If you find a horny man, you know what he wants, and most men are horny. Horny all the time. In Cannes, with the glitz and the glamour, the atmosphere is extremely sexual, from dawn to dusk and beyond, every day. There's not too much to do other than sit in the sun, watch a few movies, eat nice food and fuck. Guys, including actors, well known or not, relish the opportunity to fuck anything on two legs with a great pair of tits, and 30 inch legs that wrap around their necks. It's all part of the 'business' and it's just accepted. Now, I'm not saying that it's a perfect situation when ladies come from all over the world pretending to be older than they actually are, in fact, the teenagers, and I was one at one time, should never be allowed to attend such festivals in their capacity as a sex worker, but life is life, and everyone seems to turn a blind eye to this in favor of the fuck fest it always turns out to be. The #metoo movement sort of put a dampener on the whole scene in Cannes, but I was long gone by then and I'm sure in time it will just go back to what it was. These movements seem always to be a fad, followed by something else that then takes everyone's fancy. Now, don't get me wrong, human trafficking is something that I find abhorrent, and something I am deeply against, but Cannes was not a place where I ever saw trafficking practiced as a 'sport' if you want to call it that. Most of the girls who came were models, or liked to think they were models and even though their agencies sent them down there to meet the men who would eventually fuck them, that form of trafficking wasn't seen as something that should be frowned upon or stopped. They were there of their own free will, at least I was, so I'm presuming they were too. It's not that this sort of thing is right, I don't think there are any rights or wrongs in what I've done, it's just all about advancement, and I personally, as I am presuming the others did too, used my 'assets' to advance my life and career as I saw fit. I didn't care if someone paid me to fuck them, because I knew that one of them would help me get to the next level, maybe not the first one I fucked, but eventually someone."

Part 2
Finally in America

"When I booked my ticket, the ticket that I knew would carry me to my new home, LA, I was nervous. I had to book a return flight, even though I had no intention of using it, but because of US immigration laws and the ETSY Visa system, if I appeared at US border control without a return within a three-month period, they would flag me and they wouldn't let me into the country. Some people I knew had this happen to them and were 'deported' back to the UK, never to be allowed into the USA again. I wouldn't let that happen to me. John and I had spoken often, and with his help and guidance, we'd decided I would arrive around October 16th 2016, which would give me a month to look for work, cash based of course, before the Thanksgiving holiday, (something I'd never experienced before, but was excited to celebrate with my new found friends), and then decide if I needed to return to the UK for a brief spell or just say, 'fuck it' and stay in the US as an illegal. Many others did this, so why not me? My only problem was going to be my mother. If I became an illegal and something happened to her, I would not be able to fly to Estonia to see her, risking the threat of never being able to return to LA ever again. Remembering that there were over 11 million illegals (probably an underestimate) residing in the USA was of some comfort to me, but the thought of never being able to see my mother if she took sick or passed away, well, that was just unbearable. Decisions like that are never easy, and in the end, the comfort of having the return ticket and the prospect of John assisting me with my immigration dilemma, overruled any qualms I had of taking this massive step and putting all my eggs into that LA basket.

Before I quit the UK for good, I had many decisions to make.

What should I do with all my 'stuff'? My 'stuff' included designer clothes, bags, and accessories. I had cash in the bank, credit card debt, and other things to do that would finally bring the curtain down on the past ten years. It was a daunting task in the beginning, but once I got my head round the situations, I was off and running at full speed, dishing out clothes to friends like Alice, and sending my mother all my designer bags, bar 1, one which I decided to keep for sentimental reasons, one that Mr. Pee had given me when we first met. The rest of my 'stuff', well, it was gone in days and although I never officially closed my bank account, leaving just enough in it not to incur and fees, I withdrew about 20,000 pounds in cash to take with me to America, which was virtually all I had left from my 10 years of continual partying, but enough I believed to keep me going for a few months when I arrived in LA.

The deed was done, and with all my debt paid off, I was headed to America, headed home. My new life was already laid out in front of me, laid out in my mind at least. Hard to explain, but I knew exactly what was going to happen, from the moment I landed until today, my life has a pattern, and a pattern I seem to weave in my inner self, and then play it out in real life, virtually line for line. On the flight to LA, which I hoped would be my very last flight in that direction, my mind took me back constantly to my childhood years and those dreams that I used to have of becoming a movie star and living in the same city as Marilyn Munroe, all pipe dreams at the time, but as the BA jumbo jetted speedily towards Los Angeles on that amazing October morning, my dreams were now complete reality. Surreal in ways, but a true fact and pleasure and something I always knew would happen. Sipping my beverage and trying hard to concentrate on the in-flight movie, tears began to roll down my face, tears of joy, mixed with sadness, but tears none the less. The lady next to me tried to console me, but her efforts, although kind, went largely unnoticed. I wasn't upset with anyone, and I wasn't really sad about anything, I was just emotional, emotional beyond belief, landing some 11 hours later in the land where I knew my future lay, the city of Angels, where I was far from my past and where I would always be so close to my future.

John was there to meet me, as planned. He was delighted, and I was, comforted by his enthusiasm. Our deal was simple. We'd discussed it many times on Skype and FaceTime. I would move in with him, paying half of all the bills, including rent, whilst looking for a cash paid job. We would date, figuring out along the way if there was any chemistry between us, and if there would be any possibility of moving further than just dating. I needed a green card, but he didn't need a wife, at least not in the short term. We would fuck, and we would sleep side by side, but in my opinion, we were never exclusive, although for the first few months, it would turn out that we were.

John's place, close to Manhattan Beach, was basic, and manly, but livable, and I was grateful beyond words for the opportunity to lay down roots with his assistance and love. He was a fabulously kind human being, at least in public, working in IT and running a division of one of LA's largest corporations. John took care of me from the moment I arrived, teaching me unreservedly, how to operate in a country that at first, seemed so foreign. John had a young daughter who lived in Arizona, and although he didn't see her very often, he was fairly close to her and spoke with her often. Once I'd settled in, spending the first few days just acclimatizing, John informed me that his daughter would join us for the Thanksgiving holiday, which was about 3 weeks away, and something I was really looking forward to celebrating for the very first time. Estrella was also back on the 'scene'. She and John spoke regularly and once I arrived, Estrella began to play 'gooseberry' with us, often to our dislike. Remembering that Max had been so close to Estrella, took away some of the animosity I felt towards her continual and unwanted intrusions, but soon enough, the party invites began arriving, through Estrella of course, and soon enough I was accompanying her to movie 'get togethers' and industry networking events. But before all of this transpired, I was also out looking for jobs, something that was proving to be extremely difficult.

Each interview I went to seemed to end in disappointment when they found out I didn't have a work permit. I was sure that someone, somewhere would take me on as a PA or just a runner, anything at all that could get me an entry level position in any company, but each time, rejection after rejection, I began to think that my conception on how my life was supposed to turn out, was going to be proven wrong, as one by one, the applications ran out. In the meantime, Estrella was more insistent than ever that I accompany her to one party after another and at the same time, John was becoming irritated that I wouldn't allow him to come to photo shoots, (yes I did have a little modeling work going on), and allow him an insight into my working life. What John didn't understand, was that in the modeling business, unless you're actually involved in the shoot, you're not welcome, even as a spectator, and a silent one at that. I began to think John was losing trust in me and in us. He was pretty persistent with his requests to join me, and he became very annoyed when I refused to let him come. It was starting to drive us apart, although with Thanksgiving coming up and his daughter arriving, and our sex, although not brilliant, still continuing, we stuck it out and I remained true to him and our relationship throughout all of these insecurities he showed. Estrella, on the other hand, was a different issue.

In Hollywood, there are parties for A listers and parties for the rest, the B and C listers. Estrella, bless her soul, always believed she was in with the A listers, whereas all the time, from the second or third event she took me to, I knew she wasn't even in with the D listers. Estrella lived a life that was a lie. Indeed, I think she might have been delusional. The parties became boring and insignificant and it became harder and harder for me to agree to attend them with her. It kind of put a dampener on our relationship as she got wind of my skepticism. I was at the end of my tether with her and wanted a break, same applied to John, who was now driving me completely insane with his 'Gestapo' like questioning and his inability to understand that we were not a married couple, nor were we exclusive, even though I hadn't yet strayed. The temptation had been there, but John had been good to me and before his insecurity got the better of him, I was really enjoying our time together. Thanksgiving with his daughter was very special, as were other occasions in the first month that I'd landed in LA, but incessant badgering on where I was going and why I was going, no matter what it was I was doing, eventually got the better of my calm persona, and I knew that something was about to give.

That something was Charlie. Charlie the accident.

Charlie And His Chocolate Factory

"I knew I had the job from the moment I entered his office and commented on his custom-made shoes. Being in the fashion industry for so long, I had a keen eye for the unusual and an even keener eye for class. His shoes were just exceptional and a credit to his taste.

"So, you're not registered to work?" he asked

"Not yet, but I will be, and I need this job"

Charlie ran a logistics company, based out of a small town in the San Fernando Valley, called Encino. I'd seen his Ad, looking for a production assistant, on Craigslist, which I'd been keen to peruse in search of a job since I landed back in LA some 5 weeks earlier. Having been rebuffed so many times from so many jobs, I didn't hold out much hope with this one when I responded to make the appointment, and honestly, I'd shown up under the premise of receiving yet another rejection, but once I saw his shoes, his feet were up on his desk when I walked into his office, I knew this job was mine.

Charlie was from Canada, well-dressed and well-groomed, in his early 40's and from the look in his eyes when I sat down, ready to tear the clothes off my body and fuck me. Yes, it was another one of those instant attractions. He was reasonably tall, dark, and exceptionally handsome, and right behind his desk, where his feet just dangled, were pictures of his blonde wife and 4 young children. Our conversation continued.

"You know I can't officially employ you?" he muttered. But as he said that, I knew instantly he was considering all his options to enable me to begin work the very next day. Without too much back and forth he looked at me and blurted out,

"I'll hire you, and pay you cash, but you'll need to keep this really quiet and whatever deal we do will be our little secret. I don't want to get into any trouble." I wasn't sure if he was talking about the trouble he'd be in if he fucked me or employed me? Either way, I was hired and I was happy. At last, my life had taken a turn in a positive direction, a job, and a good one at that. It wasn't the best job I'd ever taken, but it wasn't a sex job and it paid decent money and I had the opportunity to meet people in an industry I hoped to work in. Happiness was abundant, until I returned home to John, who once again set about asking me where I'd been and what I'd been up to. I was really becoming frustrated with him and trying, in my own mind to figure out what to do about it.

My first day with Charlie was nearly a bust. I was on time, right on time, at 8 Am, as per our agreement. He never showed. I waited and I waited, and still no Charlie. I called. He answered. Apologetically stating he'd be there in 30 minutes, which then turned into another hour. Eventually he arrived and my education began, although somewhat later than I'd anticipated.

Charlie was fun to be around, and he treated me well. He had a lot going on, as did all of those people who ran similar production companies, but Charlie, well, he seemed to have a damn hurricane blowing through his office daily. I was running at 100MPH doing all the jobs that he had no time for, and impressing the heck out of him, because everything I did, I did well, and he knew it. I was limited in my expression, because although Charlie treated me like any other employee, technically I was an illegal and technically, he just couldn't. It didn't matter to me. The job took me away from John, which although sad at the time, offered the two of us a break to reevaluate one another. I wanted to marry John, for more than just the obvious reasons, security and citizenship, but something was bugging me, something I couldn't quite put my finger on, other than the fact he was so fucking curious as to my daily whereabouts. Estrella and I began having discussions on how we could move into an apartment together, and when those discussions took place, I knew that John and I had no future together and that I wanted out, and out as soon as possible, even though I thought him to be a great guy, his overbearing attitude was suffocating me. I decided to wait to see if I could reconcile in my own mind whether I should stay with John or not, and until that decision was made, I put Estrella's idea of living together, on the backburner. I wanted to give John every chance.

Charlie, in the meantime, got a job running a movie production out of

Bakersfield CA, a city about 100 miles north of LA, and he invited me to join him and the rest of the crew in Bakersfield, until the job was completed.

Bakersfield is really in the middle of nowhere and in the summertime it's hotter than Hell, it was January though, and thank goodness, winter days were of a temperature that could be easily tolerated. The job was going really well, so I believed, and Charlie was keen to utilize my office skills and my people skills, with regular intent. We got along really well, and we spent a lot of time discussing our trips from past journey's around the globe. Charlie was easy to chat with and nice to be around and I think he trusted me implicitly, because one evening, after the days' work was completed, he asked me to shoot back to LA, to Encino, to do him a huge favor. Now, remembering that Bakersfield was over 100 miles from the office and it was around 8 PM in the evening when Charlie called me to his room to ask me about this, meant I would have to drive the 100 miles there and back to be at work again for 7AM start the next day. I was sure to be exhausted, but in Charlie's own inimitable fashion, once he'd suggested I go back to Encino, he also suggested I take the next day off, giving me plenty time to perhaps complete this task and spend at least a few hours of the following day on my favorite Venice Beach, and also see John for a few minutes too!

The Task

Drive to Encino, open the office, an office that I'd never been to before, and collect the cash in the safe and bank it and bring him back the deposit slip. I was given the combination to the safe by Charlie and I began the tedious drive south to complete my task. I arrived in Encino around midnight, parked the car, opened the door and walked into a darkened room. While I searched frantically for the light switch, that smell just hit me. I knew the smell oh so well, that odor, that sweetness, that sweat, and the definite confirmation that I was in a massage studio. Lights were finally found, and yes, confirmation, as my eyes set fast on the massage table in the middle of the room. This was rather shocking to me, but at the same time, kind of acceptable too. Charlie was in the massage business? My goodness, I could smell it a mile away. The safe contained all the cash from that day's earnings, and probably several days prior to that. The odor in the room reminded me exactly of my life in London, and without doubt, this was an FBSM parlor. I could tell, and I didn't need visual confirmation either, but when I opened the safe and found the neatly stacked and named envelopes, the smile across my face was broader than a weightlifter's chest. It was funny really,

I thought I'd come home, home from where I'd always been, and it felt weird but acceptable that Charlie was in the same industry as I'd been, and although he'd kept it very quiet, and of course, didn't know my past, we had a kinship that was about to be revealed, because I knew as much, if not more about this industry than anyone on the planet, including Charlie, and when he found that out, when I decided to tell him what an expert I was in that business, it would be interesting to see how he'd react. He'd obviously sent me to perform this task without any knowledge of my past, so why would anyone, including me, know anything about his business? I was only to collect the money in the envelopes, bank the cash and return to my normal day job? Charlie was in for a major surprise.

My beach day turned into a 'thinking day'. Perhaps there was a way for me to expand, not only my trust level with Charlie, but also get involved in his massage business too. It was a dilemma for me. Do I tell him about my past, or do I keep it quiet? In the end, after a nice day sunning myself, a lovely lunch with John, who was back to his nice self, I motored all the way back to Bakersfield with my mind spinning in various directions, all very positive and all cash infused.

"Thanks for making that happen" was how Charlie greeted me when I got back. "I owe you one"

Owing me one was more than he could cope with. I wanted this guy, but I also wanted to be faithful to John, who I still hoped to marry at some point. Charlie though, now that I knew he was 'in the business', became a major attraction to me. I just could help myself. I was obsessed. Obsessed because I knew he'd understand me, well, I hoped he would. I was in that same hole, yet again, living my life but wanting something that was supposedly untouchable. His sex was within my grasp, my sex was on overdrive.

Tiana looks at me and says, "I know, I know, I'm a mess" and I couldn't agree more.

She continued. "So we finished the job in Bakersfield and we headed home. He's driving, I'm ogling, and he knows it.

"Want to go for a drink at my yacht club when we get to LA?" he asked

I was in trouble, and I was going to fuck him. I hadn't mentioned the FBSM just yet, but I wanted him inside me, and I wanted to run away too. So conflicted so confused, so horny. The fucking envelopes and massage table had turned my brain into mush. Back to the past and into the future. I just had to get part of who he was and he knew it. I didn't care about his marital status or his kids, I just wanted a fuck, a good fuck, although I had no idea if indeed it would be good or bad, I just hoped it would be satisfying.

The yacht club, situated on the west side of LA, about 40-minutes drive from Encino and about 10 minutes from John's home, was gorgeous. The opulence, hanging unashamedly from every corner or every nook and cranny. A wonderful homage to wealth, and Charlie was part of this kind of sexual overture. This wasn't small penis syndrome at its worst, this was just big boys with even bigger toys, and women who shone like beacons as you passed them in the corridors, each one prettier than the last, but all so obviously bored and unhappy. I, on the other hand, fresh and ready to party, looked like I was about to be dragged off by the Admiral, if an Admiral actually existed, back into a closet to be brushed down and sent out, cleaned up and ready to join the ranks of snobbery, where snobbery knew no boundaries. Wow, was this a scene.

Charlie took me into the bar, and we drank, not one, but three supersized cocktails, after which, I just leaned over and kissed him. It was an intentional come on, but one that didn't lead to anything more than one kiss and an offer from Charlie, keys swinging on his right index finger, to come join him on his boat for more than a quick feel. I refused. I felt guilty, strange for me, but I did, and that guilt took me from elation and wetness between my throbbing legs, to an Uber, parked outside and ready to take me back to John. Saved by common sense? I don't think so. I just took a moment to come to Jesus, and unfortunately that moment killed my libido for the night and sent Charlie into a sexual frenzy that would last more than 72 hours. We were going to fuck, we both knew that, not just fuck, but sexually demolish one another, only it wasn't going to happen on his boat or just quite at that moment.

I was obsessed with him, and he with me, and we both knew it, we both accepted it and the only remaining question was, what were we going to do about it?

Tiana fucks again, more like fucks up again, only this time, as I've told myself every time, this would be the last time. I needed Charlie to fuck me. Don't ask me why, I just did. Story of my life. I settle into a relationship with someone who helps me, (John), and then I fuck it all up. John didn't deserve this and I didn't deserve John, but hey, I hadn't done anything yet, and a kiss didn't really count.

The next two days in the office were crazy. Charlie was teasing me, and I was teasing Charlie. The back and forth banter was driving us both nuts. It was all about to kick off, as they say, and we knew it. I told Charlie I knew what his 'other' business was and he accepted the fact that his little secret was out of the bag. He didn't seem to care and in fact, it was a turn on for him once I'd revealed my FBSM past. I was in the middle of retrieving him some important documents from the adjoining office where our filing cabinets were located, it was about 4 PM in the afternoon, Charlie was on the phone but I could tell he was distracted, we both were. For the past 72 hours, I couldn't sleep, eat or do anything other than obsess over Charlie and his hidden and soon to be revealed cock. Charlie was also obsessing, I could see it in the way he looked at my tits all day and in fact I'd started to come to work in see-through tops and no bra, just to make him crazier. It worked, and as I was drawing a file from one of the cabinets, I could see through the open door, Charlie slamming the phone down and making his way quickly into the room where my throbbing poosie and I were located. I was wet, I was horny as fuck and he knew it. He came right over to me, grabbing my neck, and gently forcing me onto the floor. He stripped me naked while he released his cock from underneath his pants, and we fucked. When he entered me for the first time, I was more relieved than guilty, but when he started to fuck me, I knew I was in trouble and that all my expectations had been in vein. Charlie was crap, not just crap, but basically incompetent with his cock and after he came, which took about 35 seconds, I lay back, dripping cum from my frustrated poosie pondering the last minute or so and realizing that Charlie was nothing like the man I thought he was going to be. Then I stopped and thought for a second. Perhaps it was just that it had been the first time we'd fucked and we needed to try again, or perhaps not? My intuition, when it came to sex, was normally correct, and I just knew Charlie was my obsession and I needed to be satisfied by him as soon as possible. The funny thing was, he got up from the floor, where I still lay with my legs wide open, and mopped himself off with a tissue, then just left the filing room and went back to his office without saying a word. After a few minutes, I cleaned up and went in to join him. We stared at one another, no words flowing in either direction, contemplating our next moves.

"Perhaps we should try that again" he said, "and maybe next time we can do it in my bed on the boat?"

I didn't know what to think at that point. I was concerned on two levels, one was my job security, thinking now that he'd fucked me, he'd fire me, and the other was John. What had I done? John was still talking marriage and I was back fucking around like the old days. But between Charlie and I, the sexual chemistry was wild, and with that in mind, I decided we needed to give it another go, and do it as soon as possible. John had booked a trip to Tanzania, a business trip, and was leaving in a couple of days on his own, and I would fly out to join him about a week later and we'd planned to have a vacation doing Safari, for two weeks. I knew that when John left, I would be free to explore Charlie in greater depth, and with that in mind, I told Charlie that we not only needed to do it again, as soon as possible, but we needed to do it again and again and again, until we were both drained. That was a turn on for him, and I could see him getting erect as he sat behind his desk contemplating not only what we'd just done, but what we were about to do.

When I left the office that night, going home to John, who was a few days away from leaving for Africa, I felt guilt, so much guilt and when I arrived home, my poosie still unsatisfied, I fucked John with gusto, trying hard to make up for what I'd left behind at the office. Funny thing was, neither bouts of sex satisfied me that night, but something was about to happen that I hadn't contemplated and yes, Tiana, was about to receive yet another rude awakening.

Twice More-Then Oh Shit!

Charlie and I continued to flirt, touch, kiss and bait one another. John, in the meantime, left for Africa. I had freedom, and I loved it, sort of. I was determined to see if the sex with Charlie would improve, and what better way to venture into familiarity than by doing cocaine before fucking? Back to my old ways, but in a new place! Sad when you think back, well, sad for me because it was me who was in control, or out of control. My affair with Charlie can only be described as 'burn out' of the worst kind. He was flirtatious and I was susceptible. He was a fuck magnet and I was an even larger magnetic field. We just hit it off. Second fuck wasn't any better than the first. We went to the club, the yacht club, had a few drinks, John was already in Africa, and then we went to dinner and then to his boat. I described in great detail my previous love for cocaine, and he, being the true gentleman, he was, called his friend Eberhard, who, within minutes, was standing at the end of the berth where Charlie's boat was docked, pockets laden with cocaine. Party time! Charlie paid, I snorted and then we fucked. Again, he came so quickly, I thought I'd missed it, he was so quiet during ejaculation, but no, cum was already running down my legs and he was up and about looking for more coke. My poosie was again, unsatisfied I might add, and as high as I was, and as high as Charlie was, he proved to me that he was crap in the sack. I was smitten, though I didn't know why, and he was in love, and we were both in a ton of trouble. You know when you want something and then you get it and you really believe it's going to be good, but ends up being crap? That was Charlie and I. He was married for fucks sake and I was trying to get married. Why did I always try to destroy my life and the lives of others', just for sexual attraction? I had no idea, but I was determined to end this. I put it down to lust, but lust reared its ugly head once again, just two days later. I was about to fly out to the UK and then to Africa to meet up with John, but under severe pressure from Charlie to perform again, I decided, hey, wtf, let's just do it. No-one would ever know and one last time might be a blast, because it couldn't be any worse than the previous twice.

With that in mind, and alcohol running freely, the boat just sitting waiting for more of the same, my evening began. We got drunk, fucked for two minutes, fell asleep on top of one another, then fucked again, this time for 25 seconds. After that, I woke up, told Charlie it was over, got dressed and left. I knew I could do it, I knew I could be strong and I knew I had to intervene with my own destiny or I would be in serious trouble. And with my infatuation left behind me on that boat, I ploughed on with my life, one step at a time as I entered the taxi that would drive me right into my next crises.

John had called many times from Tanzania, begging me not to go to the UK and to come straight to Dodoma, the capital city of Tanzania, but I couldn't change my flight. Charlie, on the other hand, was begging for more sex, but I couldn't change my mind. Both men were really driving me crazy, one for the right reasons and one for the wrong. In the end, the right won out, and after telling Charlie I'd be back in two weeks to continue with our work, I was back home and packing, pondering what life would be like as a married woman living here in LA, when suddenly, I felt really sick, and that 'OH NO", "FUCK ME" feeling came rushing all over my persona. As my head disappeared down into the toilet bowl, and the vomit spewed out freely into the water beneath my head, my whole mindset changed in an instant. How could I have possibly been so stupid once again? I mean, come on, I was 27 going on 28 and every hard lesson I'd thought I'd learned, was ejected, like the vomit, out of my body in a split second. "FUCK FUCK FUCK" I said to myself, as I marched downstairs and out the front door, straight towards CVS to buy a test, a test, which within an hour, confirmed my worst fears, AGAIN!!!

My flight to London was going to be a complete headache, indeed, the trip to Tanzania should not even be happening, and these were just some of the thoughts going through my head as I began packing for my two weeks away from LA. God only knew who the father was, AGAIN! It could have been John or Charlie, but I wasn't certain, the only thing being that either one, in my opinion, would not be suitable. John had more of a chance, since I was living with him and he wanted to marry me and keep me comfortable for the rest of my life, but there was still some underlying issue with him that I hadn't put my finger on yet, but it was there, my gut told me so. Charlie on the other hand, was just a fling, a fling that ended as soon as the test read positive. Charlie would never know, he didn't need to know and anyway, I was more than certain that for him to be the father, we would have had to have had sex a few days earlier than we did. No matter what, as my clothes piled up in front of my teary eyes, willing themselves in to my suitcase, I was yet again, floored by the fact that I had been negligent and careless in my life and had now created another needlessly stupid problem, and one that should never have been created in the first place. I needed a good deal of time on my own, and the flight to London, the following day, would offer that time, time to think, time to be resolute and time to contemplate my future with John, or on my own.

Before I got on that flight, I made a quick trip to the office to make sure Charlie was on track with all the paperwork and meetings he'd let me arrange for him while I was going to be out of the country.

Charlie was already behind his desk when I arrived, normally I would be first in the office, but on this occasion, I was late because I knew that officially, I was on holiday. Charlie looked at me and he could tell something was amiss.

"Problem?" he said, quite offhandedly

There was no point in mincing words.

"I'm pregnant and I think it's yours"

There was no reaction from him, not even the hint of any surprise, nor a tinge of emotion.

"You're getting rid of it, right?" he asked.

I looked at him straight in his eyes and said, 'Fuck you" as loud as I could, walked out and took a deep breath, got into a taxi and went home.

As soon as I got home, I puked and then puked again, and then I called John to Tanzania. I woke him up.

"I'm pregnant"

There was a long pause, long enough for me to know he was in shock and not too happy, and there was silence. Then the tirade began.

"You can't be, I mean, if you are, I just don't need this now. This is not good. I am not happy, what are you going to do?"

The one liners followed one after another. He was pissed, but not once did he ask if I was OK, if I needed anything, if there was anything he could do, if I was prepared to discuss this in person when I arrived in Tanzania. Not once. I was in tears. I also didn't know whether to go on this trip or to cancel. I sat with the phone about three inches from my ear listening to John go off on a rant. This wasn't the man I wanted to be with. This was a side of him I thought existed, but hadn't yet had confirmation of my ongoing suspicions. Once he'd finished ranting, I said to him quite calmly,

"I am on my way to the airport shortly, and when I get to Africa, we can discuss this like two human beings, as long as you respect my situation and understand that you are responsible as much as me."

The phone went dead, as did my heart. I had been in bad situations before, but this was probably one of the worst ever. Totally my fault, I had been so stupid, but the fact that it was so evident that both guys just wanted to fuck me without taking responsibility for their actions, well, that pissed me off more than anything and led me to believe that I would spend the rest of my life alone, because no matter how hard I tried with people, I was always the one to be kicked to the ground and stood upon. I was sick and tired of being sick and tired, again, I knew it was mainly self-inflicted, but I had to find a way to get over this.

Abortion? Probably, well, absolutely, but I had a plane to catch so the question was, did I cancel and abort, or go and then abort?
I went.

I arrived in London, shattered, upset and confused. I was sure the baby would be aborted again, my choice of course, but somewhere deep inside me I kind of hoped that John would see the future as a family and change his wretched attitude once I arrived in Tanzania. I was pretty certain the kid was his. I had done the math and it was sort of impossible that Charlie could be the dad, though in my life, one never really knew. I knew if the kid belonged to Charlie, abortion was the only way forward, so in my own mind, John had taken over as an overwhelming favorite. Charlie would never support any child I had anyway, it was best for all concerned if I just named John as dad and moved on. In the back of my mind was our last telephone conversation. John had been a dick, a complete idiot and so condescending. This was a side of him I disliked intensely, and even though it never came out that often, the fact that he'd been that way as soon as I'd told him what was going on inside my womb, sort of proved to me that he really was one that I needed to dump and dump soon. My issue of course, immigration and what to do with my illegal status. John was supposedly my savior, but no more, unless, well, unless he'd changed his mind and attitude by the time I landed in Tanzania. I was doubtful.

London turned out to be a nice diversion. I met with Alice and a few other friends, being careful not to mention that I was pregnant. We did 'touristy' things, and went out to party a couple of nights too. I was careful about my alcohol consumption and never did cocaine, even when it was offered, not knowing if this baby was one I was going to keep. After the party was over, my journey to Heathrow airport was filled with dread. I was kind of in no man's land.

The heat, when we landed in Dodoma, was unbelievable. While I waited to get through immigration, I threw up all over the floor, obviously causing commotion and bringing attention to myself. The guards present weren't impressed, but after my explanation, they backed off and fully understood. John was waiting for me just outside of the customs hall. The conversation began.

"Hello"

There was no hug.

"Hi" he said, as he took my bag.

And that was it. Nothing, absolutely nothing. I was shocked, I was exhausted and I was feeling very sick. We got into the taxi, and sped full throttle towards our hotel. I looked at John, and he looked at me, and then it began.

"You're getting rid of it, correct?" It wasn't really a question, but more of a demand.

I burst into tears.

We never spoke for another 4 hours. He ignored me and basically dumped me in my room, our room, while he went to the bar and got drunk. I sat in bed wondering why I'd even bothered to come here, after all, it was obvious he didn't want the baby, or me for that matter. He was just so different, or maybe this was just the real him? In any event, he left me alone, came back to the room drunk, got into bed, turned round and fell asleep. The next day I made my mind up to get the hell out of dodge and go back to America.

I awoke after a few hours' sleep, went to the business center in the hotel and had them book me flights back to LA leaving that afternoon. I didn't care what Jon thought, my concerns were only for my health and to get rid of this unwanted child. I needed to get back to LA, move out of John's place, arrange a termination for the pregnancy and then find a new apartment. Simple really! I'd done it before, and I was about to do it again. Flights all booked, I returned to the room, where John was just waking up. Our plans had included a safari, and other exciting trips, all of which he could now do without my presence. I broke the news.

"I'm leaving"

He gave me a blank stare, and said nothing.

"I will go back to LA tonight, and when I'm back I will move out and find a place to stay on my own"

"OK you do that. After all I've done for you"

"Are you being serious?"

And so the arguments began. I insisted he take a long look in the mirror and that as the baby's father, he should take more responsibility and show at least some compassion, but he didn't want to know and I knew immediately, this relationship had ended. He stormed out again, probably back to the bar to continue his binge, and I packed and left. I wasn't sad, I wasn't emotional, other than being pregnant and lost in life, but I was reasonably savvy and certain I would bounce back from this, just like I had in the past.

The taxi dropped me off at the airport and I waited 5 hours for my flight to land and offload, before I was ready to board. We took off, back to London, where I would change planes, after another 6 hour wait in the departure hall at Heathrow, and then re-board a BA flight to LA, which took another 11 hours to get there. By the time I landed, and I hardly slept on either plane journey, I'd been up and on the move for more than 40 hours. I could hardly stand up, let alone walk.

And feeling like shit, making my way to immigration, confused and exhausted, my problems were about to begin, problems I'd not even thought of, problems that could almost certainly get me deported.

They pulled me over. They, being customs at LAX. I hadn't even retrieved my suitcase and they'd flagged me. I nearly pooped my pants, and without warning, 3 officers, one female, 2 male, led me into an anti-room, filled with over 35 people, most of whom were Pilipino. I wanted to puke, I needed to pee, and I started to pray. I had a huge issue, they knew it, I knew it and the other 35 or so in that room knew it as well. We were all in the same boat, all frightened and all facing deportation if the guys behind the little grey windows decided to eject us. I was in the lap of the US Border and Immigration service and I prayed to God that I would be allowed to go home, home being my house in LA that I shared with John. Oh, was I scared, so scared in fact that my life began flashing between my eyes. All my issues, admittedly self-inflicted, sex, drugs, smoking, loneliness, my parental upbringing, the orgies, my pregnancies, and so much more, came flooding into my head. I was shaking, shaking so hard, I almost forgot where I was, until I heard an officer call out a name and the man sitting next to me got up and went to window number 3. The conversation between that man and the office, which I could hear quite clearly, brought me to my senses, instantly! I was in serious trouble, I knew it, they knew it and my only way out was to pray, and pray hard. I promised God that if he let me pass through immigration, I would give up cocaine, cigarettes, sex, and all my other bad habits. I promised him that I would never get pregnant again, unless I was married to the man I loved. I promised him so much and I kept on promising, for about two hours, while I waited my turn to go up to that small grey window and chat to the officer I was assigned. They were so slow, so deliberate and not at all caring. They allowed a few to go in, and then they would take a few more away, to who knows where, but I just knew that they were the unfortunate ones, soon to be headed back to wherever they'd just come from. I hoped that this wasn't going to be me.

My name called out, my legs shaking, my nervous system in overdrive, I began that short walk of shame towards the window, where an officer, sitting comfortably behind a glass screen, invited me to get comfortable in the hard chair provided, because, in his words, 'this might take more than just a few minutes.

I was asked 2 questions.

"Why are you back in the country so soon?" I'd been away about 10 days, and "Please hand over your cell phone" More of a demand than a question, but as I sat there, shaking like a leaf, anything that came out of that officers' mouth not only seemed officious, but felt like each question or demand was just another nail in my deportation coffin.

"I went to London and to Africa on a modeling assignment and now I came back to LA to take a vacation for a couple of weeks. Is that OK?"

My words were deliberate, yet hesitant, as I thought of all the excuses under the sun that I'd rehearsed over the years while contemplating this very scenario, a scenario that had never happened before, but was happening in full color before my very eyes at that moment.

I had 2 cell phones, one from the UK and one from the USA. As the officer was digesting my previous statement, I pulled out the UK phone, which I then handed to him. He fiddled around with it for what seemed like an eternity, but which was in fact only a minute or so, realizing that it didn't get service in the USA and that nothing he tried or wanted to try would make any difference and therefore all my texts and emails would remain private. Sweat was pouring down my back, he knew it and he made the most of it.

"How long are you planning on staying this trip?" he asked.

"Maybe two weeks, perhaps two and a half. It depends on the interview? I replied

"Will you be getting paid while you're here for anything you do work wise in the United States" he smiled as he asked this.

I realized what was going on here, and I'd practiced this in my mind many times in the past, but never had to use it.
"No, of course not, I live in London, all my pay checks come from my work there. I am here for vacation only."

"How do you afford so many vacations and trips to LA?" "I'm paid very well and I'm good at what I do. Would you like to see pictures?"

He looked up, took my passport, stamped it and told me to go collect my suitcase.

I was home! My goodness was I relieved. My case was there, all ready and waiting, and so was my taxi. I'd been delayed in customs for 3 hours, all of them miserable and devastatingly tiresome. I was 6 weeks pregnant, hadn't slept for 2 days, and my heart had not recovered from the grilling I'd just been through. I needed sleep, I needed to relax, and most of all, I needed to get rid of this baby that was never going to be accepted by either Charlie or John. My taxi driver dropped me off at John's Venice Beach home, I walked in, shut the door, took off my clothes, showered, and I went to sleep for 28 hours. When I woke up, my first task would be the second most unpleasant thing I'd ever done in my life. I was dreading this, but I knew it had to be done. I was jet lagged, confused, and selfishly single minded in my purpose. Abortion it would be, but not the conventional way.

Bye-Bye Baby

I had promised God so much while I was waiting to be interrogated at LAX, so much that I needed to stay true to, so much that would be hard to stick to but so much I knew I would take care of and honor my promises made. One thing I never promised him/her, was to hang on to this child that was now growing in my belly. I didn't know what to think about that, in fact, I tried not to think about it at all. Charlie, John, the two names reeling around inside my head, but who was the father? Who cared? Not me, I told myself, as I walked in the planned parenthood office in downtown Santa Monica. After a short wait, a brief diagnosis and urine test, I was handed a small pill. No surgery this time, I wasn't far enough gone to warrant that. This was Plan B, literally.

I went home, after digesting the poison they'd given me, in front of two caring nurses and a picture of a fetus, hanging on the wall in a way that suggested I was a complete bitch for terminating a life so early. A picture that would haunt me for the rest of that day and into the next, as I sat in bed, feeling like shit and then bleeding profusely until 24 hours later, while sitting crapped up on the toilet seat, it just popped out of my vagina. Sorry to be so graphic, but the situation warrants description, for all those of you ladies out there who will read this book and might accidentally get pregnant. I want you to know exactly how it feels and what it looks like.

The pain beforehand is excruciating. It sort of builds up as the drug gets to work. There's a feeling of uncontrollable sadness as pressure coming from the inside of the belly, which meets guilt coming from one's mind. A clash of two inner titans, a coming together of differences that create an explosion of sadness and disgust. Then this bloody mass just pops out into the toilet bowl and when you look down, you see what was a baby, a life, a blood relative, and the creation from a stupid mistake, that cost someone a future. And then? And then you flush, and it's gone! It's gone from everywhere other than your inner psyche, where that child lingers for the rest of your days on earth, and probably into eternity. The surgical option is much more clinical and simpler. You go in, they put you to sleep and then you wake up. All gone! Sorted!

My life was back on track, if it ever was on any track in the first place. The question was, what was I going to do to put it on a track, or was I just going to ruin the next 27 years by repetition and ignorance? All questions that would need to wait, because as soon as that fetus 'fell out' of my womb, John was on the phone from Africa, asking for money for rent. He'd lost his job, and I'd lost all patience with him. It was time to leave, and I needed out before he returned. I started to look for places to live, and that's when Estrella and I met up again and formulated the craziest plan I'd ever come up with.

I'd found an apartment in Hollywood, not a good one, but one that would be sufficient in the short term. Estrella lived in Hollywood already and we'd agreed to meet up for lunch the same day I'd found that apartment. I hadn't yet placed a deposit, which was fortuitous to say the least, when Estrella, over lunch, suggested I move in with her. She knew what John and I had been through, and she realized I was ready for change. She also knew I needed a green card.

"Move in, let's have a lesbian affair, get married and you'll be in!" A lesbian affair? Well, why not? It wouldn't be real, but if it worked out, and it allowed us to get married, gay marriage having just been approved in the state of CA, and that got me my green card, then why not? We formulated a plan, I went back to Johns home, John came back from Africa that same day, I told him I was moving out and all he could muster was 'what about the rent?" I'd made the right decision. He hadn't inquired about my health or the baby, just the bloody rent. I packed and I left within an hour and took an Uber back to Estrella's apartment in Hollywood, where the next chapter of my life would be written. Charlie, oh yes, Charlie, was still on the scene and well aware, not only about the abortion, but also that I was an expert in FBSM, something he now realized I was better at than being his PA, and something he didn't have to worry about paying me cash to perform, since that whole industry ran on cash payments. I unpacked at Estrella's home, called Charlie and set up a meeting with him for that very next day. In the meantime, the texts began flooding in from John, begging me to return, something I ignored for a very long time indeed.

FBSM is my savior, even today, it's my bread and butter, and I'm good at it, no, in fact, I am the best! There's no one better than me. I make my clients feel special, I am able to communicate with the shyest of the shy, the brashest of the brash, and I do it with a smile and with gratitude, especially to those who have great cocks and are good looking, handsome and sexy too (these guys are few and far between BTW). I really am the FBSM queen, or as Charlie used to say, I am the slut without the slit. No one, and I mean no one, leaves unsatisfied. I have been asked many times about my technique and my ability to make an erection from the limpest of dicks. Here's the deal. I've trained so many girls, maybe 50 plus in total, on how they can make the FBSM experience sexy, fun, erotic and pleasurable. My take on the whole scene, from the 12 years I've been doing this, and yes, I still practice FBSM even today, because the cash benefits are just amazing for me, is to ensure that once that door opens and the client walks in, he's in for the best sexual fantasy experience he's ever had. I am made up, looking sexy, either in a short dress or lingerie, and I smell amazing. When that door opens and in walks a new client, or a regular, it's showtime for me and it's going to be ejaculation time for him. He knows it, I know it, and there's no place to hide. You don't have to be the best masseuse, although a little knowledge of the human anatomy does help, but in actual fact, a gentle rub on their back is all they are really looking for, along with some testicle teasing, and one or two other erogenous flirtations. Yes, I have the occasional client who will ask me to kneed out a knot or two, but that's a rarity. They all want the same thing. They want to fuck me, but know they can't, even though they're desperate to try, so they accept that a hand job release is all they're going to get while they lie on their backs fantasizing about fucking me on a return date. I tell all the girls the same thing, as I mentioned before. Look your best, be friendly, get naked and tease. After that, your bank balance will just grow and grow. When I was trained, and as you know from what I've already told you, I was trained by the best, I was always told to make conversation, smell good and look great, and with that in mind, even though there are days where I just cannot be bothered to make myself up, I have always taught those practices to those I have trained, and there have been many. When the guy on the bed is 'flipped', which is the bit of the FBSM experience they all eagerly wait for, my smile, my erotic gaze, my sexuality, has to be spot on and right in their face. I want them erect, turned on and ready to blow. As soon as I massage that cock, I want it to explode so I can clean them up, throw them out and bring in the next horny guy and do it all over again. Each ejaculation is $200, and each satisfied client is a client who will return and refer. You cannot do better than a referral. It means that you're doing something right, and most of my clients are return clients or referrals from returning clients. The secret to my success is not my tits, it's not by poosie, it's not my sexy voice, it's ALL of the above, a combination of years of experience along with my natural ability to ooze sex appeal. Charlie of course, knew all of this and he also knew he could trust me. He'd already decided I was the right person to run his little massage business in Venice and when I came out of my pregnancy coma, guilt now a thing of the past, I headed to his office on yet another bright sunny LA morning, where after a short pause to purchase coffee, we sat down together for the first time since I'd aborted the baby, to discuss the future and the possibilities of me working 'massage' for him as the boss. "Big Boss" I liked the sound of that. Charlie liked the sound of it too. He offered me the chance to manage his business, from top to bottom. I would train the girls, assist with bookings, bank the cash and keep everyone in line. I wasn't sure what I wanted to do at that point, what I did know was I needed some normality in my life. I was sick and tired of being used and abused. I had an incredible urge to be married, for more than just the reasons relating to my Green Card situation.

Estrella and I had already moved in together. She was an alcoholic, or at least on the verge of being one, and between the two of us, we'd conjured up a reason to live together and pretend we had a gay relationship in order I could apply for my residency. She had a Green card already, but I needed mine and I needed to get it very soon. I'd overstayed all the welcome I could afford in the USA, and to become legal was certainly a priority.

Estrella was also broke, something I didn't really know at the time. She worked on occasion, but she didn't have a real job. She'd sing, socialize with the wannabe rich and famous of LA, but she was a mess. She did all the drugs she could afford and she insisted that all was well in her world, but it was far from that. Our relationship had sprung from our mutual friendship of Max, and now, as we were holed up in Estrella's apartment, day after day, all she could talk about was Max. It became tedious and very boring. This wasn't the normal life I craved and I couldn't see any way that our relationship would blossom into a credible marriage, let alone a marriage that the authorities would accept as being genuine.

Normality? What the fuck was normality? I certainly hadn't found it, ever! I was now 27 and throughout all of my life, nothing had been normal, at least nothing I could quite recall. My life revolved around sex, nothing but sex, and possibly drugs, although the drugs were a kind of on and off thing with me. I was truly a party girl on the outside, but my insides? My insides ached for something other than the norm. My norm being sex, more sex and then sex again, followed by cocaine here and there. Where was the fairytale I yearned for? I had no idea, but I was about to try and find it.

Charlie was so good to me. He let me work whenever I wanted. I wasn't sure about bossing his massage practice yet, in fact, I was still trying to find my feet amongst the girls he already let work in his Venice office. I'm so used to calling it an office, but it was more like and apartment and less like a massage parlor. I seemed to fit in, but my thought process didn't allow me to contemplate becoming the 'big boss' that Charlie felt I should be. I wanted to be just one of the crowd and didn't want the aggravation of having to train the other girls, collect money, etc. My life needed to be simplified. Here I was, sitting comfortably at the edge of Armageddon every day, knowing that one wrong move and I could be deported, so what was my incentive to make that situation even more complicated by taking on more responsibility? In short, none! After the abortion I had taken time to reflect on what an unbelievably ridiculous life I'd had to date. It was really time for me to reflect and to mature. Maybe someplace out there in La-La land there would be a man, a nice man, someone I could marry, have kids and settle down with? Maybe, just maybe. And with that thought in mind, I decided to begin dating once again. Normal dating, not dating guys who I jerked off daily, although there were plenty of offers from that crowd each day. Guys would lie erect, flagpole at the ready for a hand job and would come up with the most stupid offers. "Come out with me before I cum" "If you think it's large now, wait until its inside you" I was done with all that, truly done. I decided to join Tinder, yes, you might laugh, but from all the dating Apps and sites that were on the market, Tinder seemed to be the simplest and the most effective. Everyone told me it was just an App for fucking and one-night stands. I was determined to find out if that was a true assessment or indeed, could I actually find a real relationship on that site. Charlie thought I was crazy, Estrella was too high or too far up her own asshole to make any kind of judgement, and so I just went ahead and I placed an Ad with my profile.

It didn't take long. Within 4 hours, I was matched up with 3 guys. They probably thought my tits looked like they needed some action, some of my profile pics were a little provocative, but in general, I kept everything as low-key as possible. I any event, 3 guys swiped right and so did I. It was time to have some fun.

Cameron, he was the first. Great guy, good looking, surfer type and with nice blond hair and a smile that was infectious. Lunch with him and then a peck on the cheek. Nice day out, but the thought of sex was far from my mind. Never saw him after that because I knew if I fucked him, he'd never see me again. I had this weird feeling of "OMG, I have joined the real world" as I looked at Cameron. This was dating, real dating, something I'd never really done with any kind of passion. It would take me a while to come to terms with it, but it was kind of enjoyable.

Kalum, he was number 2. Nice enough, this time a meeting at Starbucks for coffee. We hit it off, but again, something inside me told me to walk away and never see him again. So I did.

Back and forth with Charlie and massage bookings, my time for living on the edge waiting for someone to find out I was illegal, was drawing ever closer.

Derek, number 3, was great. Good looking, not at all pushy, handsome and again, a blond surfer type. He was a few years younger than me, and this time, I allowed him to take me to dinner and to the Santa Monica Boardwalk, and to a movie, total 4 dates, before I fucked him. The sex was good, not great, and it was comfortable. He enjoyed it, I enjoyed it and we became lovers, but only for a short time. I blew it by telling him the truth, that I needed to get married. He felt he was too young and he ran in the opposite direction. I was back to square one.

John was history, Estrella was history, I was now living alone, and desperate. How was I going to be able to stay in America? Every time I thought about it I wanted to puke. The situation and uncertainty was making my whole life miserable.

And then I had an idea.

Many months prior to this, my friend Leo, a photographer on many shoots I'd done, had always said he would take care of me if I was in trouble, and as a last resort, I decided to call him and reconnect. He was delighted to hear from me, and we met up for dinner. Leo was delighted to see me again and after a short session of small talk, I just got right down to it.

"Leo, I need you to marry me" I was straight to the point. "You told me a long time ago that you would, you know my situation, and I am begging you for help"

Leo balked at the thought and almost spat his cheeseburger over the person sitting behind me. He was sympathetic, but not in the least interested in helping me out. Again, too young and unwilling to give up a couple of years of his life to save mine. I couldn't blame him.

I had played all my cards. I had no trump card, no ace, no way to make this situation any better and I began to panic. My whole life had been built around living in LA and now my whole life was about to fall apart **because** I lived in LA. I wanted to cry, I wanted to hug someone, but what I didn't want was to fall back into the quagmire that had been my last 27 years. I just couldn't see any options. I was cornered, and I felt my whole world was caving in, rapidly. I couldn't leave the USA, otherwise I wouldn't be allowed back in. I couldn't get any man to marry me, I just wanted to escape, but there was no escape. Ending up on a plane back to Estonia wasn't an option, that would have meant failure, but failure now loomed on my short horizon. I was sick to my stomach, as I already said, breathless, claustrophobic, and on the verge of a mental collapse. What on earth was I going to do?

Crescendo then Climax

The thing about my life that had become evident since sitting down and going over some of my experiences, is that it takes the same direction on a regular basis and then comes back to square one, my loneliness and foolishness, of which I regret neither. I am a strong woman, a happy person, generally, but I make the same mistakes again and again, without heeding the warnings of my past. Upon reflection, all I ever wanted was a home with a great husband and a couple of kids, or did I? This story has a long way to go, long enough to make it into at least two books and possibly three. I have over achieved in the sense that my sex life has never been dull, but I have underachieved as far as my ambitions and happiness are concerned. Happiness always eluded me for more than a few minutes. Not sure why that is, or indeed, why even today, it's still eludes me. I think I find happiness, and then, it vanishes. Perhaps I am unable to be happy, perhaps it doesn't even exist, or, maybe happiness is just overrated? In any case, I strive to find it on a daily basis, and have yet to encounter fulfillment. Normality is another missing element in my life. Being involved in modeling, dancing, acting and the sex industry doesn't really lead to a normal existence, or at least so far it hasn't. I've seen more dicks than most women. I've jerked them, fucked them and swallowed them, but in the end, they all do the same thing, and that thing, that pleasurable ending for him, has not been too pleasurable for me, other than financially and the odd couple of times I've been in love. Which, by the way, have also proved to be false dawns. I dislike the term, "Sex Worker", but I suppose that's what I do. I suppose I have to get used to that term, but really I would love to discard it in favor of 'Housewife" or 'Love of My Life', only I don't see it in my future, and I certainly, no matter how I tried, didn't see it back then when I was on the verge of this mental collapse. Despite all the men I have slept with, I remained hopeful that one day a man would walk into my life with a proposal to take me away from my past, and never ask any questions as to what that past might have been. One day, not in this book, but in the next book I write, you'll see that I will find an outlet where I believed I was going to end my tortuous days and nights and settle down into the normality I have described above. That's for another time though, because my story, the one where the happy ending comes along with my knight in shining armor saving me from myself, didn't happen back when I was 27, it just became more convoluted and complicated and placed me into an up and down spiral that seemed to be continual and never ending.

Leo picked up his phone, a few days after that cheeseburger incident.

"let's meet" was all he said. The two of us went to dinner 3 nights later. During the meal, Leo told me he'd thought about things and decided he would help. He wanted to get married. My mind went into overdrive, on the one side congratulating itself for finding someone to assist, but on the other side, cautious that this would be another false dawn. Leo was an Ok kind of guy, but the spark, well, let's just say it was nonexistent. My visa had expired, I was now classed as an illegal, at the mercy of ICE and their wicked ways and running around virtually homeless and scared every minute of every day. Leo was my savior, or so I thought. We made plans, we laughed, we ate and then we went back to my 'temporary' accommodation to fuck. Leo rarely wanted to have sex with me, no wait, he NEVER wanted to have sex with me, ever, and that was a concern, but on this special night, he was well up for a good shagging. His amorous ways however, soon evaporated and his mean side came to the forefront of what became a really weird evening. He was determined to blow all the good will he'd rekindled in the last few hours by lying to me, although I have to admit, I lied to him too. He told me he wanted kids, quite how he intended to give me kids though was beyond me, unless he was an expert at immaculate conception, and I told him that I wanted him to give me kids. All lies. I never wanted his kids and he didn't want to fuck me to help me have kids. There we were, naked and lying in different parts of a very small bed, telling lies and becoming more frustrated with each other, when suddenly Leo got up and told me he needed to crap. The funny thing was, even though he was staying just that one night, he'd brought with him this vast array of different items. All his work out stuff, three changes of clothing, two bags full of toiletries, and so much more. It was so strange to look at his pile on my bedroom floor, when both of us knew it was only one night and then the plan was for me to go and move in with him. My lease was up in 3 days and I had no other plans. Leo was it. Anyway, we looked at one another, both knowing this was going to be a huge mistake, I knew for sure, Leo? Well Leo was sort of going with the flow and accepting that this was his 'mercy' deed. Help the Estonian and go to heaven.

"I need to crap" he suddenly said and off he went into the bathroom, where, 30 minutes later, he hadn't returned.

"You OK?" I shouted.

About 5 minutes later, a sullen faced Leo struts out of the bathroom. As he opened the door, the smell was unbearable.

"WTF" I said, quite forcefully.

"Em, I, er, I pooped, but it won't go down"

"What do you mean, it won't go down?" I replied

"Em, it's stuck. I cannot get the toilet to flush."

I got annoyed and decided there and then, this was it. "Get a fucking plastic bag, pick up your shit with your hands, wrap it up and then take it, and the rest of your stuff the fuck out of here!!!" By this time I was shouting and he was cringing in a cowardly sort of manner, his head bowed, his back bent up in a kyphotic state and his whole demeanor, crushed. I had no more patience for this man. He quietly walked out into my kitchen, found a bag, collected his poop by hand and packed his stuff to go. There were no goodbyes, no regrets, no feelings at all from my part. The door closed, I stood still for a few seconds, breathed a sigh of relief and then lit a cigarette. Panic, real panic, set in immediately. My last throw of the dice had fallen flat. I was about to be homeless, stateless and all alone to fight my self-inflicted demons. I had no idea what I was going to do, really no idea. I had a job, with FBSM at Charlie's place, but that was all I had. I had no car, Estrella had refused to co-sign the new lease, and my housing situation was pathetically, non-existent. I was doomed.

I began scouring Ad's for home or room rentals. My issue being, no one wanted to rent to me because of the obvious, I had no Social Security number and no proof of residency in the USA. It was a nightmare. As the clock counted down to zero and as I began to panic even more, my belongings all packed up and ready to move somewhere, I just didn't know where, I was lucky enough to come across this Ad for a room in Calabasas, a suburb of LA, situated in the San Fernando valley. It's a very nice suburb, and one that is affluent and safe.

I didn't have a car, so I took and Uber to the address given to me after chatting with the owner. He had a broken English accent and was difficult to understand, but I was running out of options and he seemed nice enough when we chatted. $25 on an Uber seemed worth the effort, and as the cab pulled up to a very nice home in a very quiet street, my hopes were raised. Perhaps this would be the place?

I had money in the bank, quite a lot actually, but all previous apartments I'd looked at, even though I'd offered 6 months' rent in advance, had poo-pooed my application after finding out that I was an illegal. I prayed that this gentleman wouldn't do the same, after all this was just a room in his home and perhaps he'd be grateful for receiving the extra cash each month.

As soon as MJ, short for Mohamad and some other name I cannot remember, opened his door, his eyes feasted on my legs and breasts. At that very moment, I knew this room would be mine, and I relaxed. MJ couldn't keep his eyes off me. He was about 60ish, perhaps Lebanese, short, semi bald, grey and, from the way he was staring, he hadn't had sex in 30 years. We chatted, he looked at my tits. We drank coffee, he looked at my tits. Eventually, we came to an arrangement, and I left, as he continued to look at my tits. The room was mine, and was ready for me to move into that very next day. I had been saved, at least for now.

MJ was a kind soul, quiet, but kind. He loved his home comforts, especially American TV> He was Lebanese, I asked him after I moved in, and he practiced the Muslim faith. He was 61, not 62 and he was single. He loved my legs and he loved to look at my tits all the time, and with that in mind, I provoked his stares by dressing accordingly. After moving in, I decided to continue with my classes in West Hollywood, dancing classes, feeling more comfortable and relaxed now that I'd found a roof to sleep under. It meant taking an Uber both ways, but it was worth it.

One afternoon, after leaving the house in Calabasas, I arrived at my place of work, Charlie's studio, to do massage, when the phone rang, and Charlie pleaded with me to meet him for an early dinner at the yacht club. At that time we were just friends, not lovers, and he was still paying me to work for him, always in cash. He sounded desperate and I agreed to meet him on condition it was food and drink only and nothing amorous. He promised me that he just wanted to talk. Liar!

We met, he tried it on, I blasted him, verbally. I jumped in a cab to West Hollywood, and I hadn't eaten anything. I was starving. Charlie had been a prick. Two drinks, a hand on my tits, trying to kiss me and hating the rejection even more than he hated his wife in Canada. Oh well, I was always going to be friends with him, even today, we still talk, but there was no way on earth he would fuck me again. I'd put an end to all of that while pregnant. Charlie was history.

Getting out the cab at the dance class studio, I made my way towards a Vegan restaurant that I loved. It was only 3 minutes' walk from where the cab had dropped me off. On the way, there was a guy, tattooed from head to toe, sitting on a Harley. I'm a total bike chick, always was, always will be, and I took an immediate like to this dude, so I stopped to chat to him. He was so cool. We chatted for a few minutes and then he joined me for a quick bite to eat. Vlad had ink everywhere, all over his face, all over his legs and arms and all over his body. I was so attracted to that, but then again, I was attracted to many different things in life, none which had yet led me to my nirvana.

Vlad had a girlfriend, and a 19-year-old son, Stew. He ran a bike store right next door to the dance studio, and after sitting with him for an hour or so, I explained to him that my life was in serious need of some stability. He listened intently and appreciated my candor too. We agreed that on my next trip to the studio, I would pop into the bike store and we'd meet up again. I never thought too much about that at the time. I had no intention of fucking him, although I really wanted to at the time.

For the next few weeks, life took a very routine path, other than with MJ. He and I were fast becoming good friends, maybe too good? We would sit and chat, go to movies, and I would encourage him to go out for dinner now and again. Honestly, it was like dragging a horse to water. He was so reluctant to do any of this, but gradually he acquiesced and we began having fun, sort of.

This relationship was very strange. MJ was 40 years older than me, and believe me, that's a lot in my book. However, once he knew and understood my immigration predicament, he suddenly wanted to help out and suddenly became even more interested in my tits than he had been from the moment I'd walked through his front door on the day we'd first met. He was now talking marriage, and I was now talking dirty to him since I saw an opening and perhaps another savior.

Meanwhile, back at the bike shop, Vlad and I had become 'good friends' and had dinner a few times. One thing led to another and I fucked him, just once, in the shop, admitting afterwards that his tattoos had been a huge turn on for me. He too was curious on how he could help me stay in the country and had suggested that one of his military buddies, based in San Diego, might be marriage material. I believed that he was just saying this so he could fuck me again, even though I knew he was attached and even though I knew I'd like to. Turned out, the buddy in SD, called me a few days later, and Asian guy called Hong. We chatted and agreed to meet, a meeting that really never happened, but that's for the next page.

MJ was now on marriage alert. He was talking traditional Lebanese, with all the trimmings. We began to have sex, occasionally, but sex it was, and I hated it. What a woman has to go through, an illegal woman at that, just to stay in the country of her dreams, well, it's not worth talking about, unless you are writing a book, which I obviously am! MJ sucked in the sack, but the wedding idea was now a reality. Vlad's buddy in San Diego, Hong, flaked out on me, so MJ seemed to be my last option. He was becoming more and more possessive. The more we fucked, the more he became weird.

"Why are you wearing such a short dress?"

"Why are your nipples showing through your blouse?"

"Why are you talking to this one and that one?"

It was unbearable and decidedly spooky too. I had to think again and I had to do it fast. Getting married to MJ might mean salvation with slow demise. I could see myself pregnant with his baby and being asked to wear the Hijab all day every day. No, this wasn't going to work, and again, it was my fault for jumping in with two feet and so little thought.

I asked Vlad for his opinion, and he suggested that I meet his son. His son? He was 19, and he seemed to be controlled by Vlad. I think the deal would have been, I marry the son so the father can continue fucking me, but that was never going to happen.

And then came the day of all days. When telling you this story, from page 1 until now, none of what I've said seems real, but I lived it and I lived it all, up close and personal. There's no getting away from the fact that I am a foolish young lady in so many ways, and that I've lived an incredible, if not terrible existence for those 27 years we've talked about in this book, but at the end of it all, this one day in particular will live in my mind and in the mind of infamy, for the rest of my days on earth. This day became my swansong of how not to live your life, and it became one of those days that you just want life to end and never start again.

It began with MJ and I having a huge fight, me packing my bags and leaving his home. I couldn't marry him and I just blurted it out. By that time, he thought he owned me, and he was wrong. I walked out at 7 AM on the dot. I remember looking at my watch, as the Uber came to pick me up, and thinking, "how the fuck do you do this to yourself on such a regular basis?"

I headed to see Vlad, who was supposed to have his son waiting to meet me. The plan was for us to talk, see what we thought about the plan Vlad and I had discussed, then more in together in Vlad's place in West Hollywood. Instead, when I arrived, this short and very angry looking, but quite pretty, Vietnamese lady stood right in front of Vlad, arms folded and spit running down the side of her mouth, like a dragon from Game of Thrones. She was ready to kill.

I got out the cab. The tirade began.

"You fuck my boyfriend. You bitch, you home wrecker, you whore!" And so it went on. After denying everything, a futile exercise, I was told in very few words, but with many expletives, that she'd pulled the security cam footage from the bike shop, having had a suspicion that Vlad was cheating on her. Low and behold, there we were, right on top of his Harley, fucking like bunnies. I was sure she was going to pull out a gun and shoot me on the spot. Might have been the best thing for me at that point, in any case, the son, son of Vlad, wasn't there to meet me, Vlad, was left ruing the day he'd met me and there I was, suitcases in hand, no home to go to and exposed to this verbal onslaught by the angriest woman I'd ever met, in the middle of a posh N Hollywood street. It was farcical. And then, as if right on cue, having just thought to myself, 'well at least I still have a job', my phone rang. When I answered it, with Miss Vietnam still screaming obscenities in the background, it was Charlie.

"WTF is going on there?" he asked.

"Oh don't mind her" I replied, "I was fucking her boyfriend and she's just found out and wants to kill me" I laughed, but Charlie didn't.

"Listen" he said, "we've just been raided by the cops, Jasmine has been arrested for prostitution, so don't come anywhere near the place. I am going to have to close it down for good. It's a complete shit show here?"

I was stunned. I was homeless, jobless and an illegal immigrant, standing in North Hollywood being screamed at by a lady I didn't know and an audience who didn't really care.

What on earth was I going to do?

Life Goes On, and On and On

The greatest thing I have found since arriving in America, is how quick and easy it is to get things done. You want a car? You buy a car and drive it out that same day. You want to eat at midnight, 7 days a week? No problem, especially in the larger cities, it's all there and readily available for you to consume. Same thing with jobs and accommodation, if you need it or want it, you can find it and you can find it fast.

As the crowd dispersed and the realization set in that I was all alone, yet again, suitcase in hand, no transportation, and no one to call who would respond with the urgency my situation required, I headed for the nearest hotel, booked a room for the night and began searching for a place to stay. Once I had done that, I reminded myself, I would then find a job. Being homeless, stateless and almost friendless, and also jobless in a strange town, well, maybe not that strange, wasn't the best of situations and it certainly wasn't the worst. I had been there before, in other cities, and survived, and this time, I kept reminding myself, would be no different. I checked into a Radisson Inn, which ended up being 25 minutes' walk from where that altercation had exploded and then subsided. I wasn't feeling sorry for myself, I was hardened to these kinds of situations and by now, and with everything that I'd gone through in my life, I was even more determined to come out the other side of this a better stronger person. These promises I'd made to myself, promises that had more often been broken than fulfilled, had to be made whole this time. I arrived in my room, shattered, and I slept through the night until late that next morning. I called the front desk and asked them if I could borrow a computer. As luck would have it, they had a small business center on site, and after showing the guy at the front desk a little cleavage, he let me use it for as long as I needed, free of charge.

I had enough cash for a couple of nights stay in this hotel if needed, but my thoughts were to find something more permanent and to find it fast. Same theory applied for a job. Remembering I was an undocumented immigrant, I was limited to what I could and couldn't apply for. Massage/FBSM seemed my best option, not only because it was all cash, but because I was good at it and could sort out 'employment' rapidly.

Craigslist, at that point in time, was my go to for most things I needed. Employment, shelter, a date? It was all there, and so easily accessible.

By 4 PM that day, I had a list of possible rooms to look at, mostly short-term leases, but without papers of any kind, even short-term, would be difficult to crack. I stayed another night in the Radisson, and then began my search for a home the following morning. I had also seen on Craigslist, an Ad for massage, and it was my intention to follow up on that later in the day. Uber was the first order of that day, taking one car after another from rental room to room, all of which proved to be a complete waste of time, mainly because of my inability to provide legal paperwork showing an entry visa into the USA or a social security number, which, of course, one could only get if legal entry for the purpose of work had been obtained from the US government. My final appointment that day was in Hollywood, and honestly, when I'd found the Ad, it had been my least favorite of all the places I was going to look at that day, hence my keeping it until last, in the hope I would find something before I arrived there. When I did finally get there, about an hour late for the arranged appointment, I was kind of mildly impressed by the façade of this old style 1930's Hollywood home. It was very 'Marilyn Munroe', very ME, and instantly appealing. I had hope!

I was shown into a lovely room by a lady who didn't really care who I was or what I had or where I'd come from. All she cared about was the cash up front and making me aware that this situation could only be for a few weeks because the owner of the home was going to remodel it and at that point in time, it had to be vacated. I found out some weeks later, after I'd left, that the home owner was on a month vacation in Africa and the lady who'd taken my cash was his housekeeper, renting rooms for cash while he was away. I didn't care less, I had a room, I had internet and now all I needed was a job. I moved in that same evening.

Hitting Craigslist yet again, I managed to locate possible massage work with a lady who had an apartment in Reseda, about an hour's drive from Hollywood. I spoke with her on the phone that evening and arranged to meet her the following morning, after being told that if I was 'any good' I could begin working immediately. "Any good?" I thought to myself, "I am the best!" and she was in for a rude awakening. If anyone was good at FBSM, it was me, I was the Queen of that particular trade! And just as suddenly as I'd found myself in the middle of a brawl on a street corner, an situation that had left me homeless and jobless, I was now back on my feet with a roof over my head and the possibility of work just around the corner. That night I slept soundly!

Ruthie, which wasn't her real name, rented a 3-bed apartment in a residential area of Reseda. It was clean, modern and filled with everything I needed to practice FBSM in a safe and healthy environment. From the moment I walked in, to the moment Ruthie offered me the job, I felt we connected. I sat and told her stories of my past FBSM exploits in the UK and in LA. She was enthralled and captivated and I could tell that she and I would get on like a house on fire. She showed me around and explained the terms of my employment.

"We have three rooms in this apartment" she said, "you will get one, for as many hours a day as you need it, you will charge what you want, make your own appointments, but, I will screen your clients, for our safety! You will pay me a rent of $250 per day. Anything you make, you keep"

Well, in my opinion, that was more than fair, and I asked her if I could get started that same day. Ruthie was impressed by my hustle, and commended me for the way I was prepared to get stuck into my work without hesitation. In the apartment, there were other girls working, some who I became friendly with as the weeks went by and others who I just ignored. One young girl in particular, I will call her Shawna, an African American lady, about 30 years old, with amazing tits and a huge ass, was not only providing massage, but almost everything else her clients demanded. She was a hustler of the first degree and would do absolutely anything to make a buck, or ten! Shawna was so open about her life and we became very friendly. She was living with her sugar-daddy, close by our place of work and she made no bones out of telling me how sexually active and perverse she was and how much money she was making each day, plus, whatever her sugar-daddy was paying her. She was raking it in. The other girls all offered their clients 'extras' too, and they all believed I was doing the same, only I wasn't. This period of time, and it was only a few weeks out of my life, was probably the busiest I had ever been, preforming FBSM. I was jerking off between 10 and 15 guys a day. We offered three sessions. One was for 30 min, (which ended up being 15 min max) and that cost $100 to $120. The next session, the 60 minute one, which was really 40 min max, was $150-$200, and the third was full sex, which Ruthie suggested we charge $500, but which I never did, and that lasted as long as it took the guy to cum, which was normally 15 minutes!. I think most of the other girls, the ones who did perform full sex, were only charging an extra $100. The money, for me, was rolling in and although I wasn't loving the job, I seriously appreciated the clients and the revenue. At the same time, I was also continuing my search for a more permanent living situation, and eventually I found a place, an excellent apartment in Torrance, just south of the LAX airport, and a place that I would share with an older gentleman.

My room there was huge, and I had my own en-suite bathroom, something I treasured. It wasn't until I left that place, and again, that was something that happened sometime after, that I realized the guy who I was sharing with was an old client. I only saw him in the apartment now and again, and it took time to come to the realization I'd seen him before, but I was sure it was him and I was certain I'd jerked him off many times when I worked at another place in Westwood, but again, that's another story for another day.

Ruthie in the meantime was making big bucks and employing more girls, hoping to expand to bigger and better things. She decided to get out of the place in Reseda and rented a huge home in Van Nuys, 5 bedrooms and a downstairs office, and up the ante!

We all moved, clients too, and the money just came flying in. I had never made this much cash in such a short amount of time. One day in particular I took over $3,000, and I felt like I was truly blessed, which I was.

We were always anxious about being raided by the cops, but out in the valley, they were pretty lenient, and the 'always expected' raid, never actually happened. One thing about working with these other ladies was that they always kept their distance, they didn't socialize and never discussed what they were doing, but we all knew. We all knew who would fuck and who would blow and who would fuck and blow. No one, however, other than Shawna, was open and honest about it, especially with me, and so my relationship with Shawna, blossomed into a nice friendship and a relationship where she felt comfortable enough to relate her inner-most feelings to me. My clientele at that time were mainly Armenians, don't ask me why, I really don't know, nor do I care, but they absolutely loved me. Recommendations were coming in from client after client and at one point I jerked off nothing BUT Armenians, for weeks on end. They were polite, reasonably clean and always paid what I was asking without ever questioning my fee. Our conversations would be brief, and their expectations, low, and so when they came, after experiencing the delectable way I concluded each massage and delightful endings, you could hear their vocal gratitude all the way down the hallway, or so Shawna told me. Shawna on the other hand, was a screamer. She would get fucked from here to the other side of LA, every day, and boy, would she make it known to everyone within shouting distance that she was cuming, squirting, or having the best fuck of her life. Only it was all a lie, as she later admitted to me in person.

"They love me darling. I make them think they are the best fuck I ever had, and the morons believe it. My tips are like my tits, huge!" she'd tell me. "the men are horrible, all of them, and they couldn't fuck their way out of a wet paper bag" she continued, "but with me, when I cum, it's fake darling, always fake, yet they think they are pleasing me., They even brag to one another about how they please me, but in the end, it's just a fuck, and I feel nothing other than the cash they put into my hand after they cum in the condom. Plain and simple, just a transaction"

Shawna was refreshing, genuine, at least to me, and eventually, if she didn't blow it all on drugs or other silly items she liked, she would become wealthy and probably purchase apartments of her own. I admired her tremendously and even though Shawna actually hated sex, yes, hated sex, she was so passionate about her work, and so into her ability to fake it, she was idolized by me and the other ladies for the short time we knew her. Ruthie, the owner, also kept her distance but had her own clients too. She was a Latino and catered mainly to that community, but never really talked about it much. It wasn't the best place I had ever worked from a friendship standpoint, but from the point of view of making money, it was by far and away the very best place I'd ever performed at.

My desperation to become a legal citizen of the United States was playing on my mind each and every day. It got to the point on some days where I would have done anything to get married to a US citizen for any reason at all, just to get a Green card. I was desperate, really desperate, and I was sick and tired of my uncertain status in this country. I used to peruse Craigslist for Ad's from men looking for wives, yes these Ad's do exist, in the hope that by chance, I might get lucky and meet someone who genuinely cared and really did want a wife to look after and to nurture and to bring into America legally and truthfully. And it was during one of my sorties on Craigslist that I decided to take the bull by the horns and place an Ad of my own. I was fed up reading Ad's from guys who were probably just looking to meet illegals for sex, and I wanted to try and weed out a guy on my own in the hope I might just get lucky enough and find someone genuine. My Ad read

"Exotic Eastern European Stunner looking for marriage and security with USA citizen."

Within 2 hours of placing my Ad, I had over 200 replies! Yes, 200 plus responses. The filtering process was interesting, but after taking some time and spending hours going through each response, I filtered it down to 3 possibilities. Even today, when I think back at how all of this happened, and remember, desperate times called for desperate measures, I lie back and piss myself laughing as to how brazen I was, and probably still am. I cannot believe I had the guts to do all of this, but I did, and although it seemed tragic to me at the time that I was actually doing this Ad thing in Craigslist, it's really funny if not hysterical now, when I remember how it all happened.

Ten Moths Of Hell

My first 'date' from the Ad, took no time to agree a to a safe place to meet. Now, remember, there are no images on any of these responses, so I had to go by instinct alone, nothing else, and words were my only guidelines, their words, not mine.

I wasn't expecting an Adonis, when Juan Carlos walked into the bar, but I certainly wasn't expecting a big fat Mexican guy either. JC, and if only he'd been the original JC from biblical times, was this huge, overweight, untidy, sloppy, and ugly man, who worked at one of LA's premiere hotels as a Valet, parking cars all day and night and probably consuming one cheeseburger to celebrate each car he managed to park that he fit into! It sounds so cruel to comment on JC in this way, but I am here to tell the truth and the truth often hurts, and from the look of JC, his pants were so tight around his waist, he was probably in pain too. He'd obviously gotten over his anorexia!! Boy was this man boring. Boring didn't even sum him up. He was dull beyond belief. He had this personality disorder, he just didn't have one! I could go on and on here and make it sound as horrible as it really was, but that would be doing the truth a disservice, it was worse than horrible! With all that being said, I decided to go to the movies and then to dinner with him. JC was just a waste of space. We couldn't converse at all, other than a few weird lines back and forth and when he began to call me Mama at dinner, while he slung copious amounts of food down his ever expandable throat, I just couldn't take it anymore. The conversation had veered to the impossible and even though I was disgusted every time I looked at JC, after our date, when he asked to see me again, I said OK and we set up a second date to go hiking later that week. Why I agreed to that, God only knows, but he had let out the bag that his dream was to be a truck driver and the way my brain works, not always the right way, but the devious side of me thought, 'well if I can help him realize his dream, then he'd be away week upon week, and I'd never see him'. With that in mind, and with JC living with his mother in Inglewood, near LAX, I decided to give it another try. We met up, went hiking and he lasted about 15 minutes before he packed it in. Exercise wasn't his forte! Where was this going? I kept asking myself that same question, but I kept thinking that something good might just come out of it, and we plodded on, not on the hiking trail, but with the dating, until finally he looked at me, and said, "maybe this can work and maybe we should try living with one another?'

Fuck me, why would I even bother? Well, desperate times....

Off we went to look for apartments, having only briefly spoken about getting married, a marriage that would enable me to live in the USA. The funniest part of all of this. JC just expected me to marry him. I don't think he ever cared that we had nothing in common and that he couldn't hold a conversation to save himself. He just presumed.

The apartment we went to look at was in West Hollywood. When we arrived there, my heart sank. Firstly, JC hadn't opened his mouth since we'd met about an hour earlier, and secondly, the place itself wasn't particularly nice. It was old and shabby, and my whole persona was now on the verge of collapse because deep down, I knew I could never live with this guy, and not only that, he'd raised all my expectations when he'd told me how nice this place would be, only to have those expectations shattered at first glance. The manager of the apartment complex was so nice. He showed us the building and then took us into a private room to do a credit check on JC. Obviously, I had no credit so the pressure was all on JC to qualify. The place was $1500 per month for rent, which meant JC had to earn at least $3500 to qualify. When the application form came out onto the managers desk, JC began filling it out. It got to the part where he had to declare his taxable income and I watched him write $1000 per month. I literally had to do a double take. I mean, who the heck makes only $1000 per month and hopes to rent any kind of apartment, especially in LA? I asked him twice, 'are you sure that's the right amount you've placed in that box?' and twice he nodded his head. The manager, who by this time had sort of given up on us as potential renters, took me to one side and said to me,

"You can do so much better than this" as his eyes rolled back into his head.

I knew he was referring not only to the apartment, but to JC as well. Advice heeded, and as we left that complex, JC was history. Poor guy didn't know what hit him. One two three, gone!

My second candidate, we will call him Ian, had texted me pic before we met up. Ian was a dreamy 6-foot-tall blonde haired God, according to his pictures, and when we met up, he looked exactly the same as the images he'd sent. He was super fit, had his own place, had two big dogs, and I thought from the minute we met up, I'd hit the jackpot on the Green Card lottery!

Our first time out took us to a hiking trail in North Hollywood. We had a blast, we even had a quick kiss and cuddle in his car after the hike was over, and then, we arranged to meet up again. Second meeting was just as good, and we ended up back at his place, no sex, but more touchy feely! I was really hopeful and becoming quite enamored with Ian, but then, as per usual, the nonsense started.

Trump was pitching up against Hillary, live on TV. We'd been out for the day, had some great fun, and now, as we sat and ate on his couch, with Ian insisting on watching that live debate. I decided to make a comment which was something along the lines of

"Politics in this country are terrible and I don't like Hillary or Trump"

Well, if Ian could have launched himself into space at that moment, he would have. His temper, a temper I had not yet witnessed, flared up to such an extent, I thought he'd blow out his own windows. He was raging, shouting at me, swearing at me, and becoming quite unattractive as his rant progressed. I am all for 'believe what you want to believe and keep it to yourself', but Ian, well, he was all for 'believe what I believe or just fuck off'

That evening didn't end well, but I persisted, giving him more than one last chance. We dated for a few weeks, had sex a couple of times, which was good sex, not crappy sex, and then, as suddenly as he'd come into my life, Ian kind of vanished. It was very strange. One day he'd call me, we'd go out, and we would have fun, then the next three weeks he'd be incognito, and ghost like. After a setting my eyes on the 'prize' the green card, I was yet again set adrift by someone who I knew wasn't for me, but who possessed most of the attributes I craved just to get my green card and settle in the US. It wasn't to be, and I never heard from him again.

The Professor!

The professor was funny, articulate, knowledgeable, kind and very handsome.

We met for the first time at a Denny's for a quick bite to eat and an introduction. He was fairly handsome, a lot older than me and friendly from the moment I walked in the door and shook his hand. The only issue I had, and it got worse as the evening went on, was that his teeth were disgusting and every time he took food from his plate, it missed his mouth and ended up either on the table or on his cheeks or chin. At first, it was amusing, but that amusement turned very quickly to disgust. After that dinner ended, I agreed to meet him for another date, hoping that his table manners would be surpassed by his amazing humor and undying kindness. He asked me to come to meet his daughter, who was coming to visit him the following weekend, but in between that, to have dinner with him in Pasadena, where he lived. We met up at a small bistro in downtown Pasadena three days later. He showed up in a Prius, a white one, and when he opened the door to get out, half of LA's garbage followed him. There were open used cans, carrier bags filled with trash, dirty old newspapers and items that looked like they'd been there for years. What a huge turn off this was becoming, but oh, his humor and oh, my desire to be married and legal. "Let it ride" I kept telling myself. Again, during dinner, his food found places to land that even Nasa couldn't find. It was just horrible, and each bite he took led to another disaster on either the carpet, the tablecloth or his chin. I was so put off by this trait, and so against seeing him ever again, when he brought out a picture of the daughter I was going to meet a few days later and then explained to me that he might be taking a new job, and one that would take him North, and that it would be great if this worked out and we moved in together and started a new life together, and oh, that humor!

We never even kissed, I said my goodbye's and promised I would come to his home on the following Friday to have dinner and meet his daughter.

I have lived in shitholes, I have lived in places where I would never keep a pig, but I have to tell you, the Professor beat all of my previous worst living experiences, by a county mile! His house was THE most disgusting place I had ever seen. Dog hair was everywhere, except on the bloody dog! The home hadn't been cleaned in years, if ever. The bath was rust, the stove covered in grease and other shit and the dog had never been bathed, and perhaps the same applied to the professor. His daughter was charming, and I loved her. In fact we are Facebook buddies even today, but that experience was one of the only highlights of an evening where I couldn't eat or drink anything for fear of contracting Malaria or some other exotic disease. We parted friends, and we remained that way for a while, but that really made the whole Craigslist experience, 3 strikes and you're out!

And so it was a return to my life performing FBSM, going out on occasional dates and searching the Ad's on CL now and then, just to see if anything else took my fancy, which it didn't. Life wasn't that bad, other than I needed a US citizen to marry me, but, if that didn't happen, there was always plan B, and plan B was for now, out of the question.

Seekingarragements.com was a site that I'd placed an Ad on many months prior to Craigslist. It's a dating site for attractive hook-ups, a site where older men would come to peruse the Ads of younger women looking for financial assistance in return for a relationship, and a site I had very little faith in. In fact, after I opened my account there, I rarely even went on to check what was happening. I got so bored with the early responses I received. Some were actually pathetic.

"Hey babe, how's the site treating you?"

"Hi have you had any luck on here so far?"

"You're very sexy, and I'm very macho, let's hookup"

I mean, for fuck's sake, who were these morons? If you had any gumption in you, as a man, you would find a better opening line that any of the above, right? My boredom led to my discontentment with seekingarangements.com, which was kind of like sugardaddy.com, only I believed it would give me an outlet to find a husband or at least someone willing to partake in discussion relating to my green card predicament. Unfortunately, as I mentioned, I had no such luck and my visits to that seekingarangements.com site dwindled from once a week to once a month to once every now and again, as my hopes faded with each pathetic reply I received.

After the debacle of my 'three' near misses on Craigslist, I decided to go online to check out my SA account and to see if anything meaningful had shown up in my mailbox.

At first, when I logged on, I noticed I had more messages than I had ever had before. This in itself was very strange and I presumed, before checking too hard, that most of the messages would be crap. I began to sift through them, one by one, slowly at first, but as my patience wore thin, faster and faster. Suddenly, and without warning, I stopped. I was shocked at first, but then after reading the headline in the Ad more than once, I became intrigued.

"If you can make a woman laugh, you can make her do anything"- Marilyn Munroe

I couldn't believe it. My favorite person on the planet, my hero, my idol, and this guy, whoever he was, had quoted her verbatim. Only a Marilyn fan would know this and as you all know, I am obsessed with Marilyn. I took my time as I went for the mouse to gently scroll over to 'read mail' icon. I kept asking myself, "Was this a sign from the heavens?" As the message opened, I closed my eyes, gaining the courage to open them just as the pointer on my mouse clicked on the wording. And there he was! In all his glory, a good-looking guy standing in the yard of his Malibu compound, inviting me over to visit and to have dinner. Although I'd had plenty of previous invitations just like this one, perhaps not in Malibu, but to journey on private jets, sail the oceans on 150ft yachts, there was nothing special about the invitation he offered up, but there was some kind of energy in the fact he'd used Marilyn's words, and those words drove me to dig deeper. I read his Ad several times, looking each time at his pictures and deep into his eyes to see if I could really determine a genuine connection. I decided I could, and picked up the phone to talk to Malibu Mike.

"This is Tiana" I told him as he answered on the 2nd ring.

From the moment he picked up the phone until the second he ended the call, I was smitten. We got on so well, discussing everything from London, where he'd also been working, to Marilyn Munroe, who he loved, to saving the planet, which we both had an affinity towards. It was marvelous, and I believed strongly at the end of that call that this relationship may have the mileage to blossom. Our date was set, and I was ready to rock and roll up to Malibu.

24 hours later, I got in my car and drove up into the Malibu hills for our arranged lunch. When I got off PCH, Pacific Coast Highway, and turned right onto Malibu Canyon Rd, the homes became even larger and cell phone service just vanished. Following implicitly the directions Malibu Mike had given me, I made all the appropriate turns and eventually, without the assistance of Google Maps, I arrived at a gate, a gate in the middle of nowhere. Punching the code I'd been given into the key pad, which was right in front of my side window. The gate swung open and I drove another half mile up a hill towards a magnificent mansion, perched on the top of a that hill, with sweeping 360* views of Malibu

and the canyon behind it. It was incredibly breathtaking, and it really was a compound. There were homes dotted all over the complex, and I could see at least another four, all large and all set back on their own land, but inside the main compound. I stopped the car in front of the main entrance to the home, getting out with my cell phone ready and willing to take some pictures of the stunning vista's that stood before me. As I did this, a man opened the front door and came out. I need time to describe this scene, so bear with me.

This man, we will call him Jeeves, was the butler, although, at first, I didn't know that. Jeeves was 6 feet 6 inches tall, skinny, kind of freaky looking, and by freaky, I would suggest Adams Family as a stereo type to describe his persona. He was 'unique' shall I say? I would have put him as a villain from a James Bond movie, someone that reminded me of Jaws, the tall guy with the gold teeth who was in The Spy Who Loved Me and Moonraker. A little shocked at what I was looking at, and surrounded by such natural beauty that are the Malibu Hills, I didn't know whether to run, smile, laugh, speak, skip or dance with joy. Jeeves made my decision very simple.

"Would madam like to join me as we walk to the house?" Jeeves was very British, very 60's and in my mind, very out of place. However, my mind was about to be changed. I followed Jeeves into the house. It was huge. In front of me, as I entered, was a massive vestibule, decorated with works of art that seemed very real and original. Andy Warhol, Norman Rockwell, Georgia O'Keefe, all hanging in tandem across the back wall, and guitars and drum sets and pianos, clearly visible in the lounge, which lay directly on the left of that entrance hallway. It was all very tasteful and all very 1960's. I could tell now why Marilyn had appealed to Malibu Mike and why he'd used her words in his Ad and I half expected her to pop out from behind a door and say hello! We continued to walk towards his kitchen, where, when I got to the door, a hippie like character called Nancy, was cooking something that smelled delicious, in a clay pot that looked as if it had come out of the stone age, on a stove top the likes of which I'd never seen before. It was massive, with 10 burners and a cast iron oven, and a flat hot plate running down its center, all of which were free-standing and surrounded by a plethora of pots and pans which would grace any five-star restaurant.

I presumed instantly that Malibu Mike must be a chef of some kind.

Jeeves and Nancy were smoking weed, yes she was smoking while she was cooking, and Jeeves was smoking because I don't think he had anything else to do other than let me in the front door, but the whole internal vibe was of a 1960's up-market frat house. When I'd opened Malibu Mike's Ad, I believed he looked like Jim Morrison from The Doors, and when he walked into the kitchen, about ten minutes after I'd arrived, I was convinced that Jim Morrison was still alive! From the way he walked to the way he talked, this was Jim Morrison reincarnated. I was floored, I was excited and I was in heaven. This was my kind of guy! And then the conversation began. We clicked, we really did. He loved what I loved and I loved what he loved. Our discussions ranged from saving the planet to vegetarianism to rock and roll to Marilyn. It was wonderful. He was drinking alcohol and smoking weed as we ate lunch, and I was sober, on water and no weed, but it didn't matter, I was convinced this guy was THE one.

I'd been in situations like this before, as you now know, but my gut told me that Malibu Mike was going to be a keeper, and one who could solve my immigration issues in a heartbeat.

After lunch, which ended up being absolutely delicious, and proof that Nancy was a superb cook, Malibu Mike asked me if I'd like to walk round the compound with him.

He took his half smoked joint and I took my bottle of water, and we walked out into the yard, where we stood in front of a giant swimming pool, and beautifully manicured lawns. Malibu Mike took my hand and he led me to the first house on his complex. Each home had its own name, and the first one was Aries, coincidently, my birth sign. He asked if I'd like to go inside and take a look, and I agreed. We entered the house and walked around for a few minutes. This home was a little more modern that the main house, but again, there was still a kind of 60's theme to everything. It was at this point in the proceedings that everything clicked in my head, and I began to realize just who MM really was. For the purposes of this book, I am not going to reveal is real identity, but when he began to undress me in the master bedroom, my realization on MM's identity made what was so obviously the inevitable, even more thrilling. He licked me all over, went down on my poosie and ate me out and then he fucked me. He fucked me gently, he fucked me with panache, he fucked me with skills that had been only a dream for me, but he fucked me for hours. He was superb in bed, making me cum, one time after another after another, until when we finished, and looked at the clock, it was after 6 PM. We'd been fucking for more than 3 hours when MM, asked if I would stay for a party he was throwing that evening. I agreed, and hand in hand, after getting dressed and cleaning up the mess we'd made, we left that home and walked some more. The grounds of his estate were so expansive, it would have taken days to get from one end to the other. It was certainly more than a compound, more like a ranch, and a ranch that went for miles. We arrived back at the main house just as the sun was setting. It was a magnificent site, viewed in private from the top of Malibu canyon, and one I will never forget. And then, and then it all went to Hell, which is not a surprise and as per usual in my life. A Witch appeared out of nowhere. Don't laugh, I am serious, a Witch, yes, she was dressed up like one, a real one, pointy hat included, showing up at the mansion, followed by another member of MM's band, followed by MM's wife!!!!!

He was married, and not only was he married, he was married to an Eastern European fashion model, wait for it, who wanted a green card and needed someone to marry her to make her legal! I nearly puked, when I found out, and although MM told me they were in an open marriage, she did what she wanted, as did he, I was having no part of this. I felt dirty and used, and I felt I needed to get the fuck out of Dodge before anything else happened that would be detrimental to my disposition. By the time all of this shit went down, the music was blaring, the Witch was preforming some kind of sunset ritual and Jeeves was lying flat, stoned out of his mind, on an inflatable dinosaur which bobbled on the swimming pools surface. It was all bizarre and so surreal. I made for my car, I made for the open road and I made moves to recapture my sanity, which I had most certainly lost in the last hour I spent at that compound. It had been one of the strangest experiences of my life and I was still no closer to finding anyone who was going to marry me and put me out of my immigration misery.

I'd thought about it for a while, and I decided perhaps I should post and Ad myself. Maybe Craigslist was the way to go again, maybe not, but after the experience I'd just had with Malibu Mike, taking my destiny into my own hands seemed the only appropriate and sensible course of action. The fact that MM had been married, and he'd fucked me, and then he'd tried to pretend that his marriage was an open one, when it really wasn't, had been distressing for me, and again, I was left holding the end of a piece of string filled with misery, a string that never seemed to end. My life was all over the place, yes, filled with fun, adventure and plenty of drama, but all over the place none the less.

Craigslist is and was an easy medium for me to post on, and so, with that in mind, I opened up my Apple Mac, and went straight to the section where all the 'fake marriage' Ads were posted, and decided to take one last look in that section before composing my own Ad. I looked and I looked and I looked. There were so many Ads, all posted with the same sentiment, "marry me and get your green card', but some were from New Jersey, some from Oregon, some from Texas, and I knew for sure, I wasn't going to relocate in any of those States. I was in LA and I was staying in LA. Desperation was for sure, killing my inner self. I really needed to get help, and I required that help in a hurry. Time had already run out and the borrowed time I was now running on was being eaten up with every passing day I couldn't get a guy to marry me. I noticed, just before I was about to close out of that Ad section, an offer from a guy in Orange County, the Ad, similar to other's I'd already looked at, suggesting that if I was a pretty eastern European looking to get married to obtain a green card, then this guy was going to be my savior. I was pretty sure it was a scam, just from the way it was written. I often could tell just by the words in the Ad if they were genuine, or a scam artist. Unfortunately, people like MM were all over the internet and would gladly say anything to anyone, just to fuck a beautiful non-resident alien, knowing that there could be no recourse from that alien lady because they had no standing without citizenship. The OC Ad that I found, looked OK, but not great, and I decided to direct message the guy.

'Is it you, or someone else looking to find a partner?' I asked

His response was instant, 'it's me', he replied.

We exchanged phone numbers and then outside of Craigslist, we began texting one another. From experience, and from the crappy times I have had meeting crappy men, it's always a red flag for me when someone discusses how rich they are or how handsome they are, before I have even met them. This is a scam, a scam to get inside my panties, I have known about this since I was 14 years old. You try to sweep me off my feet with BS and hope that you get to fuck me, then you run away. I know perfectly well when I am being lied too, and this guy, Claude, was lying to me in every text.

'Oh honey, if you and I click, I will lavish you with gifts, and take you around the planet in first class' and all sorts of crap like that. It came spouting one text after another. In the end, although I planned on not seeing Claude, I decided, 'you know what, if he's half decent, it doesn't matter what he has, as long as we get on and as long as he's not dirt poor. I was going to go for it, and I swore this would be the last time I put myself through such a situation, Yeah, right! Every time I have sworn to stay away, I always went back. I was just a glutton for punishment. We arranged to meet at a coffee shop in Manhattan Beach. He was late, I wasn't. When he showed, he was dressed rather poorly, perhaps scruffy would be a more appropriate word to describe his appearance, and that was off putting and a total distraction for me from the second we met. Not only that, but his fake French accent, which I realized afterwards, wasn't fake, but Lebanese, and probably laced with a mild dialect. He had a common French first name, at that point in time I didn't know his last name, but he exuded Arab tendencies, not French. Claude wasn't attractive in the least, and again, that was off putting. As you already know, but might not believe, I do have standards. With the old clothes, unclean look, and old shoes he wore, plus the dirt between his fingernails, I wasn't impressed and I was ready to walk until Claude began telling me funny stories. At that point I kind of relaxed and decided to give him a chance. Everyone deserves a chance, right? Claude told me that one of his friends had met a Polish lady and married her and they thought Claude should try to do the same thing. His friends had assured him that an arranged marriage was better than a 'real' one! Claude had two kids from a prior relationship. He told me he owned an air conditioning business and after talking for a couple of hours, Claude invited me to Tustin, to visit his place and go for dinner. After all the crap I'd been though in my past, a dinner wouldn't be the worst possible thing I could do, or so I believed.

Three days later Claude and I met at a Mexican restaurant in Orange County. This time, he showed up dressed more or less in the same way he had at the first date, well sort of. He had a decent pair of jeans on and a crappy shirt, but he was still a very scruffy, something that's hard to explain unless you'd actually met him. He was one of those men that no matter what he would wear, it wouldn't look like it fit him, or at least that's what I put it down to. But in my opinion, and after him telling me he was so rich, he just looked poor and disheveled. Other than that, the evening was charming and Claude picked dup the bill, which was a bonus. We spoke about marriage and yet again, he promised to introduce me to his 2 kids. He told some funny stories and also let me know one of his best friends was a great plastic surgeon in OC, and that if I needed anything done, filler, Botox, boob job….

"Have you seen my fucking boobs?" I asked him. "They're perfect"

We both laughed but Claude insisted his plastic surgeon friend would give me the best discounts ever, no matter what I wanted. When we left the restaurant, I walked him to his car, which was an old Ford of some kind, and nothing fancy. When he unlocked the door to his car, I couldn't believe what a mess it was, and just as bad as the mad professor's in Pasadena. What is wrong with men, can't they keep their cars clean? Must be something in the salty air.

We agreed to go out again.

Normally, in most relationships anyway, the first date is a 'get to know you' date. The second date is perhaps a kiss and cuddle, and the third date is sex, after a good dinner, of course.

A couple of days passed and we'd spoken a few times on the phone. He invited me back to OC and to stay at his place. We met for dinner, and again, he was dressed exactly the same, which pissed me off slightly, but nevertheless, I was over dressed and he made no complimentary dialogue regarding the way I had spruced up. I figured he was either blind or just ignorant. I knew I was going to fuck him and that eventually that night we would both be naked, so I let it go. Now, with all the guys I've slept with in my life to date, and realizing there were a few red flags with Claude, I thought to myself, do I do this or do I bail? What was one more penis inside me after all? It didn't matter. Our conversation again revolved around an arranged marriage while we ate dinner, and again, he picked up the bill, which was nice. My head was sent into a spin when Claude told me we couldn't go to his place because he'd had a fight with his ex-wife and the kids were staying at his hone, and offered to take me to a hotel to fuck. He put it more eloquently than that, but the intention was clear. Take her to a hotel, fuck her and wake up without conscience and with a smile on your face. I'd seen it all before, but desperation leads to temptation, and that green card was at that point, awfully tempting.

We checked into a real dump of a hotel, a hotel I would never in a million years book if I wanted to fuck someone and make a lasting impression, and Claude, after bragging about his wealth, was losing points quickly on the Tiana scale, as we checked in and made our way to the room.

Now, let me ask you, if you had to marry someone for convenience, and there was no attraction and you were committed by law to spending at least three years with that person before being able to divorce them, what would the main criteria be, as a woman of course, not as a man?

Small dick, cum quickly and no appetite for sex.

Claude checked all three boxes. We got to the room, we got naked, his dick was hard but tiny, he fucked me in less that 90 seconds, then fell asleep and didn't try again. I lay back thinking that this would be perfect for me. A husband who wanted a quick fuck every now and again, lasted less than 2 minutes then went to sleep with his small dick, a dick my poosie couldn't even feel when it was hard and inside me. Perfect, perfect, perfect!

We awoke that next morning. Claude was yet again full of promises. Yes, we would get married, yes, he would find me a job and a job I could do without being a legal immigrant, and yes, he would get me a new car and be the signatory on it. I was currently driving a car that Estrella had put in her name and as she and I were no longer friends, the offer from Claude was like music to my ears. However, and there is always a however with me, I just didn't believe a word he said. I was so skeptical and so over the bull shit I got from the guys I was meeting, most of the blame could obviously be placed on my own shoulders, but I couldn't understand why I wasn't able to meet someone who actually meant what they said. I realized that the world was full of cruelty, and it always seem to be placed on my doorstep, but at some point, I had to strike lucky. That point didn't seem to be that close, especially with Claude, but who knew? In the meantime, it was back to my FBSM job and long sultry days jerking off guys with fetish's and sexual anxiety. Ruthie had decided to move again, and with that in mind, I set up a meeting with her to discuss my future, and perhaps the future of my life in the USA.

Ruthie told me that her new place, in Westwood, LA, was going to become a goldmine. She was insistent that I join her and the other girls and, in her words, 'rake it in', over the next few months. She convinced me, although my life with Claude was uncertain at that point, to throw everything I had into the new apartment set up, bring in the clients and milk them dry, quite literally!

Ruthie moved in, the other girls followed, but on day one, I was missing. Claude and I had progressed to the stage where we were about to open a new bank account, a joint bank account. Yes, I was as shocked as you are now, while you're reading this. He'd convinced me that we were a perfect match, or maybe I'd convinced myself that I could tolerate him, but no matter what, the onus was on him to open the account because I wasn't legal and anything that went into the account, if I decided to clean it out, fell on his credit, not mine. I was comfortable with this. Our day together was good, and the more time we spent, the more tolerable Claude became. The next day, which was day 2 for Ruthie in her new apartment, I showed up late, but when I did, Ruthie was on me like a hot towel. She was frantic, all ready to confide in me what had happened the previous evening.

We had one lady, the laziest of all the girls who performed FBSM in Ruthies place, who was dropped off every night at the building, the old one and this new one, by her husband. She'd told him that she was a cleaner, but when she got inside, she was as naked as any of us and she was performing massage and full sex with all the clients she procured. She was always bitching about how she hated the job, but she continued doing it because this job was her only source of income and she had to prove to her husband that she was capable of making some kind of contribution to their household. We also had this text App on our phones, which was our security blanket between the clients and the apartment. The App worked like this. The client texted, but the text went through this App and then to a third party, another lady, a friend of Ruthie's, who would vet the client to ensure they weren't law enforcement. Once the client was vetted, the girl would text him back and OK the massage. If the lady performing the vetting process found anything suspicious then the client was refused service. Plain and simple. Our friend mentioned above however, took matters into her own hands on that previous evening. She'd received a text, passed it to the vetting processor , she had become suspicious and asked the client for a picture, the picture had been sent back and was blurry, so the processor said to the masseuse, I don't think you should take this client or at least ask him to send a clearer picture. This masseuse, the one who was supposedly a cleaner, took matters into her own hands, let the guy come, purely for financial reasons, she needed the money, and once he got there, let him in and sat him down in her room. The client began to ask her all sorts of questions. "How much for a blow job, how much for sex", ignoring the term 'massage' in all his requests for pricing. She, being as dumb as she looked, felt no pressure and answered the client honestly, remember, she needed the money, he said thank you and then made and excuse and headed to the front door, claiming he had a text he had to answer in private. As she walked him to the door, opening it to let him out, 5 cops rushed the door and arrested her for prostitution. The poor woman broke all the rules and then found herself carted away in the back of a Police car with a lot of explaining to do to her husband, who believed for years, she was a cleaning lady!

Ruthie was telling me this story, and while she was going through the motions, my only thoughts were, 'what if they come back?'

Ruthie believed they'd got what they'd wanted and wouldn't return. I, on the other hand, was far from convinced.

My first client that night passed off without a hitch and as the morning passed, I received quite a few texts, which I passed on to the lady who was doing the vetting process. I never did find out her name, she was always hidden in a different part of town. Anyway, I get a text from two guys at the same time, both asking for appointments at the same time. From experience, if this happens, there's always one who doesn't show, so I always made the double bookings in the hope that one would come and the other one wouldn't. If they both showed, it was first come first served, and one would become a casualty. There are always casualties in this business, either it's me or it's one of the clients. The doorbell rang and one of the appointments arrived. As he walked in, my suspicions were highlighted as he shouted my name as he walked into the apartment. "TIANA, LOVELY TO SEE YOU" as he said this, it was as if he was shouting outside and down the corridor, but alarm bells went off immediately,

A Because no one ever shouts your name when they arrive for an appointment

B No one ever shouts back outside down the corridor.

This was very strange and very suspicious.

He asked very nicely, as he walked to the massage room, if I would take his money and if he could use the bathroom. I accepted the cash, again looking at him suspiciously as he kept repeating my name. It was "Tiana, here's the cash we agreed on" "Tiana, where's the bathroom" something no one ever did. The client, who by now was looking very nervous and fidgety, went to the bathroom and when he did that, I was left holding his cash, and decided to go into the living room to give it to Ruthie.

"I think we have a problem" I told her. We discussed it briefly and Ruthie said to give the guy a chance and that perhaps this was just his first time doing FBSM and it was making him nervous. I wasn't so sure.

He came out of the bathroom as I entered from the hallway. He was till fully clothed, which, for me, was another suspicious sign he might be a cop.

"You got condoms?" he asked

"Condoms? Why would I need those?" my senses were on fire now and I knew something was up. He looked at his phone quickly, made and excuse and darted back into the bathroom. He was in there less than 30 seconds when he popped back out, told me his wife was sick and he had to leave. I escorted him back down the hallway, all the time offering him his money back, but he wasn't interested. He just wanted out. As he opened the door to leave, the cops rushed in. Ruthie told me they were the same 5 cops as had rushed in the previous night.

Ruthie was now in the hallway, I was standing next to her, back against the hall wall.

Pointing at Ruthie, one of the cops announced, "you were here last night, why are you here again?"

"I'm just chillin" she replied, quite matter-of-factly.

"And you?" they pointed to me

"I am a massage therapist" I answered, "we perform massage in here, or didn't you know?"

I was being very insolent and I didn't care. The cops assessed the situation, and then gave me a ticket for preforming massage without a license and then left. Thank goodness it was a misdemeanor, and not a felony, otherwise I would have been ejected from the USA without any hesitation. Ruthie, on the other hand, was let go. They had nothing on her. She'd just been sitting around in that lounge and they couldn't pin anything on her at all.

Thinking this was all over, as I took deep breathes and came to my senses, I was relieved that they'd accepted my excuse I was a poor student trying to make extra cash and hadn't asked for ID of any kind. But, they had fingerprinted me and I also knew that I could be subject to ejection from the country should they choose to pursue it. As per usual in my life, the shit hadn't hit the fan yet. It was only noon, on this my first day at the new place, but oh boy, what a start to the day this had been. I tried to think back through my career practicing FBSM, and even though there had been moments of madness, probably more than I could ever count, the experience I had that morning, the fear of being arrested, watching the place get raided, well, that was one of the worst experiences I could ever recall. For a few minutes, perhaps a couple of hours, the fear of God had entered my body and then, just as quickly as that fear had arrived, it subsided, and life, as I took a deep breath, carried on. Ruthie had invested a lot into this new apartment, but now, after everything that had happened, one arrest and me with my misdemeanor, it wouldn't be advisable to return there for some time. We were obviously being watched. I was certain I needed a change in career path now, or at least a diversion of some kind, and with my heart set on staying in the USA, I was going to have to be very careful on what direction I chose for the immediate future.

Ruthie and I left that apartment, which as I mentioned was situated in a decent part of Hollywood, surrounded by bars and restaurants. Ruthie had suggested we go to lunch or have a drink in one of the local bars. I had never gone out with her socially before, and since we'd known each other for a couple of months by that time, I felt it would be a great idea and give us both a chance to discuss the future. We had put our heart and souls into this new apartment and to have it all taken away from us in one foul swoop was certainly disheartening, and expensive. We had paid 3 months advance rent, money which was nonrefundable and as we arrived in the lower paring lot of the building, the guy who was our building manager, was standing there just staring at us, shaking his head. He knew we were finished, never to return, and certainly out of business. I had a feeling that deep inside he was sorry to see us go, because he loved the way we looked. Eye candy!

Ruthie, unbeknownst to me, was on Xanax. Honestly, I didn't know this because we'd never really taken the time to get familiar with one another socially before that afternoon drink. As we left the parking structure, and as she popped a couple of pills, I realized that I had been with this woman in close proximity for some time now, but that I didn't know the first thing about her. We headed for a British Pub, located less than a mile from the apartment, where, we parked up, entered and then ordered two still drinks. It was at that point in time that Ruthie opened up about her life, and we just clicked, like two long lost relatives, we hit it off.

"You're not who I thought you were" Ruthie said, as she began downing one drink after another.

"What do you mean?" I asked.

"You're a little devil, just like me and you have balls!"

As she's drowning her sorrows, spouting all kinds of insane BS about the authorities and their racist attitudes, the rest of the bar, mainly men, were listening intently to this conversation. An older gentleman, sitting about 4 chairs further down the bar to our left, who had been ogling both of us since we walked in the door, passed a $100 bill to Ruthie and suggested that the drinks were on him. Ruthie took the money and ripped it into pieces, right in front of his face. "I don't need any pimp to pay for my drinks" she bellowed.

The man was shocked at first and Ruthie was so obviously upset from what had happened to us earlier in the day, but she refused to stop drinking and was becoming more and more toxic the more she drank. Out of nowhere, a college kid started to chat to us, trying hard to calm the whole situation down. While chatting with this kid, watching Ruthie get wasted and really contemplating the end of life as I had known it, I came up with a bright idea.

"Hey guys" I said to Ruthie and the college kid, "let's go get really fucked up. I know a guy, a client, who deals in all the substances we know and love and he normally hangs out all day in this bar in Beverley Hills. College kid, can you drive?" I asked

"Yes"

"OK we are wasted, you aren't. You drive us." And as I said that, I threw him the keys to Ruthies car.

I think he was as surprised as Ruthie when I did this, but it seemed to be a good idea and we decided to bring college kid with us to get fucked up. He took us back to his place and parked Ruthies car there, the plan being that we would go upstairs, let him get his own keys, and then all bundle into college kids' car and make for Beverley Hills. We were drunk, and he was sober, but we both knew, he would be high or drunk or both, very shortly after we arrived at our new destination! Before we left, college kid shared a joint with us, but Ruthie, now so obnoxious with a concoction of Xanax, alcohol and weed, all mixed up into her blood, was just being rude, and college kid bagan to take offence.

I suggested we leave, before college kid decided to kick us out. Ruthie was just out of order, insulting everything that was good about this poor kid, and doing it with such venom. I could tell it was upsetting him. Nonetheless, we all got into his car and drove to this bar in Beverley Hills. We arrived, he dropped us at the front door, and circled around to Valet parking. We never saw him again. He vanished, and I couldn't blame him. Only problem? We had no idea where he lived and Ruthies car had been parked there. I mean, we had a rough idea, but when he took us there we were both drunk and we hadn't expected him to dump us and leave in the manner in which he did. We were kind of fucked by that point in time and had nowhere else to go but inside the bar to find my drug dealer client, Oakie, short for Oklahoma, his native state. I knew if we found Oakie, even though he and I didn't necessarily like one another, but because I'd jerked him off once or twice, he would help me and he would also make sure we got home safely. He and I had an unwritten understanding. "I look after your cock, and you keep me safe when needed" A superb arrangement which was about to come in very handy indeed.

In we marched, all guns blazing, and after about 15 minutes, and no sign of Oakie, with Ruthie downing two more shots and things getting out of hand with some of the guys at the bar, Ruthie decided to bail, and moved rapidly into the bar next door, where, when she got to the front door steaming drunk, she was refused entry by a huge bouncer, who she ended up hitting and insulting and being ejected before she could set foot inside.

While all that was taking place, I had managed to locate Oakie, and after greeting each other with a quick "Wassup", we left that bar in pursuit of Ruthie, who we found lying flat on the curb, talking to herself and begging someone for forgiveness, while the bouncer, the one who'd ejected her, was now involved in another scrap with yet another drunk Latina! This was turning out to be one of the craziest days I had ever had in my entire life and Oakie could tell from the exasperation on my face that we all needed saving. He picked Ruthie up off the ground and we all headed to his car, which was parked behind the bars.

"You ladies need a pick-me- up" he said.

We got to his car, he opened the trunk, and oh my, it was filled to brimming with every drug known to mankind. I had never seen such an array of uppers, downers, lefters, righters, highers and lowers. Cocaine, Crystal meth, shrooms, weed, heroin, Xanax, Adderall, and even baby aspirin. He had it all. It was a smorgasbord for anyone wanting to get high, low or to top themselves. I had never seen anything quite as bizarre as this, and Oakie could tell when he uncovered the gun stash, hidden behind the drugs, I was completely shocked. Machine guns, pistols, bullets, knives. This was a war on wheels, a battle front in Beverley Hills and a colossal mistake to be anywhere near, considering I'd just received a ticket for illegal massage. Things then spiraled out of control rather quickly. Oakie had suggested we do a line or two of Coke. Ruthie, on the other hand, drunk out of her skull, decided to just take a shroom from Oakies trunk, without asking him first. Well, that set Oakie off, and he and Ruthie got into it, both hitting one another, kicking one another and screaming at the top of their voices. I was under no illusion that the cops were going to appear from nowhere and arrest me and then deport me. Oakie was shouting at Ruthie, "you disrespectful whore" and Ruthie back at Oakie, "fuck you Heisenberg" with reference to the Breaking Bad TV series she'd just finished on Netflix. It was a mess.

"Calm the fuck down you two!!!" I shouted at the top of my voice, "I am not getting arrested out here, so you two just shut the fuck up and let's move on"

Silence prevailed

"I know a place we can go" Oakie said, breaking the short calm I'd manage to procure.

When he said this, we all stopped dead in our tracks.

I asked, 'where you wanting to go Oakie?"

"I have two clients, they own a huge home in Hollywood Hills, I am expected, if you know what I mean, and I know we are all fucked up, but I am happy to drive us there and we can maybe party with them, if they'll let us all in. They are in the movie business"

Well this sounded like a plan, so off we went.

Oakie drove, though I don't know how he did that because he was higher than a kite, and Ruthie, from her position in the back seat of the car, continued her abuse of poor Oakie, with unwanted verbiage such as, "you fucking drug lord", "you total pimp-master" "Life fucker", until, finally, we arrived at this mansion in the Hills, and she shut her mouth as we all gazed at a palace! It was huge, and gated and probably one of the largest homes I had ever seen. We entered through the front gate, Oakie parked up, then loaded up with a selection of drugs, which he took from the trunk of his car, and we walked casually into the home. These guys were big time. The walls were adorned with movie awards, one after another, lining up like soldiers, one more glamorous than the next. There were 4 guys in the house when we arrived, all quite good looking, all very excited to see Oakie, all staring at his two companions, especially me, because my nipples were erect, and all very ready to get even more fucked up than they were already. The crazy thing about going on a binge is that you know you've had enough, but you always want more and you keep taking more until your body just says, 'I'm done!' and decides to collapse into submission and gives out, leaving you dead to the world, but not quite ready to meet your maker. That was my current state as we joined these guys, ready to consume more of the same. We were kind of half in, half out of normality, although normality was 180* in the opposite direction from where I actually was.

All of us, the four guys we'd just met, plus Oakie, Ruthie and I, went into overdrive. We began consuming line after line of Coke, tequila by the shot, when suddenly Ruthie, bless her heart, fell on the floor, hallucinating, and talking to dead people she'd known from her past. It was all very weird and at the same time, strangely wonderful.

My phone rang. I fiddled around looking for it in my purse.

"Tiana?"

It was Malibu Mike! His unmistakable voice, kind of royal, movie star-ish, slow and deliberate and extremely well spoken, with perfect diction, was chatting to me at the other end of a perfectly good cell phone connection, but because I was so high, I felt he was standing next to me and I had to do a double-take, looking at the phone twice, just to make sure it was really him and he wasn't really standing next to me left armpit.

"Never expected to hear from you again" I slurred. It was now 4 AM.

"You high?" he asked

"Duh!" I replied.

"Got any spare you can bring over to me?"

"I'm in Hollywood Hills"

"I was just there! How funny" he replied

"I'm with my friend Oakie, and he has a shit load of anything you want, so let me know if we can come over to you. There's three of us."

"Come on over"

"See you soon"

After the call, I said to Oakie, "listen, if you want another big client, drive me to Malibu right now. This guy has mega bucks, and he's famous. He can introduce you to a ton of new wealthy clients."

Me, Oakie and Ruthie, got into Oakie's car, and stoned out of our minds, we headed to Malibu, leaving the movie guys to feast on anything they could from the scraps Oakie had sold them. This was a suicide trip and as high as we all were, and with Oakie behind the wheel, I kind of thought I was flying to heaven as we left the Hills and headed to the PCH and then to Malibu, never quite expecting to make it without dying a horrible death on the way there. It was just like the end of a movie. Sun was coming up from the east, the car was speeding towards Malibu, filled with drugs, ammo and guns and all I could think of was, if the cops pulled us over, I was headed to jail, never to return.

We made it to MM's home, and in one piece! Though I will never know how. MM was also fucked up on drugs, and he and Oakie got into an immediate negotiation for merchandise from the back of Oakies trunk. The two of them started to get into it, because MM didn't want to pay for anything, as a 'famous person' he expected it free of charge, but Oakie was having none of it. At that point in time, I began sobering up, and sobering up rapidly. Ruthie began puking up, all over MM's floor and Oakie decided to split due to MM's refusal to pay for the drugs he so craved. With Oakie out of the way, MM and Ruthie headed to the jacuzzi, where, MM was trying hard to fuck Ruthie, fingering her poosie and touching her tits, but Ruthie was having none of it. Honestly, neither of them was capable of fucking anything at that point, other than perhaps the cat, who had fled into hiding on sight of all this debauchery. They were too fucked up to have sex, or to do anything else for that matter. MM then decided to try it on with me, who I'm sure he thought was going to do anything he wanted based on our last outing. I rejected him instantly and after that, and with MM sulking, the 3 of us made our way to MM's bedroom, where we all passed out naked on MM's bed, only for me to wake up about 2 hours later, wrecked and with the worst hangover I have ever had. I knew I had to get home so I called an Uber, which took forever because of the location of the house. Remember, MM lived in the Malibu Hills, where cell reception was sketchy and where roads were unnamed. MM and Ruthie lay asleep in MM's bed, while I waited to get my Uber at the front gate, knowing that I should really wake Ruthie up and take her with me because she had no phone and didn't know where that college kid lived so she could retrieve her car. In the end I just said 'fuck it', got in the Uber, when it arrived, and made off back to Torrance to my home, where I passed out for 15 straight hours as I slept off the hangover which had consumed my whole being. I woke up with the realization that I had no job, no clear path forwards, no security and probably no future in the USA. My heart was broken. In fact, I was distraught. I had rent to pay, and food to buy, and I had no money. I had sunk to a new low and one I wasn't sure I could get out of. London had been bad, my binging, reliance on alcohol and general over indulgence, but that night, the night that began as a promising day and ended up as a disastrous following morning, well, for me, it was a new low, and one I wasn't sure I would be able to bounce back from. My stamina was sapped, my ability to recover, questioned and my continual knack of putting myself in the wrong situations at the wrong times, never ceased to amaze me. I needed a complete re-think, and I needed it there and then. The 15 hours I'd slept had only made things worse, as I awoke to tattered dreams, the fact that I'd been booked by the cops and worse than any of that, I had regressed into cocaine and alcohol like never before. This was unacceptable to me, and I was certain that with the right guidance, internal guidance, and abstention, I could still get back to where I wanted to be. The question was, where did I really want to be? It had been ten months of Hell, some of which was heaven, but most of which had been challenging to say the least, but now, with my life at a new low, and with everything I wanted to be, probably now just a pipe-dream, I needed to pick myself up in a hurry and get my life sorted out. I had run out of opportunities to do this and hoped that with a little luck, and the seven lives of a cat, my last dance would be my Prom.

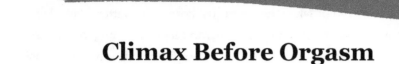

Climax Before Orgasm

Claude was still on the scene, for what reason, I couldn't tell you, and although I'd been running riot around LA, getting drunk, getting high, and getting arrested, (well maybe just ticketed and not really arrested), Claude had hung around, on the promise that we were getting engaged and then married. Although I still felt there was something very fishy about him, he'd actually finally invited me to his home, something I'd been pushing him to do for weeks, and something that I should have been more diligent about insisting on as our time spent together was becoming greater and greater. The guys from the Hollywood Hills that I'd met that night when I'd binged, were texting me continually, 'come back up here babe', 'we want you honey', and so on and so forth, to the extent that I decided I either needed to block them, or get a new phone and start again. I didn't want Claude seeing any of these texts and I certainly didn't want him to know what a crazy person I could sometimes become. My aim now? Get cleaned up and sober.

That night, the night I finally made it to Claude's place, well, let me tell you, it was one of the strangest experiences I had ever had. I was invited for dinner and as I always do, I arrived on time. He met me at the front door and let me in and as I entered his apartment, there, sitting in the kitchen, in full view, another woman! I will call her Daggers, because of the way she looked at me. At first, when those eyes met mine, I thought she was going to kill me, but as the minutes ticked by and the awkwardness between us subsided, she eased off on that horrible gaze and kind of disappeared into the background as Claude and I chatted and he showed me round the apartment. He explained to me that Daggers was a homeless lady he'd met in the supermarket, had felt sorry for her, brought her home, and given her a housekeeping job to help her out. Although that story was probably true, and I never had the opportunity to find out one way or another if it was or was not, I had the feeling Claude and Daggers were fucking on a friend's with benefits basis, and enjoying sex whenever either of them could be bothered or when they were just horny. No matter what, Daggers hated me from the minute she set eyes on me, and that was going to be an issue. I knew that my relationship with Claude had no future, but somewhere inside me, I had hope, hope that perhaps I was wrong and that it would all work out. That's why I'd been insistent on meeting his child and seeing his apartment, just to confirm to myself that the 'fishiness' I'd smelt from day one, was indeed correct, and that my ability to sniff out good from bad wasn't clouded by empty promises.

Once I'd met Daggers, I knew that Claude was never going to fulfill any of the promises he'd made me. I just knew.

"I lost my job yesterday and I have no money to pay the rent" I told him, as we exited his place and headed to dinner.

"Babe, don't worry, I will help you"

I'd heard it all before, and again, my stomach was churning knowing deep down, that Claude was full of shit.

"Daggers is moving out. I will pay your rent for this month and as soon as she moves, you can move in and I will even let you drive her car, which by the way, is a very nice vintage Mercedes."

I did see that car, and it was an old battered 1992 Mercedes, that looked as if it had been in many accidents and had never been repaired. The only thing vintage about it was the rubber on the tires, which were as bald as my poosie is today. Everything that man owned was in bad condition. It was amazing. His whole personality stank of unorganized crap.

"So, you're going to help me?"

He nodded

"When?"

A week went past. No check.

We had a joint bank account, remember? Well I called him.

"Put the money into our account" I told him.

But, as was expected, excuse followed by excuse and then excuses for the excuses, lies after lies after lies and still no money. This relationship was out of control and Claude had become the liar I had predicted. More fool me, again!

I could only help myself, no one was able to help me. I knew that from day one and I remember sitting in my home and thinking, "yes, I fuck up all the time, and yet, I bounce back. I am 28 years of age, I have fucked up more than 100 times, but yet, here I am, alive, healthy, broke, but still able to trust my instincts and survive."

Claude was dumped, unceremoniously, I might add, and I never saw him again. You'd think that after all the crap I'd been through that the last thing I would do it go back on Craigslist and look for another Green Card Ad? Well, it's me, so by now, you know me, if only a little, and woe betide the day I actually give up hope! The Ad was simple.

"Want to get married and get paid $2 million?" I couldn't resist.

I called.

We arranged to meet. I wasn't overly excited, but hey, when desperation sets in....

I waited, he never showed. I waited some more. My phone rang.

"It's me, I'm at the gas station across from the coffee shop"

"What are you doing there, come over here" I ordered

"No, you come to me"

I got up, and crossed the road, not quite understand what the fuck was going on. I got to the gas station, and there he was, a dirty, mucky, filthy looking piece of shit. How on earth did he expect any connection with a gorgeous woman like me when he came dressed like that and was unwashed and unshaven?

I just stared at him, and he knew. Oh yes, he knew I was pissed at the way he looked. Anyway, the excuses began to flow, and it wasn't like I hadn't heard any of this before.

"MY mother died in a car crash, I have been sick, my job sucks, I am not normally this dirty, etc, etc"

I just looked at him, as he motioned for me to get in his car. I was thinking "what the heck, in for a penny..."

And off we drove, to the local park, where this guy started to tell me the most unbelievable story I had ever heard.

It went something like this.

"My grandfather died a few weeks ago. He loved me, but he thought I was lost in the game of life, and he believed that I needed a woman to get me on the straight and narrow. In his Will, he left me $10 million, but to inherit this 10 mil, I had to get married before my next birthday, which is my 30th and which is in 4 weeks. If I don't get married by that date, I lose it all. If you marry me, and we do it next week, I will give you 20% of that 10 million." "Total BS!!!" I thought to myself, as I opened the car door and ran. He shouted after me, and I could hear him for at least ten minutes as I gained distance from the place we'd parked, "come back, I am telling the truth", but I knew deep down, all he wanted was sex, and if he got laid, that 10 mil would miraculously vanish. I know people think I am stupid sometimes, but I'm not that gullible.

I headed home, home to a place I could no longer afford, feeling beaten and abused by men who seem always to be filled with empty promises, promises that they hope will get them inside my panties. Everything I had tried to do to find a suitable marriage partner had failed. It had numbed me into submission and I had become kind of remorseful that I was as vulnerable as I was. In the end though, I realized that it was me, not them, those silly men, who I needed to blame. My intentions hadn't been clear enough from the beginning and I was reliant on other people's fantasies, not my needs or realities, for progression in life. I had to fend for myself and trust that the marriage and thus legality and guarantee of residency in the USA, would then take care of itself. Although I have some money in the bank, not much I might add, I needed constant cash flow to keep my lifestyle constant and bearable. I opened up my lap-top and typed in www.backpage.com.

Backpage.com, well, that's another story. If you want to know more about the guys who started that company and ended up in jail, you should Google it, but around that time, 2016, it was THE place to find escorts, massage, kink and BDSM. Everyone who was anyone in that industry, advertised there. It was the on-line Vegas for sex and debauchery.

The Ad I found was yet another lady looking for masseuses. I always gravitated to those Ad's. It was their magnetic pull on my brain. I knew I was good at it, I knew there was no great mystery in what I had to do and how I had to perform and I also knew that 99% of the time, I was safe, and free from the rigmarole that any 'normal' job might bring, let alone the stress that job could bare. Massage was my forte life. Like it or not, I was bloody good at it and not only that, my success rate at not being caught, exceptional, other than the one time with Ruthie, which I put down to sheer bad luck. I called the lady and set up a meeting.

That very next morning I drove to Northridge, which is in the San Fernando Valley, and after arriving at the destination, which took forever because of the traffic, I was in panic mode. There were cops everywhere and my thoughts immediately fell back to Ruthie and how I'd been caught. I was sure this was another trap, because everywhere I looked, I saw Police. They were on motorcycles, in cars, on foot, and honestly, although it was just a normal kind of neighborhood, with Walmart, Starbucks, Target etc, all close by, there lay a skepticism deep within me that I was going to be arrested for answering this Ad. Once bitten....

Then, as suddenly as my fears had begun, they ended, when I woke up to the realization that I was only answering an Ad, and not actually working. Nothing to be frightened of, I kept telling myself, as I dialed the phone number the lady had given me and waited for someone to answer.

"Hello" It was a man's voice, not a woman, on the other end of the line. He told me someone would come out to collect me and that I should park up somewhere close and stand by their gate. The home was quite large and looked well kept, at least from the outside.

Ten minutes, twenty minutes, and I began to wonder what was happening. Had I screwed up yet again? Then the buzzer on the gate sounded and I walked in. I entered the home, accompanied by that same man I'd talked to on the phone and I was pleasantly surprised to find a well-kept, artsy kind of home, with walls and lights that were beautifully painted and hung and a kind of 'sparkly' appearance, and by sparkly, I mean, good vibe. It just didn't look like a massage house, and believe me, I had seen enough of those to know the difference. I was impressed. There were a couple of cute dogs in the hallway and the man who'd let me in told me to have a seat and play with the dogs because the boss was still asleep! "Asleep?" I asked.

"Oh yes" he said, "be patient, she'll be with you soon, I am her assistant."

I sat and waited again. The dogs were nice and by this time, all thought of the cops had vanished from my mind. I knew this was a safe place and I knew it wasn't a set up.

And then IT came out of the bedroom. I say IT, because I didn't quite know if she was an IT or a They or something else. She, and we can call her a she for the sake of continuity, was over 6 ft tall, she had rock hard massive boobs, bright neon yellow hair, no eyebrows, a crooked nose, a cigarette dangling from her mouth and this silk dressing gown, that started at her bum and finished just above her boobs, and was only half tied, leaving only the imagination to figure out her gender. She walked out and walked right past me, ignoring me completely, entering her kitchen only to have the briefest of conversations with the guy who was her assistant, and then coming back towards me with a half-smile that read, "who the fuck are you'

"You're pretty" she commented, as she took a seat next to me, "very pretty"

"Thank you" I replied.

"When can you start?

"Today"

"Sweetie, tomorrow will be fine. Can you send me some pics of yourself and I will place some Ad's and can you come back tomorrow around this time? We don't start until 2 PM in this house, so don't show up early"

"I can do that. What kind of pics do you want?"

"Raunchy" and with that comment, she got up and went back to bed. As she was about to close the bedroom door, she shouted, "you'll make a fortune here"

And that was it! I left. I went home, took the pictures, texted them to her and waited. I was back in the FBSM business.

I showed up that next day, and again, was made to wait at the front gate for more than 15 minutes. This time I had a good look around the outside of the home, noticing the security cameras which were positioned everywhere. I hadn't seen them when I'd come the day before, but now, with a little more time, I scanned the place before the gate buzzer sounded and nudged me out of my day dreaming. Again, I entered the house and was asked to sit on the couch. As I sat, more and more ladies showed up, until there were five of us, all sitting comfortably in the lounge, where we'd been moved to. The boss lady, well, she was still asleep, and one of the other girls decided she would show me round the house. There were 5 bedrooms, including the one where the boss slept, a jacuzzi room, a kitchen, 4 bathrooms and a lounge, where we all sat watching movies. I waited an hour, and then 2 hours and then three hours and not one client came in. I waited another hour and then the boss lady appeared, dressed exactly the same as she was the day before. It was like Groundhog Day. Still no clients arrived. It was now 5 PM.

"Eh, I am just going to pop out and grab a bite to eat" I announced to anyone who cared to listen. No on replied. I left.

I walked out of that house and I never went back. I got in my car and drove home, and do you know, not one person called me to ask where I was and if I was coming back. It was so strange, so strange! I'd sat there for hours, waiting for something to happen, and so had the 4 other girls. No one showed up. It had been a weird experience, so weird, and yet, I had sort of known to expect the unexpected, especially when it came to dealing with people who were strange, and this lady had been strange. How could they run a business like that? How could it be that after I left no one called to see if I was OK? It was bizarre. Backpage.com, and again, the Jobs Wanted section, open on my laptop at 7 PM, I noticed an Ad for massage ladies to do outcall. I didn't like outcall because it limited the number of clients I could see in a day. At least with in-call, the clients are supposed to line up one after another, but with outcall, although there's a little more money for each massage, the driving time back and forth all over LA, cut into massage time and it made little sense financially. But, with everything that was going on in my life, I needed money, so I made the call. In 48 hours I'd gone from being high to being unemployed, to being employed to be unemployed and back, once again to employment, although, not in the exact job I desired. Two days floating around LA to different hotels, homes had me exhausted and disillusioned. The clients were OK, but not great, the money was crap, and by the time I included gas and my time traveling back and forth to different parts of the city, I just wasn't making money. My whole persona was being dragged down by my inability to make things happen. The clients were nice enough, but the compensation for the work I was doing and the travel, just didn't cut it. With that in mind and my continual perusal of all the Ad's on line and in Craigslist, I found another possible place of employment one night, when, after calling a number from an Ad on backpage.com, the lady at the other end of the phone, asked me to come for an interview. The place was an apartment block in Lauren Canyon, and she'd asked me to pop over for a chat and some coffee. The fact that she's been so pleasant and polite on the phone, led me to believe that this time, I may have found a nice stable set up in which I could apply my skills and begin making money again.

I drove to Hollywood and found the apartment block, surprisingly nice,

I might add. I rang the bell, was buzzed in and as soon as I walked into the apartment, I felt like I was home.

The place was spotless, modern, quiet, and comfortable. The lady in charge, Esther, made me very welcome. From the moment we met, we hit it off, although her inability to concentrate on anything for more than two minutes, drove me nuts. She definitely had ADD, and to top that, she was a perfectionist, like no other. This was a professional setup. Three rooms, all with massage tables, all clean and nicely decorated. A jacuzzi room, again, beautifully apportioned with Italian tile and mirrored all the way around. After the tour, we sat down and Esther discussed money with me. She had already mentioned that this was truly and 'upscale' massage facility, and that she never allowed anyone who didn't pre-screen to enter. It reminded me a lot of London and Justin and Julia. This lady was clear and concise with her instruction and ran the place military style, with orders given and taken in the manner they were received. We discussed money. Wow! She was more expensive than any place I had been before and my cut would be larger too. She had rates for massage, massage with body slides, and finally, the works, massage with body slide and then jacuzzi. It all seemed good to me. My interview had taken two hours, a complete joke, as any other place I'd ever been to took no more than ten minutes, but the perfectionist that Esther was, accompanied by her ADD, had elongated the interview into a disproportionate marathon.

She wanted pictures, but the pictures needed to be perfect. She wanted me dressed in my best outfits, and nothing else would do, and she wanted to control every movement I made, to make those perfect pictures even more perfect!

Her whole persona was just neurotic. It didn't matter what it was, either my pictures, her cell phone, the trash, other girls who worked there, Esther just talked shit about everyone and everything. I knew there would be issues somewhere down the road, but it was a question of when and not if, I would leave this place. For now, I was in, and ready to make some dough. This was a great area, affluent, and my expectations had been raised by the possibility of an upscale clientele, and also the hope that although Esther was nuts, actually, quite intolerable, I would be able to put up with her and her perfectionism, while I built up a list of clients to help me, what I believed would eventually lead to my branching out and doing FBSM as a solo practitioner.

I began in earnest. My line up was back to back and based on the images that Esther had posted of me, I had no problem attracting men who were rich, and men who were even richer. The great news was, I was busy, busy jerking off anyone who could afford me, and also anyone who couldn't, as long as they paid in advance. Just pay the money and take the choice, a motto that kept a roof over my head and my immigration issue at the back of my mind. Esther however, was proving to be more of a nutcase that I ever believed. She would fire girls for no reason, she would hire for even less reason, but in general, she left me to my own devices, probably because I was bringing in more business that anyone else she hired. She ran two shifts, 11 AM to 6PM and 6PM to midnight, the latter being the busiest of the two and that's the shift that I ended up working, more often than not. The company, I mean the other ladies who worked there, were fairly decent, none though had anywhere near the personality I had, nor the ability to lure the rich men in, turn them around and keep them coming back again and again. I was so good at that, excelling beyond all expectations, other than my own!

About 6 months passed and one afternoon, I went to a dance class in Venice Beach, before my evening massage shift began at the Laurel Canyon apartment. I had just finished and was walking across the street to get a juice when my phone rang.

Malibu Mike! No fucking way. I pondered for a few seconds on whether I should actually answer, all kinds of thoughts of our cocaine binge and sex sessions quickly running through my head. I'm sure he just wanted a quick fuck, but who knew? Right? "Yeeeessssssssss" I said, as I drew out the Yes, sarcastically.

"How are you darling? Where are you?" he asked.

"Venice Beach" I responded.

"Me too!!" he shouted excitedly

"Where are you?" I asked

He told me, and as he told me, I looked up at the street sign above my head. I was on the same street!

"What are you doing?"

He told me he'd been hanging out for 3 days on a cocaine binge, pharmaceutical cocaine, the best kind, and that he'd not slept, eaten or washed in that time.

"Want to come over?"

I stood on that street corner and thought about it. I had been sober and off all drugs for more than 6 months. I had been making great money. Straight and narrow and decisively right, were my mantras at that point in time, but something inside of me just said, DO IT. It kept saying DO IT, and so I did it.

"OK I am coming over. Address?"

I walked about 200 yards, found the home and knocked on his door. Malibu Mike answered, and boy, was he high? His ass was higher than his elbows. He looked like shit, smelled like shit and even talked like shit.

"Come on in?" he motioned.

"No, you come out. Let's walk" I suggested.

"OK, to where?"

"I don't know, but you look like crap and fresh ocean air can't be anything but good for you at this point in time"

He left the house, leaving the front door wide open and we began to walk.

"What the fuck are you doing Mike?" I asked, with a concerned look spread across my face

"I found a new inspiration, and I am writing music again. I came out of a very bad place in my life and now I'm so inspired, I have been revitalized"

"You looked fucked, not revitalized" I told him.

"I know" he replied," but honestly, my songs are fabulous, I am really on to something here."

"Who's home is that?" I pointed back in the direction we'd just walked from.

"A friend of mine, Albi", Mike sat down on the edge of the closest wall to take a breather. Honestly, he looked like he was about to keel over and die. "You want to meet him? You'll really like him" and as he said that, he winked.

'Poor Mike' I thought, always trying to be someone he wasn't, only this time I thought he'd gone too far. I feared for his safety and well- being, and I suggested we head back to the house.

The door was still ajar, and we walked in. The lounge area, the first room you entered after crossing over the front door threshold, was huge. There was a pool table, flat screen TV, about 75 inches wide, empty beer bottles, empty vodka bottles, and just about empty bottles of every alcohol I could imagine, strewn across the pool table and the floor. This looked like party city and it was obvious to me that a man, a single man, owned the home and just didn't give a hoot about what it looked like, having never bothered to clean up for what looked like weeks.

"So, who's your buddy?"

Mike grabbed my hand, squeezing it tightly and he marched me up the stairs. We walked into the master bedroom, and there, on the bed, lying half naked, was a gorgeous 26-year-old man, who had so obviously just woken up.

"Albi, meet Tiana" Mike said.

Albi got out from underneath the sheets and oh boy, what a body this guy had. I was in love and I immediately realized this situation might just get out of control within a very short period of time.

"Nice to meet you" Albi came over and hugged me, and my poosie just dripped poosie juice, right into my now, soaking panties. Mike could tell I was horny and although he was trying hard to chat to me, my attention was solely focused on Albi.

Albi and I chatted for an hour, while Mike passed out on the bed. We had so much in common, and we hit it off in a way I hadn't done with any man in such a very long time. Albi offered me a line of cocaine, and although I didn't think I would snort it, I did, well, I did half a line, which was enough to take the edge off of things while Albi and I became acquainted.

"What do you do for a living?" I asked him, after having gone round the houses talking about all kinds of shit for an hour or so.

"I'm an entrepreneur" Albi said, and he said it with such a casual tone in his voice, that for just a fraction of a second, a look of misbelief and skepticism must have been evident on my face.

"I AM!" he said with a reinforced shout, obviously seeing the doubts in my gaze. "What kind of entrepreneur?" I asked him.

"Well, it's a long story and one that I don't want to get into right now, but if you let me buy you dinner tonight, perhaps I will reveal more."

It turned out that Albi was a drug dealer, but not just any drug dealer, Albi was one of the largest drug dealers in LA, although that fact wouldn't come to light immediately.

Back at Laurel Canyon, things were going from good to not so good. Same old story. The Madame, Esther, a total fucking nutball, was hiring and firing like it was going out of fashion. One day there would be a flavor of the moth, the next day, she'd be gone. The only thing that seemed to stay constant was her love of me and my ability to make great money there. I had been there about 7 months, I'd met some amazing people, even some of the girls who had worked there were great people too and I could never figure out what motivated Esther to fire the one's I believed were just doing their jobs and making everyone money. Esther made little sense to me and as the months progressed, her demeanor and inability to concentrate on matters at hand, drove me to distraction. There was a lady called Jackie, Esther's kind of right hand lady, who took care of all the paper work for Esther, took pictures of all the ladies, handled screening and also performed massage too. She'd been with Esther many years, assisting in all aspects of the business, and then one day, about 5 moths after I had joined, she serviced a client called David, the strangest of characters, and a man who wanted to be 'rubbed out' by every single one of the ladies working for Esther. He'd come to all of us for FBSM, finally accepting that Jackie would be his last 'conquest', which we believed was because he'd always had a crush on her. Anyway, after seeing Jackie, David refused to see anyone else, and insisted on seeing her and her alone, every time he came in, which was about once a week.

We had a strict no sex, no finger in the vagina policy in that apartment, a policy that Esther imposed rigidly. We were told that men touching our tits was fine, but anything else was out of bounds. This was so alien to me. Any other place I had ever worked, it was up to the girl what she did and how much she charged for extras, but Esther would have none of that. Then one afternoon, Jackie called in sick, and David, upon arrival was told he'd have to see someone else, which didn't please him one little bit. Another girl, a lady from Brazil, filled in for Jackie and when the session was over, she told Esther that David had tried to finger her, stating that Jackie always let him do that and that if she didn't allow it, there would be no tip.

Esther called David and the two of them went at it on the phone for over an hour, after which, Esther slammed the phone down and demanded that Jackie be called in to talk to her in person.

Esther couldn't handle the fact that David like Jackie more than any other girl, and the next afternoon, when Jackie came into work, Esther canned her ass out the front door faster that she could walk. It was so strange. Jackie had done little, if anything wrong, certainly in comparison to the other places I had worked, fingering was absolutely expected and allowed and never refused. If a client wanted to do it, you let him, no harm done. Esther was never going to thrive without Jackie's presence in that apartment. When I asked Esther what on earth she was thinking by firing Jackie, I could tell that Esther was not only jealous of Jackie but was furious that Jackie had crossed a line, a line so ambiguous, I had to laugh out loud when Esther explained her reasoning. She was just so paranoid and as time went by, this paranoia got to me and I realized that it was almost time to move on, AGAIN!

Be My Fuck Buddy

Although doing outcall hadn't been a preference for me, and even though I was working three nights a week at Lauren Canyon with Esther and the crew, I had kept the outcall gig that I'd set up before meeting Esther and once or twice a week, I would receive texts to go to hotels or homes in LA, not only to service regular clients, but also to visit newbies, most of whom were visiting from out of state. It was a good gig, outcall that is, when it needed to be, and meeting nice interesting wealthy people never did any harm. I was making money at night and often during the day. My relationship with Albi had turned into more than just admiration too. Going back to that first meeting, where I'd snorted a half line of cocaine with him, seemed like an eternity ago, but honestly, the two of us had met up two days later, when I was in Venice and he called to ask me to dinner. Remember the pool table in his lounge? Well, when I'd arrived at his place, walked though that front door, he's ripped off my clothes and we fucked on his pool table for over an hour. The sex with Albi was fantastic, amazing and deliciously satisfying. He'd taken me like a real man, fucked me in all holes and then cum in my mouth, not just once, but twice, and that, well, that was the beginning of our 'fuck buddy' relationship, a relationship that was still going, two months later.

How to keep a guy as a fuck buddy.

1 After sex, get up and leave. If you stay, a relationship is what you're looking for.

2 Never regret anything you do together. The raunchier the better. Regret only leads to remorse.

3 Offer up your body occasionally and make it clear he's not exclusive. Giving him the opportunity to be with you every day is a relationship.

4 Be very casual and coy with your adoration.

5 Fuck like crazy when possible.

After my first sex session with Albi, I received a call from my outcall booker to go to a date in Pasadena. I was still swallowing cum when the phone text came through.

"Who is that?" Albi asked.

"A booking" I told him, as I began putting on my clothes.

"Booking for what?"

"Wouldn't you like to know?"

"You're leaving me after we just had the best sex ever?" He was kind of upset.

"Yes, I need to get to work, I have things to do."

At that point in time, Albi had no idea what I did, after all, we'd only known each other a couple of days, but I knew that as I left his house, he was pissed, and I had no intention of telling him anything more than I had already. He could be my fuck buddy for now, nothing else. This might have been one of the smartest choices I ever made, because as time went on and I realized what Albi did for a living and just how much trouble I might have gotten into had I continued having a relationship with him, today, I may have been a single mother with visitation rights to a husband housed in a penitentiary in Nevada. In the meantime, as that fuck buddy partnership evolved, I was working and seeing Albi about once a week, and all we did was fuck and I'd leave. Each time it was the same story. Great sex, get dressed, exit stage left. It suited me, and I realized, that it didn't suit him. But oh well, that was his problem, not mine. Drug dealing was something to be avoided, sex, especially sex with Albi, was addictive. The funny thing is, the half line of cocaine I did with Albi at the first meeting we had, when Malibu Mike intoduced us, was the very last time I did cocaine, ever! It's been 2 years, and I haven't touched it since. After a couple of months of repetitious sex, great sex, I thought perhaps there may be a way to make this into a relationship after all. We decided to chat about it over lunch one sunny afternoon, at a Mexican joint near Santa Monica. Albi expressed his fondness for me, over a couple of Corona's and some fish tacos, and I thought, 'why not give him a chance?'

We ended up back at his place, in bed fucking like bunnies once again, and then, after he and I had both been satisfied, several times, we lay together, cuddling, and I was just becoming a little bit more comfortable with the thought that perhaps Albi and I might just become a couple, a proper couple, when his doorbell rang. A guy came in, dropped off some cash, and pick up some drugs. Albi came back to bed, then the doorbell rang again, another guy, more cash, more drugs. This went on for two hours. 10 guys, ten wads of cash, ten drug pick-ups. I looked around the apartment, there was cash and drugs everywhere, and I mean EVERYWHERE.

That's when I sat back, propped up on a pillow in the bed and realized that Albi had a massive drug business, a HUGE drug business, and a business that was perhaps more lucrative than I believed. I was torn. Albi was a drug dealer, an outlaw, a bad boy, I was of a similar personality, living on the edge, always in trouble, always looking for something that wasn't there. Maybe my dreams of living a life in Hollywood with my husband and two kids was just a pipe dream, and nothing more than that? Perhaps I was born to be the wife of a drug dealer, a cad, a man who never kept to the rules? Who knew, but as I watched this scene unfold, the mules, one after another, collecting their pay load, paying Albi and then leaving with a package of drugs, I wondered what I was going to do? Should I stay or should I go?

I was falling for Albi, I really was, and I knew he loved me too, even though he'd not said those exact words yet, I just knew. I was in trouble again, but good trouble, and things were about to become even more interesting.

How To Keep A Guy As A Partner

1 Tell him you love him

2 Stay in bed after sex, licking him from top to bottom

3 Share life's adventures together and let him know you are happy

4 Don't ever refuse him his deepest fantasies in bed

5 Stay in tune with everything, all his needs and desires, and then fulfill them, regularly!

Back in Lauren Canyon, Esther was really driving me nuts. I was raking it in, big bucks every day, much more than any of the other girls, and often I made more than all of them combined, but no matter what I did, Esther found fault.

"Your toe nails don't match the color of your fingernails!" she'd scream

"Your hair needs washing" she'd suggest

"Where did you buy that dress? It's inappropriate" she'd judge

This ongoing tirade of insults and suggestions never stopped. It wasn't just me who felt her wrath, everyone did. Such a shame really, because this was a great place to work at. The clientele was superb, the apartment was gorgeous, but Esther's continuous bickering was killing the whole vibe for me. You know, in general, when working in such an environment, it's normally the girls who are really bitchy to one another. It's a competitive issue I believe, and one that I rarely, if ever, get involved in, but with Esther being as bitchy as she was, and the rest of the team all willing to take whatever she threw at them, moral was crap most of the time, and there seemed no way to fix this. I presumed that as per usual, I would stay a while and then politely leave for pastures new. That day was edging closer and closer, and with Albi and I becoming closer and closer, the two situations were about to collide and create one large volcanic eruption.

Albi bought a boat, a nice boat, a boat that we could go out into the Pacific Ocean and enjoy pleasant afternoons just sailing around, fucking on deck and in the one bedroom, luxurious I must say, that was situated underneath the main deck. Delightful times, mostly spent licking one another from top to bottom and then feeling our bodies entwined while the boat gently bobbed from side to side in the, normally glass-like waters, that surrounded our little part of that great big ocean. The drugs kept moving out of Albi's home, with roll after roll of cash coming in, all on a daily basis. This really bothered me and the last thing I needed was to get arrested as an accomplice, should his place ever get raided by the cops or the DEA. My affection for Albi had grown from pure sexual desire, to adoration and love. I was smitten, and ready to tell him this, but in the back of my mind there was a nagging little voice that said, 'he doesn't have a job, he's a drug dealer, get the fuck out'

I tried to ignore that voice, I really did, but his marvelous love making skills, our fun times out and about together and his wonderful, gorgeous, sexy penis, well, you know how it is?

"Want to go out on the boat today?" Albi asked when he called me one morning.

"Yes, but I need to be at work by 6" I told him. We'd become so close, that

Albi now knew what I did to make money. The best thing was, he didn't care. "As long as you don't fuck them, I'm down with it" he'd told me. After all, he was in no position to critique my job preference, and he never did.

The boat was moored in Marina Del Rey, and at 11 AM that morning, we boarded together, lunch and a couple of bottles of wine in hand, ready and willing to have another great fucking session out on the ocean and accompany that session with some nice food and even better wine. We set sail. It had been a couple of months since this relationship had begun and although we'd been intimate, both sexually and mentally, there was still a lot I didn't know about Albi, and indeed, perhaps I didn't want to know? As we were sailing out to the spot we would drop anchor and begin fucking or eating, or both, Albi, who always piloted the boat, looked at me and suddenly said,

"I'm going to Mexico next week to visit my dad, he owns a ranch near Acapulco, would you like to come?"

I sat up, shocked.

I didn't know his dad lived in Mexico, not did I realize Albi was Mexican. This took me by surprise. I'd jerked off many Mexican dudes over the years, and Albi didn't fir the bill. His skin was as pale as mine, and coming from Estonia, my skin is very pale, and not only that, his penis was circumcised. I had never met a Mexican with a circumcised dick, ever! Albi could tell something was up, and he asked me, "you ok?"

I snapped out of my thought process and smiled.

It was time to tell the truth.

"Albi" I said, "I am unable to leave the country because I'm an illegal immigrant"

I waited for his reaction, which came faster than expected.

"Illegal? Then let's get married" It was more a statement than a question.

My heart sank, that little voice in my head was getting louder, telling me there was no question that a marriage would never work with Albi. No matter how much I thought it might, how tempted I was, I just knew it would be the wrong choice.

Albi spoke again, "anyway, at the border they never ask for much, maybe just a driver's license'

"Albi I can't take the chance. I would love to come, but I can't. I am so sorry. I will try to think about the marriage thing while you're away, but for right now, just fuck me, and fuck me hard." Albi willingly obliged. We fucked and we drank and we fucked again and then we headed back to the dock so I could make my 6 PM check in time in Laurel Canyon.

When we finally got off the boat and secured it, we headed to the car. Across from our car, I noticed this black SUV, don't ask me why I noticed it, I just did, saying nothing to Albi, as we both got into his vehicle and headed off back to his apartment where my car was parked. I looked in my side mirror, the SUV was pulling out with us, and then it began to follow us. Still I remained silent. This was really strange and I started to panic. That little voice in my head echoed out loud, "I TOLD YOU SO" again and again. That SUV followed us all the way back to Albi's home, and as much as I wanted to say something to him, I kept my mouth closed for fear of looking silly. Yes, that sounds silly to say, but my whole thought process was, I needed to get out of this now, and not wait a single moment longer. I could feel the noose tightening, and with that SUV following us home, that noose felt like it was about to close for good and suck the life out of me.

Albi went to Mexico to visit his father later that same week. He was away around 10 days. When he returned, things weren't the same. I think he'd had a chance to think about our relationship and when he got back and we had sex that first time, it was crap, forceful, unimaginative and cold. He was someplace else when he came, and I was lying with him on top of me, with tears running down my face, knowing that Albi had gone. Fuck buddy to lover to another Ex, all in the space of a couple of months. I could never explain to him how I felt because I knew it would never make sense to him, and honestly, why would I want to be the wife of a well-known drug dealer? I didn't, and wouldn't and I couldn't. Albi and I had sex one more time, and the same thing happened. It was cold and calculating. The love had been sucked out of us, and sadly, when that sex session was over, I walked out the front door of his apartment, and I never went back.

It took me months to get over Albi

I was back at work, in and outcall, and lots of it. This process, get up, wash, go to work, come home, wash again, go to sleep, repeat, made me think and think hard about who I was and who I actually wanted to become. I was obviously trying too hard at moving in the wrong direction and nothing seemed to fit. My French friend Claude was still on the scene, though for what particular reason, even I didn't know or understand, and every time I went close to Venice beach, something I did regularly, either to walk, surf, or just hang out, I was just around the corner from Albi's home and so desperately wanted to pop in, call him, of slide under the covers with him and make passionate love, but again, I knew I couldn't and I also knew that this abstinence, if that's what you want to call it, was just driving me insane. My mind harked back to my days in London, and I began to count, if that's humanly possible, all the guys I had performed FBSM on over the years, which came to a staggering total of over 5000 men. Out of those 5000 men, maybe only 3 or 4 or perhaps it was only 2, had meant something to me, something more than just sex. Amazing to think you have the privilege of meeting so many guys, yet 99.9% of them are just wasters, or men who I wouldn't give a second glace to. Yes, each one of them, or at least the majority of them, had always left my presence, satisfied and in love, not knowing that they, contrary to their own beliefs, had meant absolutely nothing to me. Men always ask me

"Are you turned on?" when I am grasping on to their erect cocks, but the fact of the matter is, I am never turned on. I perform a service, a service to bored rich guys, fat ugly guys, guys who cannot get it up, guys who just want a cheap thrill, guys who have turned 18 and can't get any poosie on their own, guys who are married, guys who are single, guys who want to just chat, guys who have no personalities, guys who think they can fuck me if they offer enough, but out of all these guys, only 2 or 3 have managed to get past 2nd base and fuck me. Yes, when I perform, I am wet, but that's all a trick, a misconception, where lube is my savior. When I look at a man's cock, I feel nothing other than he needs relief and needs it fast in order that I can take his money and then kick him out. I have had the same experience since I came to the USA. I've met and serviced around 3000 men, of which 2, at a stretch, meant something to me. My deepest thoughts and wishes had tried, up to that point, to ensure my security and future, through marriage, and so far, had failed miserably. My best efforts to succeed and all the time and momentum that I believed I had gained, were once again, washed up on an empty shore, a shore that seemed at that moment in time, to be completely abandoned and void of any certain future, and that future, balanced precariously on the edge of an immigration precipice, was now looming large to the point where success seemed to be nothing but an impossible dream. And then, and then it happened again.

The call, from a gentleman who lived near Venice Beach, was for my outcall service. We made an appointment and I left for our meeting with my heart beating just a little faster than normal, knowing I was headed back to where Albi lived, although not in the same street, it was close. Jibril was a doctor, a handsome, dark skinned gentleman, of Arab descent. His rugged features, enhanced by his tanned skin, and beautiful lips, yes, they were a magnificent addition to his fit a sculpted physique, made for the introduction, as I walked through his front door, to be kind of embarrassing for both of us. He could see, and I could tell, there was a definite and instant connection. The massage got underway in his living room, where, by request, he'd asked me to rub his shoulders before we went upstairs to his bedroom. Jibril was in the middle of a very messy divorce, he had two kids and his wife had custody. His house was magnificent, and the king-sized bed in the master suite, very comfy. As we both stripped off, Jibril was in a daze, looking up and down at my nakedness, trying hard to look me in the face and not right at my tits. We took our time, chatting stroking, whispering, stroking, laughing, and finally, as he came, smiling at one another as the wanton to kiss, passed by awkwardly with the reduction in size of his now empty penis and balls. We had definitely made this weird attraction come to life and before I left, Jibril asked for my phone number and offered to take me to dinner. I loved that idea, and although not quite over Albi, this, I thought would be the first step to recovery and putting Albi in my rear-view mirror.

And so, once again, my life took another turn and dating with Jibril began, at first, with just dinner and a massage at his place, but after a few weeks, those massages turned into smoking weed, massage and then fucking, great fucking. We were entwined nightly, his fit and athletic body, most welcoming, and delightfully satisfying as he would enter me and make Albi, a thing of the past, and this time, for good.

My massage days, both in and outcall, were still financially rewarding, with new and returning clients keeping my bank account in the black, and at night, more often than not, Jibril would keep my libido intact, by satisfying me with great sex and wonderful conversations. He was a lovely guy, lovely that is until one evening, we'd just fucked for an hour or so and we'd retired back down to his living room, when Jibril did something I'd never seen him do before, and something that completely shocked me. He took out a pipe, a glass pipe, and filled it with crack cocaine. At first, I had to look twice. I was so confused. I remember asking myself, 'what the fuck did he just do?' and then after that, asking him directly, "What the fuck was that?"

His response, so casual, so direct, so matter-of-fact. "It's crack, want some?"

I sat down on his couch, my mind, yet again in turmoil. I had left Albi, a drug dealer and was now with Jibril, a drug user, not only that, he was a doctor too! The following day he had surgery, and I asked him, "Don't you think this is a bad idea with surgery at 7 AM tomorrow morning?"

"I do this all the time" he replied.

I walked out. I didn't hesitate, I just walked out.

"Where are you going?" he asked, as he ran after me.

"You are doing crack cocaine and you have surgery in 8 hours. I don't want any part of that" I said, as I got in my car and drove off, never calling him again, never answering my phone when he texted me, and never wanting to have any part of a life with someone who was taking drugs. Again, I knew in my past, I was no saint, but to get out of my past, I had to have a clean future, and Jibril wasn't going to be part of that future. I just, once again, ran away, spending the next day's contemplating who the fuck I was and why I got involved with idiots like Jibril, all the time, not just once or twice, but time after time. I realized that I had to change my whole life, not a part of my life, but everything in my life, the problem being, how do I do that? I was soul searching for weeks after that, crying on and off, beating myself up about my inability to make my life whole, scared shitless that I was an illegal immigrant in a land that I now loved and eventually coming to terms with the fact that I was living my life on the precipice of that great unknown, unknown to me, and that unknown? Stability. Fuck buddies were great, for a while, but it was time to move on and find a man who would keep me, not just fuck me.

Where Do I Go?

My phone rang one afternoon, as it did every afternoon, and morning and evening and often even during the night. When men were horny, they were horny and an erection didn't wait for sunrise, sunset or mid-afternoon heat. It was erect and my clientele wanted serviced when service was required. That service was dictated mostly by blood flowing to their insatiable members. A client once told me that the only thing that stopped him in his tracks was his erection. When he got one, it needed to be taken care of, either by someone like me, his wife or his right hand. 'There was just no way around it', he explained, 'boner means I no longer want to be a loner' "So eloquent" I replied, with both eyes feigning both lack of interest and incredulity. My clients were anything but a rare breed, composed of the wealthy, the poor, the smart and the uneducated, all with one thing in common, a desire to be fucked, to get fucked or to go fuck themselves. The nonsense that I have listened to over the years has been incredible. The narcissism, the misogyny, and homophobia, compounded by every single pick up line that man ever wrote, has molded me into this oblivious, yet often caring individual, who realizes at the end of the day, as long as they pay, I really don't care who they are or what they do or where they go after the cum in my hand. They can say what they want, try anything they want, within my rules, and cum as many times in as many different ways as they want, but in essence, they are all the same, horny fuckers in need of a little excitement in their lives, whether that life is fulfilled or just boring and mundane, they arrive, then they cum and then they pay and they leave, mostly with a smile on their face.

I rarely picked up, I preferred texting, but on this occasion, I answered. For various reasons, I have to be very vague in my explanation of the events that followed, but on the line was an extremely well-known basketball player, residing in Beverly Glen, in a gated community, who'd seen my Ad, and asked if I would come over to his place and perform FBSM. At first, his name meant nothing to me, but I always research people or phone numbers after talking or texting with prospective clients, for my safety as well as theirs, and sure enough, this man was who he said he was. I got in my car and drove to Beverly Hills.

Well, after passing through the gate to his community, I was completely blown away by the homes that I saw as I followed his directions while salivating at the prospect of getting inside one of these mansions. At the end of a cul-de-sac, stood the home I was about to enter, and boy, was it massive.

Athletes in America are revered, and this guy, we can call him Sporty Jim, was one of the most famous of all, in his sport. Even I knew who he was, and I was from Estonia. I was welcomed in graciously, and thus began a very nice friendship, and one that would last for a month or so. Sporty Jim loved what I did for him, as do most of the men I service, but Sporty Jim, well, he was smitten. After I finished that first massage, he called me the same evening and asked me to come back the very next day, which I did, and then the next day and the next day, by now, you must be getting the picture? We never had sex, but his needs were certainly taken care of. By the end of that first week, we were really good friends. Sporty would tell me about the other players on his team, their likes and dislikes, who drove him crazy, who he thought would be a success, who he believed would never make it. It was the off-season, and Sporty was prepping for the upcoming kick off to the 2018/19 program, which was only a few weeks away. After. Couple of weeks of going to his home, Sporty asked me if I'd like to become his personal masseuse and travel with him around the country while the team played all it's away games. I loved that idea, not only from a travel perspective and getting to see the rest of the United States, but financially, Sporty's offer was simply amazing. "And of course, you'll get to go to Canada too" he offered up with some excitement. The deflation on my face, when he said this, was so obvious that Sporty asked what he'd done to upset me. "I am an illegal" I told him, "and I cannot leave the USA"

Sporty Jim was so understanding, sitting me down and asking me to tell him what it would take to make everything right with immigration and the offering to try to find me a willing partner to marry me. I was so grateful for his impute, but I also knew the chances of him helping me out were slim. Our relationship was extended by another couple of weeks and then his training program and team commitments interfered with what had become, our regular schedule and Sporty Jim, vanished into the void that LA can often become. When I say vanished, perhaps I am being a little harsh, we kept in touch and he always told me he was 'working' on getting me hitched. By this time, I was staying away from all temptation, sex and drugs and alcohol and I'd sworn to myself that self-healing in the form of complete celibacy, was the only way forward, and if, God willing, I was to meet the right guy, it would happen by chance and not necessarily be forced. I was still working in-call at Laurel Canyon, in fact, I had been there coming up on 18 months, despite Esther's tantrums, and my outcall business, which I ran myself, was thriving too, as was my bank account. Yes, I received calls from idiots now and again, but that was to be expected. One particular idiot, told me he was a famous baseball player, and for a month, after chatting with him regularly on the phone, before we'd even met, convinced me that he was going to be the best player in the world, pay me a fortune to massage him every day and carry me off, around the globe, as his wife no less!. Yes, these things still happened, even with the internet for immediate ID back up. When, to my own detriment, and despite having so many reservations, I actually did go and meet this clown, he was nothing more than a perverted gawker who got his rocks off trying to con woman in my profession. For what reason? Who knows. I never saw him again though.

My immediate aims, staying clean and away from all men, proved to be the right decision, and for almost 8 months, I was alone, healthy, stable, and financially secure, living a life that really suited me at that time and healing gently from all those relationships which had promised so much and yet delivered so little. My psyche, since I had been a child, led me to this point in my life, a sexual object, with ALL men, a model, a desirous human being, and one who'd now seen a thing or two in her short life and was very very worldly indeed. The big question was, what on earth was I supposed to do, stuck here in America, with no place to hide and nowhere to go other than back to Estonia, something I didn't even want to contemplate. That was my last resort, or the option that would be thrown at me if the government of the United States ever caught up with me, which I knew was a complete long-shot. Yes, life was there to be lived, but lived where and how? My dreams, my LA dreams, my whole life's purpose, hanging in the balance because of red tape, paper work and an inability to find a man to marry me and take responsibility for me as his wife. I kept thinking, 'where are you?' but he never seemed to arrive, and as we have seen, when I thought he'd actually presented himself to me, he was no better than the last guy who'd done the very same thing, and often worse. "Where would this all end?"

I was about to find out, and again, find out, the hard way.

HE walked into the apartment at Laurel Canyon, my 6 PM massage. As soon as that door opened, I was in love. My legs buckled, my heart skipped a beat, my whole body ran wild with anticipation as this 'creature', this beautiful man crossed the threshold from his outside world into my grasp. It had been about 8 months since I'd dated, kissed, and slept with anyone, but as soon as Doug walked through my door, I knew my celibacy was about to end.

Doug, what a true specimen of a man. What a hunk. What a phenomenal human being.

He undressed, this blond God like titan, all the time gazing straight into my eyes. This was indeed magical, this, I decided, was the way love was written into all those chick flicks I'd watched over the years, and this, I'd decided, was going to be the best FBSM I had ever performed on any man, ever!

Doug and I just hit it off from the moment we began chatting, (I'd hit it off instantly with men before, lots of men, but this seemed different), until the moment 'the flip' arrived. He was from New Zealand, and was stationed in LA for a few months on business, although at some point he believed he'd need to return to New Zealand, he loved LA and was doing everything he could, to arrange a longer stay. I divulged, grudgingly, although perhaps it was deliberately, my own pathetic situation to him, and he was very understanding and appreciative of the angst that this had been causing me. He just got me, he really got me, understanding me completely, or so it seemed. I was ready to jerk him off. It reminded me of the movie Pretty Woman, with Julia Roberts, only this was me, really, it was me, and I was flying, flying into another world as Doug, and his erection, spoke to me just as Richard Gere, sans erection, had spoken to Julia.

"You don't need to do that!" he exclaimed, as I made for the erection with my right hand.

"You don't want to have a release?" I asked

"No, I want to take you out to dinner and then talk more and then make love. I don't want a quick wank-off in this room. It's not what I'm about. It's not what we are about."

I think it was only the second time in the past 8 years that an erect man, laying face up on my massage table, had refused a hand job from me.

"Well, when's the dinner appointment?" I asked him, smiling as I did, and giving him that 'Tiana' look, that look which, if read correctly, said, Feed Me and the Fuck Me!

Doug knew that look too. I could just tell. We clicked, and we'd clicked big time.

'How about tomorrow lunch?" he suggested.

"That works for me"

We planned to meet at Santa Monica pier at noon and go from there, but before Doug left, our lips were entwined in some of the best deep French kissing I had ever had with any man, ever!

Our tongues darted and teased each other, as his hands cupped my buttocks and his covered erection made me wetter than the Pacific Ocean. I knew when I got wet like that, there was no doubt in my mind Doug and I would be very compatible in bed, and I could just feel my poosie juice oozing into my panties. This was wonderful, too wonderful to believe. But yet, this was real, so real.

He left, eventually, and I calmed down, and then I Googled him. It turned out, thankfully so, that he'd been telling me the truth. Everything about his background checked out, which made me even wetter! I couldn't wait to see him again, and I barely slept that night, the anticipation was unbearable. I took the following two days off from work, knowing I would probably spend them in bed with Doug, and made my way to Santa Monica, to meet him for lunch, already nervous with anticipation and a little bit of dread, thinking that my luck, often bad as it was, might just take a turn for the better that day.

The sun was bright in the midday sky and the pier was busy with tourists and locals alike, but there he was, Doug, my Doug, all spruced up and waiting for me at the spot we'd agreed. We hugged, kissed for a minute or so and then headed to lunch, where, over a few bottles of water, and a couple of salads, we renewed our deep connection with ease.

Lunch flew past, followed by a quick walk on the beach and then, just when I expected more, Doug made an excuse to leave.

"You're leaving?" I asked, sounding pissed off and confused. I had expected sex, great sex, but he didn't seem interested and that annoyed me to the point of exasperation. There I was, in the middle of a Santa Monice sidewalk, my panties oozing sexual anticipation and my hormones crying out for a good fucking, and Doug was ready to leave? This made no sense. Had I misjudged the situation?

"Next time babe" was all he could say, as he hugged me, and wished me a pleasant day, and then walked off. What the fuck!!! Doug called me later that evening, and we spoke for a half hour, at which time he pointed out that he'd had to run because of a prior engagement, and that, honestly, there was no one else in his life and no one he wanted to be with more than me. It went in one ear and out the other. I'd had too many disappointments in my life to really care. We arrange another date, two days later, and this time, after a very brief lunch and some mind games back and forth over a few glasses of iced tea, Doug ushered me into an Uber, and we drove back to his place, where, with music blaring, clothes discarded, and sexual arousal at its peak, we proceeded to make love for more than 4 hours. I swear to God, I orgasmed more than 20 times, and he came inside me at least 3 times. It was by far and away the best sex I had ever had in my life, and I know I've said this before in the previous chapters, but what happened that day changed my perception on what love making really could be. I was blown away, and so was he. We just fucked and fucked and fucked, until he was empty and I was dry. Doug, at 28 years of age, was at his peak. Me? Well, I was lying there enjoying his peak. He fucked me in positions I'd only ever imagined and some that I didn't believe even existed. He was a true fucking machine, with a very nice penis and a thrusting motion that just made my clitoris scream in ecstasy. I just believed all of this was meant to be, and again, compatibility, between two consenting adults, played a huge part in the chemistry we now shared. This relationship blossomed over the next few weeks. We were inseparable, but in the back of my mind, I knew at some point Doug would vanish back to his home country, and I would be left in the USA, which again, is where I'd always wanted to be. Doug knew all of this, but faster than I could count to 5, we were falling in love with one another.

At Laure Canyon, my work was become so mundane and not that I didn't appreciate the income, but since Doug had entered my life, it all seemed so meaningless. He knew what I did for a living and I'd begun to let him into my life, slowly passing on some of my experiences from the past, all of which he took in his stride and didn't really seem to care. My eight months being celibate, had unleashed the beast that lay deep inside me and Doug was the sole beneficiary of this wanton desire that had been dormant for so long, and he was also enjoying every moment of it, appreciating my candor, my love making skills and my ability to make him feel like the king he deserved to be.

And then, and then it happened again. My outcall business was still flourishing and I'd received a call to go to a home in Marina Del Rey. When I arrived, with nothing but Doug and the sex we'd just had on my mind, and a relationship which was now around 3 weeks old and one of the best I'd ever enjoyed, I had no idea what was about to happen, as my car pulled up to the front door of a cute little cottage style home, two blocks from the ocean.

John opened the door, ogling me as I introduced myself, and shook my hand. Ogling me in such a manner, I presumed he'd fucked me ten times already, and that was before I'd even crossed the threshold. John, oh John. A fit, 40 something hunk of a man, who, under normal circumstances, I would have fucked on the spot, but my circumstances were not normal, and once the thought of fucking John entered my head, led for sure by the way he was staring at me, guilt, guilt towards Doug, filled me with a sadness that I'd even had thoughts about fucking John in the first place. His home was amazing, and we hit it off instantly. He had 2 kids, an ex-wife, and a desire to live his life as if it was 1999. In other words, party central. That was the case until I walked into his home, when, by his own admission, he fell in love instantly and decided on the spot, he was going to marry me, something I didn't find out about until several months later. John and I conversed for over 2 hours about anything we could cram in, within the time limits my fee would allow, and I must admit, knowing how sensitive and genuine a human being John was, left me with such a conflicting feeling as I left his place and headed home for another gargantuan sex session with Doug, who was waiting patiently at my place, erection in tow, ready and willing to make me happy another 18 to 20 times that night! "How'd it go sweetheart?" he asked, as I marched in the door, guilty that I'd even had the audacity to give John the come-on.

"Fine" was all I could say, as he rose from my couch and trundled over to lay a huge embrace on my person. We kissed, hugged, kissed again, and then I just blurted it out, from nowhere.

"You going to stay here or go back to New Zealand?" I asked him. This was a conversation we'd skirted over the past few weeks, but the conversation had never been as direct as the question I'd just asked, which kind of rolled off my tongue so nonchalantly.

"I haven't thought about it in great detail" he responded, with a kind of surprised look on his face. "Why do you ask?"

"You know why I'm fucking asked Doug. I love you, but I am scared you'll pack your bags and fuck off back to New Zealand without me, and really, truly, I want to stay here, and I would love you to stay here too" I was laying it on thick and fast, spurred on by my new-found feelings for John. I needed to know where I stood. John was single and American. Doug was single and from a different country. I was single and illegal. I had to protect myself, remembering the saying, 'I love you, I love me, but I love me more'

He continued, "Let's not discuss this right now and let's for sure, not spoil this sexy mood" He kissed me again. My legs buckled with joy. We fucked and I forgot all about our chat after my 10th orgasm of the evening. I was content, and he was fantastic! As I lay in bed, my eyes closing tight and my body ready to fall asleep, I wondered where I was going with any of this, I wondered if Doug was really the one, and I also wondered, as was my usual MO, if I was going to, at some point, fuck John and ruin everything yet again. My body shut down, I fell into slumber land and all my worries just carried forward into tomorrow.

The End Without Any Beginning

Why is it that a beginning always has an ending, but yet, an ending never has a beginning? John and I met two days later. He'd called again and asked me to come over. This time, it was different. I walked into his house, he hugged me, and then attempted to kiss me, tongues entwining, something I didn't resist. At least if I did, I don't think it was for more than a Nano second. Kissing led to touching, which led to sex, good sex, not great sex, and my question was then confined to history. I knew we'd fuck, and honestly, there was little guilt left in me after Doug had refused to answer my question, 'will you stay or will you go?'

It seemed so final. My relationship with John, beginning, my relationship with Doug, without an ending, and no decision on where either relationship might end up.

And so, a merry-go-round of multi-partner sex and deceit began. As it began, my thoughts were solely on MY future, not either one of theirs. In life, as I already knew, there are always casualties, and one of these guys was going to end up as a casualty, and, I thought, 'as long as it's not me who ends up broken hearted, who cares?' Simplifying the way I looked at life was always best for me, and this, now complicated situation, complicated solely by me of course, was never going to be simple.

John and I began seeing one another regularly, he wanted a massage and then sex, and often he would take me to lunch and then we would have sex again., I would then go home, contact Doug, make some lame excuse about not being able to see him that day, my poosie already having been serviced by John, and then call John to tell him how much I liked him and wanted more from him.

Here were the benefits and drawbacks from both relationships.

1 Doug, not knowing if he would stay in the USA, was my soul mate, and best lover ever.

2 John, a US citizen, offered decent sex and guaranteed stability, if we got married, and at that point, marriage hadn't been discussed.

3 Doug was easy going and had no ties

4 John had 2 kids, admittedly, no issue for me right now, but who knew what would happen in the future.

5 Neither man cared what I did for a living, but John was definitely the more jealous of the 2.

6 I loved Doug, I just knew I did, but John I only liked. I liked him a lot, but I didn't love him, at least not yet.

Oh, what a twisted web I was weaving, and the thing was, I felt bad, but not that bad enough to stop doing what I was doing. It all reached a boiling point about 6 weeks later when Doug and I were lying in bed. We'd just finished a monumental session of some of the best love making I'd ever had, and we were spent, both of us, totally exhausted. I was becoming mentally drained, having to remember which man like what position and offering both Doug and John, equal opportunity in bed. It sounds bad, but it was kind of fun until this one afternoon, John was entering me doggie style and I inadvertently suggested, quite wrongly it turned out, that he didn't like to do it that way. Stopping suddenly, and withdrawing his penis, he looked at me at said, "Are you fucking the right guy?" I laughed, realizing my error, because it was Doug who had this issue, not John, and trying hard to recover my faux pas by telling John I was joking. It all passed off without much more of a thought from him as he re-entered me and fucked me hard for another hour, but my mistake had shown me what a tightrope I'd been walking and that I needed to put an end to this 'double-dating' as soon as possible. It was decision time, not only for me, but for both of them too.

Back at my place I confronted Doug.

"Doug, are you going to leave soon for New Zealand?" I asked, pouting as I did so. I knew if he said yes, I would be devastated. I loved Doug, I really did, but I was also aware that he couldn't give me my fairy-tale ending, the ending I so craved, marriage and kids and a home in LA.

"Funny, I was going to chat with you about this later tonight when we went to dinner, but now seems as good a time as any."

My ears pricked up and a feeling of dread washed over me, expecting the worse.

He continued.

"I've been thinking a lot about us recently and you know I love you, and you know what my situation is too. I cannot stay in the US and have to return to New Zealand.."

I was listening intently, all the time waiting for him to come out with the words, 'you're dumped', but he kept on talking and those words never crossed his beautiful lips, as he finished off by saying, " ... and I think it would be great if you came with me to New Zealand and we made a life for ourselves out there. You'll love it, my parents and the rest of my family will love you too and I think we could be very happy out there"

Most of what he'd just said washed right over my head, my mind stuck on 'move to New Zealand with me'

WTF, I was born to live in LA, why would I move to NZ? Indeed, why wouldn't I move to NZ? I had never been there, but I was always told it was the best place on earth to live. Was this Doug proposing to me? Was he just asking for a continuation of an already fabulous relationship, and let's see where it goes? I had no idea how to respond, and so, as I always did, direct and straight to the point, I turned around and faced him, both of us fully nude and gazing lovingly into one another's eyes.

"Are you suggesting I give up on my dreams and move to a country I've never been to just to see what happens between us? Knowing that if I do this, and it doesn't work out, I can never get back into the USA again, ever!"

Doug looked at me, and without blinking, he said, "yes, yes I am"

"What if I say yes, and we get there and then we fall out over something? Where do I go then? What security do I have?"

"None" he replied, "but you know how we feel about each other, don't you think it's worth the effort to see if we can make it work?"

"Well, yes, but again, if it doesn't work I am going to have to go back to Estonia, to a life I didn't like and to a country I don't want to live in"

"Well," Doug continued," what would it take to persuade you to give my idea a try?"

"More commitment" I snarled

"You mean marriage?" he asked

"Yes, marriage, kids, a home, and all the trimmings"

Doug looked at me, and then the magic words came out of his mouth.

"OK, I agree, you're right. Let's go to NZ and get married and settle down. I love you and you love me, so let's do it!"

I was blown away, completely overawed by this suggestion, and lost for words, so lost that I got out of bed and went into the bathroom and pretended to sit and pee. While doing this, tears began to roll down my face, and trust me, these were not tears of joy, these were the tears of fear, fear of the unknown, fear of losing out on my dream, my dream of living in America. I did love Doug and I'd have to think long and hard about his offer, but for now, sitting on that toilet, Doug banging vigorously on the door asking of I was alright, it wasn't the right time. I wiped away my anxieties, washed my face and came back out into the bedroom.

"Sorry about that" I said, "It's all a bit much to take in and digest"

"Completely understand." he said, "take your time and we can discuss in a few days. I'm not leaving for a month at least, so we have time."

"Time?" I just looked at him, "I've been an illegal immigrant for 3 years, and have been counting the days until I got caught, which, as each day passes, seems less and less likely, and here you are, offering me everything I always dreamed of, other than a home in the country I believed I would always live in, and you think I have time?" I was crying now. "I don't have time. I have nothing here, other than an illegal life, and if I come with you, will that change? How do I get into New Zealand? Will you guarantee that we will get married? What if you change your mind? Time? I don't have time Doug; can't you see that?" The tears rolled down my face, torrents of salty frustration, tumbling towards a floor that deserved better that my misery.

"I won't change my mind and we will sort it out. We have at least 4 weeks, and in that time, we can discuss the best way forward for both of us. And one more thing, I will not leave you." He seemed adamant and completely honest.

We hugged and then got dressed and as we were about to leave for dinner, I received a text from John, how ironic!

CAN YOU COME OVER RIGHT NOW?

I looked at my phone, and sent a response

SORRY I AM BUSY

I pushed send and Doug asked, "Important text?"

"Just another job" I replied at which point my phone buzzed again with Joh's response

ITS URGENT

"Doug", I looked away as the following words came out of my mouth, just in case he knew I was lying, "I'm sorry, I have to take this job. It's a regular and I don't want to let him down."

No problem" Doug said. "Call me when you're done.

I texted John back.

I AM ON MY WAY.

That drive took an hour because of traffic, even though the distance wasn't too great, and on the way over to John's, all I could think of was a new life in New Zealand with Doug, a happy marriage and kids perhaps? But it was New Zealand, and not LA. LA was my dream, and I kept going back and forth between my dream and my reality. The reality, an illegal status and little hope of resolving that, overwhelmingly outweighed by the prospect of a new life in a new country with the man I loved. Did I really have a choice in this matter? No, my mind seemed to be made up already. I had to accept the opportunity that Doug just offered me, and I had to give up on my dream. It made sense, it was the right thing to do and far from being the most logical person on this planet, at that point in time, my whole body was letting me know that I needed to follow my gut and get out.

John opened his door and gave me a bear hug.

"Thanks for coming so quickly." he said, "I hope I didn't interrupt your evening?"

If only he knew.

"What was so urgent?" I asked. Knowing what Doug and I had just discussed made the guilt I already bore, even worse and really, I was hoping that John had had enough of me and wanted to tell me it was all over. Or that he's met someone else and was kicking me to the curb, just in time for me to leave without trace.

Instead, he ushered me into his lounge, poured me a glass of water and asked me to sit and say nothing while he talked. I was now curious and again, part of me expected the 'you're wonderful, I love you, the sex is great, best person in my life' speech, 'but we are done and you can fuck off'

It didn't come. Instead I got

"Tiana, I have loved every minute of our two months together, you're special, you're the best thing that ever happened to me. I love you and I want you to move in with me, we can get married and we can live happily ever after. All your immigration issues will be resolved, all your past will be washed away and you and I can have a great time traveling, making babies or doing anything else you would like to do. I have been thinking about this for days now, and I know you feel the same as me."

If only he knew!

"Take my offer, let's sort out your life, my life and therefore our lives"

For the very first time in my entire life, I was speechless. I couldn't even breath. How many girls get two proposals like that in a lifetime, never mind in the space of 2 hours? Was I dreaming, or what this indeed what I deserved? It was like a game show. 2 contestants, both with good intentions, vying for the beautiful model to whisk away, just like Cinderella, and make her happy, forever more. But on this occasion, there had been no script, no ulterior motive and only genuine intent from both interested parties, Doug and John.

"Sweetie, are you OK?" John asked.

I was in deep thought, not even listening to him, knowing that for 3 years, 3 long years, I had begged borrowed and stolen to try to make this happen, and it had just happened twice! Not only twice in the same day, it seemed like it had happened twice in that same moment and that time had stopped and God, if there is one, was upstairs laughing his or her head off, saying, "there you go Tiana, you got what you wanted, not make a choice and make sure it's the right one!"

But God had given me two very different options. One, with a man I love, to move to a country I didn't even know, and the second, with a man I cared deeply about, but didn't love, to stay in the place I had dreamed about since childhood. What a dilemma, what a turnaround, what a nightmare.

First things first, and John, who was by now standing right above me, on tenterhooks.

"Wow!, John" I said, feigning delight. "I just don't know what to say"

"Say yes" he laughed

"I mean, I want to, but I also want to think about this and discuss it further. You've taken me by surprise, and honestly, I thought you were calling me here to dump me, not to ask me to get married"

"No, I would never do that, I love you" he said. I just couldn't tell John I loved him, because I loved Doug, not him.

"John, let me think about this. It's all I ever wanted..." he interrupted me as I was speaking,

"Yes, I know. I know it will save you, your immigration status, and it'll make me very happy too."

God, my heart was torn into a thousand pieces. What a situation to be placed in. I also wanted out of his home urgently, just to think, but I realized John wanted more and was expecting sex at a minimum. I had to come up with a reason to leave.

"John, don't take this the wrong way, and please realize I am so so grateful to you for your wonderful offer, but when you texted, I was just on my way to bed because I am not feeling well. Would you mind terribly if I left and went home and we can talk in the morning?"

"Stay here" he said.

I was afraid of this, but I told him that I needed my own space for the night and that he'd blown my mind with his proposal, so it'd be best if I just went home. Reluctantly, he agreed.

I gave John a hug and left.

Driving home, I checked in with Doug.

"Hi Doug, I am headed home, I will see you tomorrow"

"Come and stay here" he said

"No, I don't feel great, and I need my own space" This was Deja Vous in all its weird glory. Doug understood and after we chatted for a few more minutes, I disconnected the call, drove home, still in a daze and went to bed. I just couldn't sleep, my mind in turmoil, but when I laid back and regurgitated what had just happened, I was incredibly honored and proud that these two guys, albeit in the same night, had both offered me almost everything that I wanted. Yes, just like an unfinished jigsaw, there were little pieces missing from both offers, buy hey, at least I now had offers, offers that were, for the most part, very appealing. My issue now, was which way to turn?

And turn and turn is exactly what I did. Up all night, weighing up the pros and cons and going over and over what I should and shouldn't do. Both Doug and John were two exceptional human beings, but I knew that either way, this was going to be a lifechanging decision that I didn't want to screw up. If I did, it could mean years of misery.

The sex with Doug was the best ever, but New Zealand? Did I really want to try to live there? All my life my ideal destination had been LA, and if I gave up on that dream, would I ever be happy? On the other hand, I did love him and it wouldn't be so bad spending my life with the man I loved, would it? Or, would I be miserable, knowing that the love I felt, would probably dissipate over time, as in all marriages, and then I'd be left with the possibility of having had children and living in a place I didn't really want to be. Or, by that time, would I love New Zealand more than I love LA? Then there was John, offering me everything I ever dreamed about, including staying in this city that I adored, but, I didn't love him. I liked him, and maybe, in time, I would love him, but my intuition told me that would be a long-shot. John would take care of me for sure, and I supposed there was always divorce if it didn't work out with either man, but the lure of a green card after marrying John? Well, that was really an added bonus for me. I really wanted to stay in America. I loved America, and the fact that I would have to marry a guy I didn't love, wasn't too much to expect because I figured most marriages were like that anyway. Rightly or wrongly, my choice would have to be made with my own expectations sorted out in my own head. That night seemed to drag on for days, as these thoughts would not leave my head and one way or another, I realized that very shortly, within days, I would need to make up my mind and follow my decision for better or for worse, literally!

Never Alone

For the next 3 weeks, I slept with John on one night and Doug the next. It was really mind blowing, and for all sorts of reasons, most of which were mental, my and inner self torn to pieces. Can you imagine lying with the guy you love, having great sex, discussing a future together in New Zealand and then the next thing doing the same thing, but without the love, knowing staying with that guy kept you in the town that you loved? Seems crazy now to even think about this, stupid in fact, but that was the truth. Monday, Wednesday and Friday, I was at John's home, (weekends were for John to spend time with his kids), and the rest of the week, Doug and I were together. Doug's tenure in America was coming rapidly to an end and the pressure from him to decide on our future together was becoming unbearable. It wasn't as if I was incapable as a person to decide what was right for my life, I was normally really competent when it came do doing just that, and Doug knew it. I could tell that something inside him felt there was an underlying issue and that I wasn't being straight with him, but I kept reassuring him, "It's not you, it's the thought of going somewhere I've never been and not being able to return if it didn't work out"

He kind of understood and even though he continually pledged undying love for me and for us, he was becoming more and more pissed off that I was prolonging something that he felt should have been sorted out weeks ago. "I need to book you a ticket to come with me" he would say

"My parents can't wait to meet you'

"I have started to look at apartments in Auckland"

And it went on and on and on.

With John, it was slightly different. Although he'd expected me to jump at his offer of marriage and as three weeks had now passed without me responding to that offer, his patience was definitely tested when each time he'd say, "any progress?', meaning, had I made my mind up yet, with the response from me being, 'just give me time', he'd roll his eye balls as if to say 'for fucks sake woman, I'm offering you all you ever wanted, what the fuck are you waiting for?', but actually saying noting, showing more patience than he ever needed to. And honestly, he was right. He felt I was leading him on, and I could understand that completely. The last thing I wanted to do was upset either one of them, and it seemed I was well on my way to killing both deals, without actually making one of them come to fruition, something that would be impossible for me to live with for the rest of my life.

Three weeks and one day into this fiasco, I finally came to a decision, but even though I'd decided, I was still conflicted. I just presumed that conflict would stay with me forever, and no matter which way I chose to go, the guilt of not choosing the alternative option, would weigh on me forever.

Preparations began.

It took me a few days to get my things together, call my landlord and cancel my month to month lease, and do all the other stuff that needed to be done, before finally, and still somewhat uncertainly, I was ready to go.

My new life was about to begin, and, it was about time too! I had waited patiently, perhaps too long and too patiently, for this moment. From the tender age of 5, LA had been in my mind, my heart, my future. My dreams had been of Hollywood, Marylin Munroe, all those movies my mother and I used to watch together, my love of clear blue skies and sunshine, huge wide boulevards, lined with tall thin palm trees, the aroma of BBQ continuously wafting through musky, often polluted air, the Pacific Ocean so large and intimidating, yet also so inviting with pelicans skimming over whitecaps and flying gracefully just inches above it's sometimes, glass-like, surface, and endless soft sandy beaches which became so special to me and played a huge part in my life after I arrived. Comforts I always enjoyed and which are now indelibly ingrained as memories, all of which will stay with me for the rest of my life.

From day one, in Estonia, I had looked forward to living a normal life, because, as you have read in this book, my life has been anything but normal. From the beginning of my modeling career when I was 13, to my introduction to sex, orgies, drugs and more, my life, to date, had been a rollercoaster ride, with huge uphill climbs and even steeper descents, some of which I never believed I would ever emerge from. I have been bullied, coerced, conned, taken advantage of, fucked, both physically and mentally, many times over, and I've always got back up on my own two feet and survived to live another day. My whole being and the things I have done, have been entirely at my own free will, and when I've succeeded, I have been fortunate enough to enjoy that success and reap the benefits that go hand in hand with all the hard work that success brought me. I've traversed back and forth across this planet, subsidized only by my intentions, mostly good, and always sincere. I have searched high and low for a man, a man to look after me, to bear children with and a man who will care about me for the rest of my days, knowing that not always is this guaranteed. Now, at the end of this journey, that man hopefully exists, but yet again, only time will tell if that ending, a happy ending, comes to fruition.

With my bags packed, my new life about to begin, my mind was set on taking this new direction to the next level, a comfortable and manageable level, a level that remained constant for the new part of my journey, a journey that presumably would also have twists and turns, only this time, not so vicious or severe. Yes, the dawn of a new day beckoned, as my front door closed for the last time and my body relaxed, accepting that what had begun as a dream, had actually finished as reality. The truth of that reality? I was never going to end up alone, and I was soon be made the happiest lady on this planet.

All Marriage Is a Lie

The wedding was brief, so brief in fact, I didn't even realize that the official representing the State of California, had finished her part of the ceremony. I say ceremony, but I use that term in its loosest of terms. My wedding was a complete farce, and one that my mother, who never attended, would have balked at. Yes, I needed to be married, and yes, I wanted to be married, but did I need and want it to be like this? My head was elsewhere, as that golden band was placed on my ring finger. I was thinking, "I know what I'm doing here, but do I really want to be here at all?" And the poor guy I was marrying, did he know what a ride he was in for? I knew in America, I could get divorced as easily as I could get married, but for now, I was placing my faith in a man I hardly knew, although a man who I believed would take care of me forever, should forever even enter into my mind as a state of permanency.

There was no honeymoon, no party, no presents, no congratulatory speeches, we just exited the courthouse and made our way into what would become, a kind of normalcy, although I would again use that term in its loosest form. I moved in, and he made room for me. It worked, kind of, but our relationship began with a lie, and it continued with untruths, many untruths, for the remainder of the time I was with him. He had no idea that I was still working. I had made up a story that on weekends I would shoot porn, not as a cast member, but as part of the crew. I always wanted to get into movie production and he knew that, so this 'fairytale' I'd made up sat well with both of us, whereas the truth, well, let's just say, FBSM was back in my life from the moment that ring went on, to the moment it came off, which was each time I entered a hotel room and had a line of clients waiting to be 'rubbed out'. It took 2 months for me to cheat on him, three months to do it more than once and then by the 6th month, nothing mattered to me except being unfaithful to a man I'd married, but to a man who was crap in bed, had a small dick and came in seconds. I hated it, hated it all, but there was that little matter of a green card, my dangling carrot, my incentive, that safety net which would guarantee my longevity in the United States, and for that reason, and that reason alone, I persisted with the sham my marriage was and the disaster it would become.

On another note, my FBSM business was fabulous. I would work 3 days a week, and take acting classes two days a week. I was making good money, money which I hid from my husband, (well not all of it, but some of it, in case of emergencies), and money that would pay our bills in the long run because unfortunately, my husband lost his job and I became the breadwinner. I enjoyed what I was doing, all cash, no grief and sometimes great sex, most of it casual. My clients were made up of regulars and newbies, some nice, other's not too memorable, but clients all the same. I had a routine. My routine ran something like this.

Place Ad on rubratings.com or privatedelights.com or one of the other sites.

Take appointments and vet clients

Book hotel somewhere outside of LA.

Arrive at noon to check in at 1.

Begin seeing clients around 3 PM until midnight and then from 8 AM until noon.

Check out

I always got a room with two beds. One for fucking and one for sleeping. I never slept in the same bed I worked on, even though most of the guys never fucked me, the sheets would be soiled from their cum and my massaging oils. I also always tried to negotiate with hotel reception to be at the end of a corridor or somewhere in the hotel which was away from the elevators, just to maximize privacy for all concerned. This was something I learned over several months as I grew into learning how to look after myself, because I understood very quickly that my other half had little intention of doing this for me. Life had always been this way, no matter who I lived with, who told me they loved me, who had made me pregnant, I always took care of it myself. I didn't need assistance, I just knew how to survive.

And my business began to thrive.

He arrived late, only about ten minutes, but late all the same. My husband had just called me to see how I was doing, I was abrupt, not wanting to talk to him at all, but finding time and patience to go over the niceties, 'yes I am fine", 'yes it's been busy" and finally, repeating what he'd just said, 'I love you too", although, quite honestly, that was a bigger lie than telling him I was involved in a production team shooting porn movies in Simi Valley. The HE I am discussing took my breath away, no, wait, he did more than just take my breath away, he made my legs wobble too, and my nipples erect at the same time, although as we already know, my nipples are mostly always erect, something I am really proud of. HE was 6 ft 4, blond hair, blue eyes, and fit, and honestly, the rest didn't matter. I just stared at him and he stared back. It had been some time since I'd had sex, even being married hadn't guaranteed regular sex, and anyway, my husband's cock was minute. HE, yes him, the guy in my hotel room, looked like he was ready to shag me from the moment the room door had opened, and he and I knew that, although he was about to pay for FBSM, more was definitely in the offing. He stripped, I stripped and the fun began. We just hit it off, just like the old days in London, when a client would arrive and we would have so much in common and end up fucking. This guy was one of those, those being a very fuckable man, a man who instantly turned me on, a man I could date and a man I really wanted.

The massage began, the conversation never ended and when the 'flip' arrived, I massaged his cock up and down and round and round but he didn't pop. He didn't want to, or so he said, and he didn't want to fuck me, or at least that was my impression, but underneath his coy attitude, I felt there was more to be had, that MORE, being intimacy of the penetrative kind. Patience is a virtue, so they say, and as he was about to leave, he asked me out on a proper date. He lived 40 miles south of where we were at that time, and I readily agreed. I hadn't told him I was married, there was no point just yet, but I knew that should this blossom into full blown sex and debauchery, that secret would eventually have to come out in the open.

We began texting one another. We began flirting, and we both knew where this was headed. I made a point of Googling him, and was surprised to learn that his main occupation was working with retired folk in a home close to San Diego. This was not what I'd expected from a man like him, but, oh well, I'm sure he was good at it and if truth be told, my ambitions of meeting a super-rich guy were probably exaggerated anyway.

We met up a week later, walked on the beach in San Diego, and the usual things that happened to me when I was attracted to someone, happened once again. We held hands, we kissed, we had lunch and then we went to his place to fuck. Fuck? It was unbelievable! I know I've said this before, probably too often in this book, but this guy knew what to do. He fucked me in a way that my husband could only dream of. I hadn't had sex like this for many years, and after orgasming for the 13th time in a row, I actually wondered if I had EVER had sex like this before. We lay side by side, spent, and with thoughts of my husband and the guilt that I would feel when I walked into our home that night, running constantly through my head, I got up and told my new fuck buddy the truth.

"I'm married"

Silence

"Nothing to say to me?" I asked him

He didn't.

I left. He texted. We agreed to see one another again, after he'd told me that my being married had taken him completely by surprise and he was lost for words. And so, with a few texts back and forth, this extra-marital relationship began in earnest.

And he wasn't the only one.

One week later, another client entered yet another hotel room I'd booked, and once again, after the sparks flew back and forth, I agreed to see this guy again, but under differing sets of rules than San Diego boy. This guy was older, maybe in his 40's, and had 7 kids with 4 different women, but he was wealthy and he looked after all of them. I don't know what to say other than he was gorgeous and the attraction was there. We set up another massage date, not a dinner and fuck date. Maybe I was learning? San Diego boy and I were seeing one another once a week, then twice a week and even though he'd accepted my circumstances, deep down inside me I knew it wouldn't last.

7 kid guy on the other hand, well, he was looking forward to his next massage, already texting me regularly, and being extremely suggestive. I quite liked that, but I was also being very cautious. He had all these kids, and that was an interesting scenario for me, even though he was single, and I was still married, I knew that I wasn't going to have kids with my current husband and

I also knew 7 kid guy wanted more. Would that be so bad? I kept asking myself that question. Having a kid with a guy who already had 7, well, that could be an issue, but if it worked? Anyway, that day, the day of his next massage and our second meet up, ended in disaster because the hotel wouldn't let me check in early, and by the time I got to my room, I had put him back and hour not just once, but twice. He didn't show, not because he didn't want to, because he couldn't make it any other time. I thought I'd pissed him off, but seemingly not, because he's still on my case every day asking for another appointment. In the meantime, San Diego boy dumped me. And then, THE PILOT showed up.

I stay in one of two hotels, unless both are booked, in which case I have a third option. Each one is rated in order of personal preference and choice number 1 is my go to on 95% of the times I am out and performing my trade. I set up in the room, take out all my oils and such and always have a few condoms available close by the bed, just in case....

My clothes are few and far between, only because I have no need for anything, just a night dress or perhaps a nice top and skirt, just in case.....

And then there's my makeup and hair products, but that's a story in itself.

Having had the same booking system for many years, the guy sees the ad, sends a text, I verify him and then make the date, or not, and after agreeing the fee, which is also emblazoned on my Ad, we trade names and I hand out the name and address of the hotel I am staying at. When the client arrives, he texts, I send a reply with my room number, he bypasses reception and heads straight up to wherever I am and then we do our little dance and he leaves. Simple.

My phone buzzed. It was another possible appointment. We sent texts back and forth. We agreed to meet, we agreed a time, I sent the hotel address. I received a response that I'd never received before, in all the years I'd been doing this, this response was totally unique. I crying with laughter emoji.

'WTF' I thought to myself, and texted back one word, PROBLEM?

SAME HOTEL I AM STAYING IN! came the reply.

What were the chance of that? It honestly had never happened to me before. Most men were coming from work or from home, but this guy was staying in the same hotel and was prepared to come and see me no matter where I was? I just happened to be 3 floors underneath his room.

We made a time and he showed up 5 minutes early. I got to the door and he just stood there, ogling me, transfixed by something he'd seen the second I'd cracked the door open.

"I am in love with you!" he blurted.

"Sure you are sweetie" I said, trying to be as coy with him as was humanly possible.

"I am" he said, as he walked into my room, unable to take his eyes off me.

He stripped, I stripped, we began the process, massage, chat, more massage, more chat and then he flipped. I liked what I saw, I also loved what he was telling me, and it seemed we had quite a bit in common. I rubbed him out, he came, I laughed, he smiled, and then he said to me,

"Want to shower with me in my room?"

"Hmmm, NO!" I replied

"Dinner then?" he offered

"I am booked through until 8 or 9 PM and the restaurant closes at 9 so maybe or maybe not" I was still trying to be coy, but there was something about him that I really liked.

"OK, let me know" he said, as he finished dressing. "I'm in room 1012"

Well, for the next 3 hours, all I could think about was Pilot guy, each man who came and left my room was just a blur, and all my energies were centered on this proposed dinner. He was texting me in between massages, and I was texting back, and then, finally, as my 7PM guy left at 7. 40 PM, (I'd sort of kicked him out to enable this dinner to happen with Pilot guy), I called room 1012, and told Pilot guy to meet me in the restaurant. We had a very nice time together and after we'd eaten, I knew he'd try to come back to my room, so I made it very clear to him that I was going to drive home to sleep and that I would be back again tomorrow to meet him if he was still in town.

"I am here for two days, so come around 10 and we can spend the day at the hotel pool"

I liked that idea and I agreed to meet him the next day.

At noon I appeared.

"Where have you been?" he asked

"Keeping you waiting" I smiled.

One thing that I have always had a superstition for is dogs. It's about the only thing in my body that makes me feel this way. Some people, well, maybe a lot of people, believe that when they see a black cat walk in front of them, it's good or bad luck, depending on what country you come from, but me, on the other hand, I have always believed that if my path is crossed by a Dalmatian, yes, a Dalmatian, it is very good luck. Don't ask me why this is the case, but I think it's got something to do with watching that Disney mover 101 Dalmatians, when I was a kid. Anyway, at several times in my life, crucial times, I have been in situations when a Dalmatian has crossed my path and the person or persons I was with at the time, or the things going on in my mind at that precise moment, all seem to work out or come to fruition, hence enforcing my belief that Dalmatians are a good thing.

Here we were at the poll, the sun was blistering hot, we had a couple of drinks on the way and Pilot guy was telling me he had a kid and that he was divorced and that I was the most beautiful lady he'd ever met in his life, and at that very moment, he pulled his cell phone out to show me a picture of his little boy, and WTF! A Dalmatian was standing right next to his kid.

"Is that yours" I asked

He nodded.

We had sex within the hour, not great sex, but really good sex, and then we ate dinner together and then we had more sex. When he left that next morning, he asked to see me again. I agreed, my hopes buoyed by that fucking Dalmatian!

Then came a call from what turned out to be one of the strangest situations I have ever had in my entire life. It was a text that kind of turned my eye. Nothing really out of the ordinary, but it was polite, structured and quite different from the usual text I received. Normally the guy will just state quite simply, "Hey, are you available? Rates please?", expecting my standard response, dishing out the relevant info before going one step further to screen him, but on this occasion, I received a full paragraph, enquiring, intriguing and fortunately, very polite. I looked at it long and hard. Cops? Nah, it was too eloquent, so I decided to reply. The guy, Alf, was quite clear in his instruction. He knew what I charged and wanted me to come to him home, which as it happens, was only a mile from where I used to live, in West Hollywood. I told him I would be there within two hours, to which he responded that he was excited to meet me. I showered and got dressed and made my way North, up the 405 and then along Pico and into Hollywood. When I arrived outside his home, I was quite impressed. It was a very modern building, obviously new construction and it had this gate, which I thought looked ugly and out of place on such a nice looking home, which was electronic and of course, shut tight. I texted him from the curb, where I'd parked up, informing him I was here and early and that I was in no rush so he could take his time. He responded very quickly, stating his wife would be right out to open the gate and that I could park in their driveway.

His   wife??
I was confused, very confused.

He, like every other one of the men I serviced, was surely expecting a massage with a 'happy ending', but with the wife in the same house? It didn't take her long to appear, and when she did, I was duly impressed. She was gorgeous. About 5 foot 3 inches, blonde, slim, beautifully dressed in a white summer frock, and lovely white high heel shoes and to top it all, she had the whitest brightest smile I had ever seen. She opened the gate and waved me in confidently. All this time I am thinking, 'does this guy really know what I do for a living?"

When I got out my car, his wife, who we will call Mary, came right over and gave me a huge hug. "Thanks for coming all this way" she said.

I could tell that something wasn't right, from the moment she touched me, I could smell the effects of excessive cocaine use written all over her eyes, and as Alf, the husband, exited his front door to greet me, it was clear he was on the same high as her. At that stage, I was in two minds whether to go inside or not, but with Alf carrying my donation, plus a huge bonus, in his left hand, I knew that money, on that particular day, would rule. I entered their home and this is what happened next.

"We want you to massage the two of us" Mary said

"No problem."

"Me first," she continued, "then Alf, and the donation.." she pointed to the cash I still had in my hand, "should cover ALL the extras" she emphasized the word ALL, making me think that they wanted to fuck me, which, by the way, was never going to happen, well, at least in my mind it wasn't.

I followed her upstairs, where she slipped off her dress and bra and panties, keeping her heels firmly attached to her feet, and proceeded to lie naked on her bed, a huge bed, and probably one of the largest beds I had ever seen. She had beautiful soft tanned skin, and a completely shaved poosie, perfectly manicured hands and feet and she'd tied her hair up in a bun, all ready for her massage. "Get naked" she demanded.

Well, it began, as it always does, with her on her tummy and me massaging her back. Alf sat on a chair, about three yards away, snorting line after line of cocaine, with Mary, asking me regularly, if I wanted to join in the party. Although tempted, I simply refused. While I am massaging her and Alf is snorting coke, he also has his pants off and is rubbing his cock, which looked soft to me, underneath his boxers, trying hard to get aroused. From what I could see though, his cock wasn't cooperating, and Alf was becoming more and more frustrated and snorting more and more coke.

The flip arrived and Mary turned around and whilst exposing her perfect tits, rose colored petite nipples and shaved poosie, she smiled and asked me,

"Are you OK with 'getting me off', using two fingers?"
"Sure"

I went for it, moving my fingers slowly at first, around her clit and then suddenly driving them deeper and deeper into her poosie. She was loving every moment of this and Alf, although completely into what I was doing, still had a 'stranded' penis, and mega frustration, egging his wife on to cum, and to cum quickly.

"Can I kiss you?" Mary asked me.

Well, I don't normally do this with women, but I agreed, telling her that it would cost her more. She quickly nodded her acceptance of my new fee and our mouths met, at first softly, but as my fingers grinded more and more inside her poosie, our passion became extremely vigorous and intimate. With a huge scream, Mary came, and as she did, she squirted poosie juice all over her clean bedsheets, writhing up and down at the same time, as if rocking on a boat that was ploughing through a storm at sea. She was really engrossed and totally lost in that moment, which, for me, was quite interesting, because I too felt it as being breathtaking and quite a turn on. Alf however, now very high and very loud, shouted over to his wife,

"Right you, it's my turn, get off the bed"

Mary did as Alf commanded.

She was so beautiful, and I had no idea what she was doing with this guy.

Alf was now naked, his tummy on the bed, and I started massaging him.

"Let's just cut to the chase" he said, as he turned over, exposing his cock, which was still soft.

"Mary, let's do this!" he shouted, even though Mary, his wife, was standing right by the bed.

"Do what?" I thought to myself. And then the fun began.

"Rub my cock" Alf ordered.

"OK, no massage?" I asked again.

"No, just rub it"

I took my oil, began lubricating the stem of his cock, and as I was about to start rubbing him out, Mary got up on the bed, she was still naked and gasping, and the 'porn' began.

"Alf, I was out with this guy, Rod, when I was 15 years old," she began, "and we went to the movies, and inside the theatre, as the move was playing, he started to play with my tits, squeezing gently on each nipple and bringing all poosie juice to the boil, and then, as we became more passionate, he placed on hand under my skirt, and felt my virgin cunt...."

As I was listening to this, and as Alf was listening to this, I could feel his cock growing and growing and getting harder and harder. This was totally weird, but it was doing it for him, no doubt he was now erect. Her stories continued and I continued, for at least twenty-five minutes, and all the time I am thinking to myself, 'I thought I'd seen it all...'

Mary's stories got wilder and wilder and Alf's cock was enjoying each and every word she was spouting, until, just as my hand was going to go numb, he exploded and his cum run down my hand as his body went into convulsions of ecstatic pleasure. It was over. I was exhausted, he was high and completely gone, and Mary as lying on the bed kissing Alf's bare chest and stroking his forehead, saying, "there, there, there Alf"

I'd been there over three hours, but I had a $1000 in my hand and the two happiest clients on the planet. But the story doesn't end there. They became regulars, and each time I went there, they paid me more money, and each time she began narrating her sexual exploits, none of which I knew to be true or false, and I didn't even want to ask, he would go from zero to hero and cum all over the place. Every one to their own, right? A couple of months into this regular trip, I received a text from Mary confirming yet another time and day to attend yet another session. I arrived on time, and Alf, who I always texted when I arrived, came out of his home looking rather surprised at my presence. I could just tell by the look on his face that I wasn't expected. He opened the gate and directed me into the driveway.

"Did I get the date wrong?" I asked him, as I got out of the driver's seat and began my walk towards him for a quick hug.

"Mary told me today" I said, as I looked at her text on my phone and showed it to Alf.

"Ah", said Alf," Mary was called out of town and probably forgot to cancel, but it's OK, come in and you can just work on me"

We went inside, and upstairs to the bedroom. By now I knew the drill and I undressed, as did Alf.

The massage began, Alf, as I could see from the residue on the bedroom table, had already been at the cocaine, and was well-gone. By the time he flipped, he'd already suggested that as Mary was MIA, I should tell him stories from my sexual past because that was the only way he would cum. I began, and after the 3rd tale of sex and debauchery, depicting the time my poosie was rammed by two cocks at the same time, Alf was still soft. It wasn't working, he knew it, and I knew it.

"You want do snort a line with me?" he asked. I refused.

"Please don't tell Mary I couldn't cum, with you?"

"No, I won't" I replied.

"It's the coke. It makes it harder for me to ejaculate, and her stories always help, but I don't know why yours don't"

"It's not important Alf, I won't tell, I promise"

He tipped me $200 and I left. To this day, Mary has no idea what happened, but every time I go there, it's the same story, she gets off on my two fingers and he cums buckets after she gets graphic with her past. Whatever turns you on I suppose, and who am I to judge?

Pilot Man and San Diego Guy

It's funny how things turn out. I met both Pilot man and San Diego guy, performing FBSM on both of them, although not at the same time of course! Both were happy to come and meet me, and both were happy to leave happy and then date me, but when San Diego guy vanished into the cold blue ocean of men who have dogged my past, Pilot guy hung around, making it clear, although it took him a couple of weeks, that he loved me. We had been inseparable for weeks. We did everything together, and he even began teaching me how to fly, something I always wanted to learn to do. I had invited him to my apartment, something I never did with any man, and now, out of the blue, he had invited me to visit his parents' home in Washington State, again, something I thought I would never do with any man. This was getting serious, and even after just 6 weeks, I began to have feelings for this man that I had never had for any other man before him, even though we were two completely different people. I also knew that he hated what I did for a living, and though he'd never said so, I could tell he resented the fact that I had naked guys in my bed every day of the week, ejaculating on my hands, my arms, my body, and sometimes my ass. I believed that as I'd met Pilot man doing this very same thing, and although he had every right to his opinion, and again, I reiterate, he'd never complained to me once about what I did, I just knew it rankled him because of some of the questions he'd ask me after we'd fucked and were lying in bed naked together, but, in my opinion, he had no right to be upset but it mattered not. As far as our relationship was concerned and when he blurted out "I think I love you" for the first time, and I told him the same thing in return, I knew that this relationship was perhaps going places. Damn that fucking Dalmatian.

Then one afternoon, completely out of the blue, a text from San Diego guy, a man I hadn't spoken to in months, appeared on my phone.

"Hi, just driving through Irvine and was thinking about you. Hope you're doing well"

It floored me, and my first reaction was, "FUCK YOU", knowing I wasn't going to respond. He'd vanished from my life without any warning or reason, and as suddenly as he'd vanished, he was back? Fucker, and Fuck him!

I thought about it for two day, and then I made the decision to text him back, a simple text, "I am good, Glad you're OK"

His response was swift.

"I'd love to see you"

My response was even swifter

"Why? You just ran off and never discussed with me why you did it or where you were going. Why would I ever want to see you again?"

"Well, I had my reasons. You were married and I didn't want to get involved and now I feel differently and I miss you"

I thought about this for a few minutes and replied

"OK that's fair, where and when do you want to meet?"

Two days later, we met and we chatted, and then we chatted some more. I could tell though that this was going nowhere in particular, rehashing the old and predicting what the new would never become, and so, after several cups of tea and something to eat, San Diego guy was history and my new life, with Pilot Guy, became the reality I was to follow for the foreseeable future.

Pilot Guy offered me hope, something that had never left my soul, but which somehow became stronger every time he and I sat down and talked, ate dinner or made love. There was a certain positivity when I was with him, something I hadn't received from many men in my life, if any at all. We planned our future daily, even though we knew, the future was always changing. Pilot Guy also accepted that my life had to include FBSM, something I was good at, really good at, and he also knew that he'd met me only because of this and nothing else. With a certain amount of courage, I dropped everyone around me, men that is, and decided that I would make a real go of it with Pilot Guy, and to this day, we are still an item. My divorce was finalized and my apartment was now being shared, although not daily, often twice weekly, when Pilot Guy came into town. We traveled together around the USA, following his crazy schedule, and I got to see different parts of the country while he worked. I would place Ad's in the local papers of whatever city we ended up in, and while he flew, I performed FBSM to the populous of that particular town. It worked, and I have to admit, I was happy. I met his family, on more than one occasion, and even stayed with them, sleeping comfortably in the same bed as Pilot Guy while his parents slept next door. We grew to love one another deeply, in fact, I can honestly say, my love for him is greater than with any other man I have ever met, and yet, there is no pressure from me to him or him to me, to make that love more permanent and settle down together. If I spent the rest of my life with him, I would be OK with that, and if I didn't? Well, that would be OK too because I have learned, on multiple occasions, there's always someone else, no matter how lonely or isolated I feel, that somebody seems to just appear, and the next relationship begins. For now, though, I am set on Pilot Guy and am content with the way my life has ended up.

With my FBSM career in a never-ending progression and never being short of clients, either now, or regular, I see no reason to end that career in favor of any other job. I enjoy my freedom; I love being naked in front of strange men, I think I must have real exhibitionist tendencies, I love the money it brings and most of all, I love the thrill of a man becoming hard when I am in control. Until any of that changes, or until circumstance determines that it's time to give all of that up, I shall remain, the secret masseuse.